MONEY PLAYERS

The Amazing Rise and Fall of Bob Goodenow and the NHL Players Association

Bruce Dowbiggin

KEY PORTER BOOKS

Library and Archives Canada Cataloguing in Publication

Dowbiggin, Bruce
   Money players : how hockey's greatest stars beat the NHL at its own game / Bruce Dowbiggin.

Includes index.
ISBN 1-55263-810-3

1. Hockey players—Salaries, etc. 2. Hockey players—Labor unions. 3. National Hockey League—Finance. 4. Hockey—Economic aspects. I. Title.

GV847.4.D68 2006   331'.04179696264   C2006-901792-1

The publisher gratefully acknowledges the support of the Canada Council for the Arts and the Ontario Arts Council for its publishing program. We acknowledge the support of the Government of Ontario through the Ontario Media Development Corporation's Ontario Book Initiative.

We acknowledge the financial support of the Government of Canada through the Book Publishing Industry Development Program (BPIDP) for our publishing activities.

Key Porter Books Limited
Six Adelaide Street East, Tenth Floor
Toronto, Ontario
Canada M5C 1H6

www.keyporter.com

Text design: Marijke Friesen
Electronic formatting: Jean Lightfoot Peters

Printed and bound in Canada

06 07 08 09 10 5 4 3 2 1

MONEY PLAYERS

By Bruce Dowbiggin

The Defence Never Rests
Of Ice and Men
The Stick: A History, a Celebration, an Elegy

To Carl Brewer and Sue Foster

—both deserve a place in the Hall of Fame

Contents

"The value of all things contracted for is measurable by the appetite of the contractors, and there the just value is that which they be contented to receive."
THOMAS HOBBES

"Man is an animal that makes bargains; no other animal does this—one dog does not change a bone with another."
ADAM SMITH

"A verbal contract isn't worth the paper it's printed on."
SAM GOLDWYN

Introduction

Q: How many NHL executives does it take to screw in a light bulb?
A: Just one. But it'll take him 301 days to do it.

NHL commissioner Gary Bettman is fond of saying that his league has the best fans and the best game in the world. Which begs the question, if you have the best game, then why don't you have more fans? Outside of Canada, where hockey is an obsession, the NHL is still a regional phenomenon in the United States with pretensions to glory at the national level. The reasons are many: cultural, structural and financial. Hockey has remained the ugly duckling from the north, still waiting to blossom into a swan for the attention of Middle America. By the time the first edition of *Money Players* was printed in the fall of 2003, the league had squandered multiple opportunities to capture a larger share of the North American market through expansion, failed television ventures and obstinate leadership at the club and league level. The style of play had degenerated into more clutching than the senior prom; the vicious Todd Bertuzzi attack on Steve Moore had repulsed many casual fans and—as the subtitle of the book indicated—the players and their union had beaten the NHL at its own game by winning mammoth salary increases. Power had devolved to the players.

The best way to understand the salary spiral of the 1990s is to see the NHL as a real-estate market. In every city there are neighbourhoods: upscale, middle class, blue-collar, and better-lock-your-doors. It's bad news if your neighbour grabs the first lowball offer he hears and runs. Likewise, it's great news if a neighbour plays hardball and gets 20 per cent more than the market price for her shack.

So it was with the NHL. You have many neighbourhoods: Franchise Player Park, Sniper Street, Enforcer Road, Fading Veteran Way, Goalie Crescent, and Blueliner Boulevard, to name a few. The value within these properties is determined by the best—and worst— deals consummated by the players who reside in those neighbourhoods. For fifteen years, the NHLPA—led by Goodenow—and the player agents had repeatedly dominated the teams in setting these market values. *Money Players* documented this process.

Faced with this laundry list of misery in the fall of 2004, the NHL decided first to crush its players union, the NHL Players Association. In this respect, Bob Goodenow, the NHLPA executive director, complied by boxing himself into a negotiating corner with an unequivocal refusal to accept a salary cap. As can be seen by the new subtitle—*The Amazing Rise and Fall of Bob Goodenow and the NHL Players Association*—the players widely overestimated their hand in the labour market. At the first signs of stress, many abandoned Goodenow's hardline in return for a paycheque and an end to the public criticism. As a result, the league regained the whip hand in labour matters. To its credit, the NHL made the first serious attempt in seventy-five years to restore skill to the game. Certainly the early impact upon scoring was encouraging, leading many to speak of a "new" NHL on the scoresheet if not the TV ratings race or on the balance sheet.

Whether the rules change works will only be shown over time. Wily coaches understand that while scoring grabs headlines, defence still wins Stanley Cups. The same can be said for the impact of the new collective bargaining agreement with its salary caps, revenue sharing, and escrow payments. While it was widely celebrated as a panacea in the early days, the truth is we just don't know if small markets can sustain superstar salaries any better under this new CBA than under the previous agreement. Or whether successful small markets will retain their star players more easily than they did under the old deal. The rush to keep franchise players such as Brad Richards (Tampa), Jarome Iginla (Calgary), Rich Nash (Columbus) and Joe Thornton (San Jose) away from free agency by offering very rich deals at lengthy terms indicated that many managers were still operating under the mindset of the old CBA. The best guess on small markets is that the smart managers, such as Brian Burke, will succeed while the chronic goofs in other cities will get caught and devoured in the web of this CBA, too.

As for the apparent demise predicted for large markets, there's conflicting evidence here, too. Toronto was initially hobbled by losing $30–40 million from its payroll, going from centre of the universe to universally scorned. Chicago spent unwisely and performed poorly. But Philadelphia hardly qualifies as a small market, and through judicious pruning of their costly veterans and excellent player development of young talent they were once more under the new CBA. Detroit, too, cut deeply from its peak at almost $80 million and remained the NHL's best team in the regular season thanks to its fertile farm system and scouting department.

In short, the people who prospered under the old rules through player development and judicious spending are likely to prosper under the new rules. And until the shattered players' union recovers its equilibrium, any incentive for improvement in the NHL will have to come from the league itself or outside forces.

I want to thank Jordan Fenn and Jonathan Schmidt of Key Porter for having faith in completing this project that began five years ago at Macfarlane, Walter and Ross. And thanks to my agent

Linda McKnight for helping them to see the dream. While some material has been updated since the original printing in 2003, the core of the book remains true to the initial manuscript. The book is now being added to the curricula of sports management courses across North America, and it is our hope that it will serve as a reference point on both hockey and the sports business for a long while.

Bruce Dowbiggin
Summer 2006

$$\boxed{1}$$

The 2005 Lockout: Goodenow's Swan Song

To the untrained eye, the press conference at Toronto's Westin Harbour Castle Hotel on July 28, 2005, was simply an orderly transfer of power at the helm of the National Hockey League Players Association. On a day that barely suggested hockey, with stifling heat and smog sitting heavily on Canada's largest city, the press and TV networks had been hastily summoned to an afternoon meeting in the air-conditioned lakefront hotel. On the dias in the ballroom sat the newsmaker, Bob Goodenow, the executive director of the union since 1991 and a formidable force in the hockey business. As he faced the press, many hot and cranky at the short notice, the hockey world was still recovering from the whirlwind signing of a new collective bargaining agreement between the NHL and NHLPA the week before, one that ended a year of turmoil and pain in the league. Perspiring TV camera operators and newspaper photographers scrummed for the best shot of a man whose name had rarely been out of the headlines in Canada the past few years. Flanked by the union's leadership and senior staff, Goodenow's face betrayed little emotion—as it had done almost every day since he succeeded Alan Eagleson as the leader of the world's best hockey players. Inscrutable, unfathomable, unapproachable and assertive, Goodenow remained an enigma to many of his own members, let alone to the outside world as he began to speak beneath the omnipresent NHLPA logo.

A week before, on July 21, 2005, the day the new CBA ended a 301-day lockout of his members by owners, the fifty-two-year-old Goodenow had described the unique challenges that lay ahead and of his own anticipation for tackling a new economic plan for the NHL. But less than a week later, the message was very different from the American-born labour lawyer. He was stepping down, allowing his deputy, Ted Saskin, to assume the executive director's position. "I sat down with members of the executive committee, and we talked about the future," he began. "The decision was made that it would be best if we made the transition now. . . .

"There's the old saying, when it feels good and it looks good, go ahead and do it, and that's what we've done. . . . I have no plans for anything right now. I'm going to take a few months off and think about what I might want to do in the future." When pressed on why his plans had changed so rapidly in less than a week, Goodenow elaborated, "My contract would not have made it through to [the next CBA]. We all said rather than have a change that we knew would happen down the road, now's an ideal situation with the new agreement to have one person step in and form the strategy. I said that was fine with me."

And what about his contract, the one that he'd renegotiated before the lockout, the one that still had almost three years to run at $2.6 million a year? "What we've worked out is an accommodation that's satisfactory to everyone," he said. (Probably none more so than to NHL commissioner Gary Bettman, Goodenow's mortal enemy for a decade, who stopped celebrating long enough to damn him with faint praise: "I have always respected Bob's tenacity, passion and professionalism, and I wish him well in his future endeavors," read Bettman's press blurb.)

Watching as the NHL's worst nightmare quietly slipped from the scene after fourteen years of confrontation were Goodenow's lieutenant Saskin and NHLPA president Trevor Linden of the Vancouver Canucks, the two principal negotiators for the union since the 2004–05 season and playoffs had been cancelled in February of that year. Both made the kind of appreciative noise that accompanies such a sea change in an organization.

"What Bob has done to the organization and for the players has been absolutely outstanding, and we're all tremendously appreciative of it," said Saskin, a licensing lawyer who'd come to the NHLPA to promote business opportunities for the players and was now about to assume the executive role at their union. "Obviously there's some very large shoes to fill in terms of the job that's been done, and there's a lot to be done in the future."

"Every NHL player has benefited enormously from Bob's leadership and dedication," echoed Linden, whose own career spanned the Eagleson and Goodenow regimes. "He has been a tireless advocate for the players, and he dramatically improved the players' situation in every respect....Bob built the NHLPA into a first-class organization, and we are all very grateful to him." Indeed, with Goodenow as NHLPA head, player salaries rose 250 per cent, from an average of $276,000 in 1990–91 to roughly $1.8 million in 2003–04. More than that, he'd given them self-worth and a true advocate in the face of domineering ownership, no small thing in a business where house unions were the rule, not the exception, for most of the NHLPA's forty-seven-year existence.

But the warm words and tributes this summer's day scarcely disguised the rancour within the NHLPA during recent months. After vowing solidarity forever on the issue of a salary cap in their industry, the players had been crushed in negotiations for a collective agreement, agreeing to virtually all of management's major issues. However great his stature, Goodenow was being made the fall guy. Despite the fact that he probably lacked the constitutional authority of the Players Association to do so, Linden had effectively fired Goodenow the previous weekend and offered the executive director's job to Saskin at a price to be largely set by Saskin

himself. To get Goodenow to leave quietly, Linden had had to guarantee the former Harvard hockey captain almost all the money left
him on his contract. The two men, who'd worked so closely on running the union before and during the lockout, were scarcely talking
before Linden's pre-emptive strike. The firing, supported by some
but not all the executive board members, would drive a permanent
wedge between them. To those who'd seen Linden as Goodenow's
puppet, there was rich irony in the pupil firing the master.

The bitter break between Goodenow and Linden culminated a
chaotic period for the previously invincible union. Goodenow,
who'd successfully led the NHLPA through two previous labour stoppages in 1992 and 1994–95, had warned his membership about a
long, tough road when the league padlocked the arenas in September
2004. Boston owner Jeremy Jacobs, the hawkish power in the NHL's
Board of Governors, had set the tone for a PR war against supposedly rich, spoiled hockey players. "It's been suggested that perhaps
the game would be a whole lot more interesting if people skated
harder every game as opposed to just mailing it in," Jacobs told
the Boston media. Based on such bullish noises from ownership,
Goodenow had forecast that it might take anywhere from eighteen
months to two full NHL seasons before the owners would be willing
to negotiate fairly. In the early days of the stoppage, it seemed players were united behind his strategy. "The bottom line is, if they want
a hard [salary] cap, we'll sit out for the rest of our lives," Toronto
Maple Leafs union rep Bryan McCabe told the *Toronto Star*, "If
they're not going to budge off of that, there's really nowhere to go."

But as the NHL's lockout of its players dragged on month after
month into 2005, players abandoned their earlier commitment to
Goodenow's lengthy timetable. Many began saying Goodenow was
out of touch, that he had ruled by fiat for so long that he could not
take the temperature of his membership. Legendary player Bobby
Orr, now a player agent, claimed Goodenow (and Bettman) were
putting their own agendas ahead of the game. A faction headed by
Linden and Saskin, tired of Goodenow's strategy of attrition and the

public assaults of owners and fans alike about "greedy players," began making noises about compromise on the inviolate salary-cap issue. Players losing millions and seemingly ignored in the union's strategy, complained publicly and privately about the union's insistence on fighting a salary cap when both the NFL and NBA had them.

High profile stars—many of whom shared Linden's agent Newport Sports—tried suing for peace behind the scenes with the league, going around Goodenow. More and more, Goodenow was left out of the loop as the union dramatically dropped its long-held opposition to a salary cap in an effort to rescue the 2004–05 season at the last moment. Slowly, an owner-friendly deal was carved out after the union's collapse on the salary-cap issue following the cancellation of the Stanley Cup for the first time in eighty-eight years. A humiliating CBA containing virtually all of the owners' demands was reached in July 2005, 301 days after the owners had locked out their players on September 15, 2004; at that point, Goodenow could barely be said to be in charge.

The confusion at the top was reflected in the players' comments after the deal. "My feeling is I'm confused and disappointed," lamented Lightning defenceman Brad Lukowich. "I thought the players were tougher on this."

"Why did we sit out all year to do this?" asked Flyers forward Turner Stevenson.

"Am I mad? No. I want to get back to work. But at the same time, I'm just a little disappointed that it went this far to play poker and to have someone call your bluff," said Matthew Barnaby of Chicago.

With a new CBA containing humiliating salary caps and links to league revenues for salaries finalized in principle, Goodenow was suddenly a man on an island, supported by only a small coterie on the NHLPA executive council and in the membership. Faced with a nasty public fight with Saskin and Linden for power and a CBA he privately repudiated, Goodenow accepted his fate when Linden terminated him in the days after the CBA was signed. But the price of impulsively ridding the NHLPA of its leader had been formidable. Despite the fact that the union lost over a billion dollars in salaries for 2004–05 and that all existing contracts were rolled back by 24 per cent, Goodenow was to receive almost all of the approximately $7 million he was owed through the end of his deal. It was a huge price that would enrage many in the membership who'd lost millions thanks to Goodenow's lockout leadership. Added to the inflated $2 million salary Saskin demanded for himself, NHL players were paying out a small fortune to their union officials to accept the NHL's bidding.

Linden's actions in summarily dismissing Goodenow and handing the job to Saskin subsequently set off a civil war within the NHLPA as well, pitting teammates against each other over the direction of their union. Saskin supporters, anxious to distance themselves from the disastrous results of the lockout, claimed Saskin was the right man even if his hiring process was flawed and so let's move on—as if it were a hockey game they'd lost, not a struggle for a stake in their business. When dissidents refused to consent to Saskin's hiring, a late-night conference call was held to coerce the opponents into voting for the hire—even though the vote violated the union's constitution. Next, a mail-in vote was staged with thirty-seven ballots being sent out to teams and NHLPA executive members. Though nine voters abstained and four others voted against, Saskin trumpeted the vote as a resounding confirmation of his leadership.

Still, opponents, headed by former NHLPA vice-president Trent Klatt, did not disappear. They demanded to know why a union that had meticulously hired Goodenow after a lengthy search had not followed the same scrutiny when it gave Saskin the job without examining any other candidates. Or why Saskin had been awarded a hefty salary increase even as the NHL's average salary dropped by 40 per cent thanks to the deal he'd negotiated. As players began seeing escrow payments as high as 11 per cent clawed back from their paycheques, more voices joined the group asking questions of the new NHLPA brain trust. Perhaps the most passionate objector was former Chicago star Steve Larmer, who resigned from the union to protest Saskin's hiring. Larmer was a survivor of the Alan Eagleson era when the NHLPA was a house union and Eagleson—as executive director—lined his own pockets at players' expense. More than most, Larmer knew the struggles to make the NHLPA a legitimate bargaining unit for players and the price some had paid to make it so. "I am proud to say I worked for one of the most powerful organizations in pro sports," he wrote, "but what has happened over the last nine months and more so in the last ninety days has led me to make a tough decision. I feel I must resign.

"I am resigning because this organization has taken a giant step backwards, back to the days of Eagleson where a select few made decisions for the group. Where there has been misinformation and denial of information to the players which is totally disrespectful. This is something that I and many others worked so hard to get rid of in our organization and it has all returned. This is wrong. Honesty and transparency should be the foundation of this organization and that has been torn away. I remember the Eagleson days when the PA was ruled by the minority and the majority was kept in the dark. Our group of players challenged it, demanded change and received it. We all vowed that those days would not return but lo and behold they have.

"[W]hat has taken place since Bob was let go is unacceptable. No matter how you look at it, it shows a total disregard for all of the players... I feel that under the present conditions with all that is happening I cannot be associated with what is going on."

Marvin Miller, the godfather of sports unionism who turned the Major League Baseball Players Association into a powerful force, ridiculed the union representing hockey players. "The whole thing smells bad," Miller told the *New York Times* in December 2005. "You have a so-called senior adviser who takes the leading role in making one of the worst settlements imaginable and then becomes director of the union." Miller concluded that, "It tells me really what I've known all along. And that is that the NHLPA has never been a legitimate union at any time."

Klatt and about sixty players (including Chris Chelios, Eric Lindros, Ed Belfour and Dominik Hasek) took their grievances to the U.S. National Labor Relations Board and the U.S. Labor Department, where they were turned away on jurisdictional grounds. Later they filed a lawsuit in U.S. court. Then they announced they'd take the case to court.

The capitulation in collective bargaining and the public squabbling over Saskin's accession to the head of the union was a dramatic collapse for the union and Goodenow, its guiding force. When the original edition of *Money Players* went to press in October 2003, they were considered a virtually unbeatable combination, going from strength to strength at the expense of spendthrift owners and inefficient general managers. Goodenow had reversed almost a century of financial and emotional control of his members by owners, turning a house union under felon Alan Eagleson into a formidable opponent for the NHL at the bargaining table. Twice before, Goodenow and the players had schooled owners in the art of negotiating at both the union and the individual-player level.

They'd achieved the turnaround by converting a player's loyalty to the dressing room into a loyalty to the NHLPA as well. Mike Liut, former all-star goalie and now an agent with Octagon, experienced that brotherhood bond in thirteen seasons with St. Louis, Hartford and Washington. "There's no hiding in hockey," says Liut. "There is great symbolism in the fact that the first thing a player does when he enters the room is strip down to his underwear. You're naked in front of your peer group. They know who'll compete, who'll throw snow, who'll take one for the team, who can think out there, who can play, who's limited in these areas. You can't hide from your teammates."

So loyalty to the room is prized above almost every other virtue. What you see here, stays here. For years, this almost Masonic code of secrecy had been a stumbling block for the players. No one exchanged salary information. No one fraternized with players on other teams. No matter how wronged, how humiliated, you sucked it up silently, played the game, and disappeared from the scene with little fanfare. An intractable owner trades you across the continent on your kid's birthday? Deal with it. Your ribs are cracked but there's a four-point game in Chicago tonight? Bite the bullet. Your own union leader Eagleson tells you that you don't belong in the game? Tough.

When NHL players finally got rid of Eagleson as their union boss and united behind Bob Goodenow, the fanatical zeal of the room— so often an impediment—suddenly became a strength. With proper leadership the NHLPA became one of the most cohesive labour organizations in North America and a target for the men who owned and ran the NHL. The mere mention of Goodenow or the squadrons of player agents in the field set management's teeth on edge. And why not? The days of the sweetheart labour deal, orchestrated by Eagleson, were long gone. Bolstered by a strong union and trained agents, NHL players had beaten the owners at their own game, seizing control of hockey's economics.

Before Goodenow, the players were at the mercy of the owners' dictates. As they confronted the owners' lockout in the fall of 2004 many were wealthy beyond their dreams and had bargaining clout employees in other walks of life can only envy. Salaries topped out at $10–11 million U.S. a year and even the median salary of $800,000 a season was a king's ransom in comparison with the meagre stipends of years past. They'd also been helped by an arrogant, inept NHL management class that personified the old Wall Street maxim of "bulls get fat, bears get fat, but pigs get slaughtered." Awash with easy money from expansion, TV, naming rights and merchandise sales, ownership had squandered millions on dubious signings and questionable strategies. The resulting escalation of salaries had swung the pendulum in the players' direction for the first time in NHL history.

As a result, players had gained self-esteem and confidence they'd never known when a bad game, a bad play, could send them to the minors forever. A new, fairer balance had been introduced under the iron hand of Goodenow, which grew progressively more powerful as the twenty-first century arrived. And while some chafed beneath that iron hand, few wanted to interrupt the party. Until the fall of 2004. In the pages that follow, you'll discover how this astonishing transformation of the NHLPA came about and how it was shattered in the cancelled season of 2004–05.

2

The Education of
Bobby Holik

The stone walls of the old courthouse in Kingston, Ontario, shimmer in the summer heat. Not even the cooling breezes off Lake Ontario can lift the humidity that smothers this former colonial outpost on Canada Day. On the old cricket grounds in front of the courthouse, people move from one pool of shade to the next as the sun rises to bake the city.

At a restored Victorian home behind the courthouse, early-morning heat radiates from the flagstones of the patio where a lonely figure contentedly puffs his pipe. Gilles Léger is the director of pro scouting for the New York Rangers, and on this most unhockeylike of days he's on an errand from his boss, Rangers general manager Glen Sather. Léger was here the previous night, and, after a few hours' sleep at the neighbouring Hochelaga Inn, he has come back to play the waiting game.

It's been a week since Robin Big Snake and his family returned home from Toronto, dreams of glory set aside for the time being. Much of the NHL has trooped off to rest exhausted bones and frayed nerves, but Léger is eager to restore the Rangers to the playoffs for the first time in many years. Rangers fans and the voracious maw of the New York media demand action from Sather, who arrived in

Manhattan with much fanfare in June 2000. Two years after tackling the GM's post, Sather has seen his glory stolen by the Rangers' cross-river rivals, the New Jersey Devils, and the revived Islanders out Nassau County way. High-profile trades for Eric Lindros and Pavel Bure have fizzled. Anything less than a playoff appearance in the spring of 2003 and Sather will be considered a failure in the flash-frozen world of New York opinion.

Like Sather, the unassuming Léger has been around hockey most of his life. If there's a sense of urgency in the balding super-scout, it's impossible to detect as the sun climbs above the trees. This year, Canada's birthday also happens to be Independence Day for the NHL's unrestricted free agents, and Léger is patiently awaiting the opportunity to tell Bobby Holik, Tony Amonte, and Mike Richter why they should be wearing the blue, white, and red of the Rangers next fall.

Léger will not speak directly to these unrestricted free agents. He'll address their agent, Mike Gillis, the former Boston Bruins and Colorado Rockies player who lives in this perfectly appointed heritage home. Gillis is upstairs in pyjama bottoms and T-shirt, drinking coffee and checking voice mail in the un-air-conditioned room that serves as his office. While other agents work from lavish suites, served by squads of assistants, Gillis works alone in the spare room of his family home at an antique wooden dinner table. His tools are basic: laptop, cellphone, office phone, fax machine. The decor is restrained as well; there are no photos of Gillis grinning beside clients such as Holik, Bure, or Pavol Demitra, no scintillating action shots of Amonte, Mathieu Dandenault, or Markus Naslund. There are rustic paintings of Quebec winter scenes on the walls, and wine catalogues and notebooks piled about the floor. The only concession to his trade is a neat stack of NHL jerseys on an heirloom chair by the door. From the whirr of the oscillating fan in the corner, you'd be hard pressed to identify this as the lair of a man who wrote $39,450,000 (all figures in U.S. dollars) in NHL contracts in 2001–02.

The frugality of Gillis's operation draws a crack this morning from Islanders GM Mike Milbury, once Gillis's teammate in Boston. "He just left a message," smiles Gillis from behind the desk. "He says, 'You're such a cheap prick to not even have someone answer your phone. Call me!'" Milbury's profane, mocking malevolence is typical in the macho world of hockey, and while Gillis is hardly a jock type any more, the boyish banter of the dressing room still brings a smile to his usually impassive face.

Gillis has reasons to smile today—millions of them. The forty-four-year-old player-turned-lawyer has been looking forward to his clients' becoming unrestricted free agents under the terms of the NHL's collective bargaining agreement. As of today, they are free to reap the kind of salaries that make NHL management figures weep and ordinary people shake their heads. Gillis, who sold his business to Assante Corporation, a financial-management company, in 2000 and now works under their banner, was up till three in the morning, handling phone calls and awaiting offers from teams eager to bid on Holik, Amonte, and Richter. There were no early bids, and now Gillis has awoken to scan the morning market for hockey stars.

Adam Oates, he notes, is a surprise early signing. The veteran centre inked a two-year deal at $3.5 million a season with the Mighty Ducks of Anaheim just after midnight. A brilliant set-up man with more than 1,000 career assists, Oates has been recruited to feed passes to superstar Paul Kariya, who's been languishing in mediocrity with the Disney-owned team. To get Oates at the trade deadline, the Philadelphia Flyers had sacrificed goalie prospect Maxime Ouellet and two first-round draft picks to Washington. But after being eliminated in round one of the 2002 playoffs, the Flyers have let Oates walk to the West Coast for nothing. This leads many to wonder what Bobby Clarke, the Flyers GM, has to do to get fired.

The salary the Ducks have agreed to pay the forty-year-old centre has Gillis licking his chops. NHL commissioner Gary Bettman has again promised restraint and sobriety in bidding for unrestricted free agents this summer, but Gillis knows that local market forces will cause many owners once more to ignore Bettman's call. He knows that a flood of platitudes and outright bribes from desperate teams will flow to his clients this day. And he knows that Léger, a former NHL GM, is not waiting on his patio to work on a tan.

As he sips coffee, Gillis learns that the Rangers have offered the first blandishment of the day. At the homes of Holik, Amonte, and Richter, delivery companies have brought crystal Tiffany apples and dvd players loaded with a "welcome to New York" message from Big Apple luminaries such as David Letterman. Meanwhile, Dallas owner Tom Hicks (the man who signed Alex Rodriguez to a stunning $252-million contract to play shortstop for his Texas Rangers baseball team) is loading Stars general manager Doug Armstrong, special assistant Guy Carbonneau, and head coach Rick Wilson into a Gulfstream 5 jet to hop across the continent for visits with their free-agent targets, reportedly including Holik and Amonte. It all augurs well.

But Gillis is in no hurry to finalize a contract before lunch. "We've got to let everybody get in there and throw punches," he says. "First you create a market, get a few offers on the table. Then you stand back and let them fight it out." There have been accusations from Amonte's old boss, Chicago's crusty owner Bill Wirtz, that the entire contract process with his soon-to-be-ex-captain has been orchestrated in advance by Gillis. Wirtz, once the powerful chairman of the NHL's Board of Governors, claims that Amonte will sign for $7.5 million a season with the Stars and that people are fooling themselves if they think otherwise.

Gillis bridles at this impugning of his professional integrity. "Bill Wirtz is full of shit. He had every opportunity to sign his captain to a fair contract, and now that he's losing him, he's trying to blame others. I can't stand that stuff."

Perhaps Wirtz, one of America's richest men, feels he can intimidate Gillis, or at least salvage some credibility with his season-ticket holders, who've watched the Blackhawks become a bad joke under his stewardship. If Wirtz does try to bully Gillis, it's likely to be a

futile move. Despite a six-year career in the NHL, Gillis is no senti-
mentalist. His role as an agent is not the culmination of a boyhood
fantasy or some thwarted dream of athletic glory. He's not in the
profession to hobnob with his old pals from his playing days. He
often counsels his clients on how to maximize their talents—and
paycheques—at the NHL level: "Sometimes you have to take a step
back or sideways to get them to understand their own game," he
says. A man whose clientele is almost completely made up of players
disaffected with their previous representation, Gillis has orchestrated
celebrated trades for Pavel Bure to Florida and then to the Rangers
in the glare of public criticism. He has traded barbs and epithets with
the toughest GMs—some of them former teammates or opponents.
He states his goal succinctly: "Maximizing compensation is the first
and foremost part of my job." If Gillis's career were a movie, it
would be *Unforgiven*.

"The agent business is full of guys with big balls," says one high-
ranking NHL management figure. "But Mike Gillis has the biggest
balls of all."

You can probably thank his former agent and union leader, Alan
Eagleson, for Gillis's intransigence. Eagleson and Marvin Goldblatt,
the accountant at Eagleson's Sports Management company, handled
every aspect of Gillis's career from the time he was drafted out of
Kingston of the Ontario Hockey League by the Colorado Rockies in
1978. Gillis paid Eagleson's standard 10 per cent for contracts and
financial management. When Gillis's father died, Goldblatt said he
became "a surrogate father," advising and supporting him. His
injury-plagued career ended in Boston on September 22, 1984, when
he fractured his right ankle in a scrimmage. After doctors told him
he would never play in the NHL again, Gillis decided to retire and
collect the $275,000 (U.S.) in NHL and NHLPA disability insurance to
which he was entitled.

He intended to use the money to help finance his legal education
at Queen's University in Kingston. But Goldblatt informed him there
were problems with the claim: the insurers were balking at paying the

settlement. Gillis was devastated. Eagleson eventually told him he would need to employ legal and accounting help to pressure the insurers (who also happened to be Eagleson's friends and the guarantors of the mortgage on his flat in London, England). The NHLPA boss bragged he would bring in another pal, Supreme Court Justice John Sopinka, to help obtain the money. Eventually Gillis was informed that Eagleson had been successful. For a fee of $41,250, Gillis would receive his payout. Though unhappy to have to pay for what he felt was rightfully his, Gillis accepted the deal and moved on.

There it might have rested if not for the work of groundbreaking journalist Russ Conway of the Lawrence *Eagle Tribune*, a newspaper in the Boston area. Conway had learned that many former Eagleson clients, including Pat Quinn, Dale Tallon, André Savard, Bill White, and Willie Huber, had been charged questionable fees by their agent and union leader to process disputed claims. Conway contacted Gillis to find out about his experience. The young law student rejected Conway's allegations about Eagleson and Goldblatt, whom he trusted implicitly. He and his wife, Diane, wanted to put the incident behind them and get on with their life in Kingston.

When Conway's research was picked up by the *Globe and Mail* in 1994, however, the Gillises decided to look into their old files in the basement. What they found shocked them. The $41,250 in "legal and accounting" payments had in fact gone to Kingsmar Holdings, one of Eagleson's companies, not to outside experts in the U.K. and the U.S. Worse, it appeared that the fees were unjustified. Gillis's insurance comprised three separate claims and, according to the contract, acceptance of one meant that all three claims were valid. Stung by this betrayal, Gillis launched a legal action, suing to recover the amount skimmed by his former mentor and agent, who by now was under investigation by the FBI and the RCMP. Eagleson countersued Gillis for $244,000, hoping that the prospect of a hefty legal bill would scare off his former protegé.

Eagleson discovered what Bill Wirtz was now learning on the Amonte file: Mike Gillis has a stubborn streak. Gillis engaged the services of Charles Scott, Q.C., a star litigator at Tory Tory Deslauriers and Binnington, the firm where Gillis had articled. Scott, who has represented everyone from the big banks to Harold Ballard's daughter, is not a man to be trifled with in a courtroom. Undaunted by Scott's reputation, Eagleson refused a settlement and pushed his countersuit. A trial began in Toronto in September 1996 before Justice Joseph O'Brien. The high-powered Eagleson, pal of prime ministers and captains of business, intended to face down a young man who could lose everything should the decision go against him.

At issue was Eagleson's credibility. Documents showed that Gillis's claim had already been approved by insurers when Eagleson told him he needed legal help. Although there was no evidence of billing during that time, Eagleson insisted he'd verbally warned Gillis that "the meter was running" on his services long before the claims were green-lighted. Eagleson's evidence rested largely on pencilled-in Daytimers, the testimony of cronies, and the intimation that Gillis was simply a malingerer who tried to take the disability money under false pretenses.

If the trial had a pivotal moment, it grew out of a February 13, 1984, appointment Gillis had had with Dr. Charles Bull, a friend of Eagleson's for forty years and one of the physicians who confirmed Gillis's medical disability for insurers. Bull testified he remembered an early-morning appointment and that Gillis had then gone on to Eagleson's office where, Eagleson claimed, he'd warned Gillis about his mounting legal bill. But Gillis and his wife, Diane, contradicted Bull's testimony. She recalled they'd timed the doctor's visit to coincide with the sleeping times of their seven-month-old son, Max. The boy, Diane Gillis testified, had been cranky that morning, and she'd been embarrassed by the ruckus he was creating in the waiting room. When Mike's forty-minute exam ended, she told the court, they'd gone straight to her mother's Toronto home to settle her son, not to Eagleson's office. She told her husband he "was on duty" with Max the rest of the day. This, noted Judge O'Brien, was "more than mere differing recollections." But whom to believe?

In the conflicting testimony, it was the evidence of a young mother trying to cope with a fractious son that stuck with Judge O'Brien. "I find Diane's evidence on this point vivid and persuasive," he said. On this key recollection, O'Brien believed the former player, not his glib former agent and union boss. Indeed, O'Brien thought little of Eagleson's evidence and behaviour. Eagleson at one point admitted lying to Gillis about getting Sopinka's help while dissembling to the insurers about the amount of the claims.

In his finding, the silver-haired judge observed that Eagleson had demonstrated "an ability to mislead and lie with documents in his testimony. . . . I concluded cross-examination of Eagleson demonstrated he was attempting to mislead the court and he had also attempted to mislead Gillis." O'Brien also witnessed the famous hat dance seen by so many players who'd been denied help by their union leader. While acknowledging the work Eagleson did put in getting the claim approved, O'Brien said Eagleson "never gave Gillis any details of what he was doing nor did he explain in what capacity he was working. . . . Eagleson was wearing a number of 'hats' at the time—acting as director of the NHLPA, player agent, lawyer and friend/advisor. There was a great deal of cross-over activity in connection with all these roles."

As for Goldblatt's performance, O'Brien "found his alleged lack of recollection astounding." The judge awarded Gillis the $41,250 his former agent had skimmed, plus interest, plus $30,000 in punitive damages. Eagleson was also ordered to pay $446,000 in legal costs. Eagleson disputed the legal bill, but Judge O'Brien pointed out that it was his own "laboriously calculated" counterclaim that had lengthened the trial and increased the court fees. As Charles Scott succinctly put it, "Because Eagleson was so greedy trying to screw Michael out of $41,250, it cost him $520,000."

Gillis took little satisfaction in bringing Eagleson to ground (it was the only time the former NHLPA director ever gave evidence on the stand in the seven years between the start of the FBI's investigation and his pleading guilty to six criminal charges in 1997). He had lost the mentorship of Eagleson and the deep personal friendship with Goldblatt. He'd also risked his financial future to expose Eagleson as a liar and a cheat. But few in the hockey world bothered to attend the trial or stand behind him in his moment of need. Both in and out of court, Gillis had to listen to intimations that he was a shirker, a quitter. Moreover, NHL establishment figures such as Serge Savard were suggested as possible witnesses for the disgraced Eagleson.

Had Gillis's mistrust of the NHL power structure not been solidified by the unhappy end to his playing career, it was carved in stone by his emotionally draining, three-year legal ordeal with Eagleson and the deception of his friend Goldblatt. There's no hazy nostalgia, no cozy chumminess, no "for the good of the game" platitudes in Mike Gillis. Not for the first time, the NHL had created its own worst adversary.

In Gillis's view, Bill Wirtz was a part of that recidivist hockey culture when he suggested Gillis was breaking the collective bargaining rules by arranging Amonte's signing in advance—the old bully-boy tactics. After Wirtz's blast, one thing was clear: none of Gillis's prize clients was going to end up in the livery of the Blackhawks.

One of the first calls Gillis receives on Canada Day morning is from client Bobby Holik, at home in New Jersey. After twelve years of being told where to play, the bruising centre will finally call the shots this day. Informed that no offers have materialized so far, Holik is philosophical. "I took a risk that I wouldn't have a good season or that I might get hurt. Why shouldn't I wait a little longer?" he says by phone. "I'm a believer in happy family, happy player. And happy player, happy team. So if my family is happy with this deal, it will be good for everyone." Holik has been resisting the overtures of Devils GM Lou Lamoriello for months now (Lamoriello had made an offer of $8 million a year the previous day), and he's prepared to wait one day more to hear what value other teams put on his services. "He tried to come to me in February to talk about a deal,"

Holik says, "but I said, 'This is when I'm playing hockey. Talk to Mike.' I even heard he was trying to get my dad [legendary Czech star Jaroslav Holik] involved, but I put an end to that right away."

Holik, Boston forward Bill Guerin, and Toronto goalie Curtis Joseph are the prized players in this year's crop of unrestricted free agents. To some, the notion that Holik (who had 25 goals and 29 assists in 2001–02 for the Devils) might set a new salary benchmark is an unfathomable mystery and indicative of all that's wrong with pro sports. The thirty-one-year-old, six-foot-four, 230-pound centre is no prized box-office attraction. He's not seen in the company of Hollywood starlets or international financiers. His career scoring totals equal about three of Wayne Gretzky's best seasons. He's a frank interview and a hard worker, but if people wanted to see hard work, they'd buy tickets to the production line at General Motors. Yet Holik, Gillis suspects, will be ardently pursued by as many as a dozen NHL clubs, all convinced that the native of Jihlava, Czech Republic, will help them replace Detroit as Stanley Cup champion next June.

Why such keen interest? Holik is an implacable, intimidating foe with massive legs and a torso harder than hickory. He has reduced offensive stars such as Toronto's Mats Sundin to near catatonia in the playoffs, wearing them down with brute strength and punishing two-handers on the arms, wrists, hands, and stick. Like most Europeans, Holik rarely fights; but this doesn't mean he's soft on the opposition. A night battling him in the slot is like a night in the ring with Lennox Lewis. Such players have always been a hallmark of winning clubs, going back to meat grinders such as Bert Olmstead, Gary Dornhoefer, and Clark Gillies. "He battles, he's not afraid," says Devils captain Scott Stevens. "He's courageous, he uses his size well. Is there another player in the league like him? I don't think so."

Most in the NHL agree. Other teams also like the fact that he has a chip on his shoulder the size of Ellis Island because of his treatment by Lamoriello. While Stevens, Patrik Elias, Petr Sykora, and Martin Brodeur received much of the credit for the Devils' two Stanley Cup wins in 1995 and 2000, it was Holik's fierce dominance at centre ice that gave his more celebrated teammates the room to manoeuvre. With Holik as sheriff, they felt secure walking the streets. Lamoriello admitted as much in the weeks leading up to July 1. "I have nothing but the highest admiration for the things Bobby has done for this hockey team. If I'm able to put my players on the order of importance, there's no question I put him on the highest level."

But subordinating his offence to do the dirty work did not translate into dollars for Holik, who began his NHL career in 1990 with the Hartford Whalers (now the Carolina Hurricanes). "Lou likes to play the angles," Holik had explained the previous November. Seated next to his wife, Renee, and agent Gillis in the lounge of the Plaza Athenee Hotel in Manhattan, wearing wire-rimmed glasses and an open-necked shirt, he recalled the way the club rewarded Stevens and Brodeur with handsome new contracts. "Lou could have had me [in the summer of 2001], but I wasn't high enough on his priority list. He had to take care of other people first. So I've decided I'm going to wait and see what happens on July 1." Told Lamoriello had nothing but praise for him, Holik smiled thinly. "Lou will tell you all sorts of nice things. He doesn't like agents. He's been trying to drive a wedge between Mike and me. I've been with Mike for ten years, I trust him with everything. Last year, I didn't have the leverage. This year I do. It's all about the bottom line."

Adding to Holik's determination was his salary arbitration in the summer of 2001. After hearing for years that his sacrifices for the team would be rewarded, Holik was crestfallen when, during arbitration, the Devils pointed to his modest scoring statistics as a reason to lower his salary request. "Nobody respects Bobby's contributions to this team more than me," Lamoriello remarked later. "But you can't just give the money away." Instead of the $4.2 million a season Holik was seeking, he was awarded $3.5 million. His teammate Sykora, a flashy Czech who is much less vigilant than Holik defensively, also went through arbitration that summer. While any hockey student would tell you Holik's contributions to the Devils were more important, Sykora was awarded roughly the same salary by the arbitrator.

As he sipped a soda water in the Plaza Athenee, Holik recalled that decision. "It took me a few weeks of talking to Mike to sort things out. I needed time to absorb everything. To put it in perspective. When the season started, I think I'd done that. Some of my teammates may have had questions about my commitment, but I think I answered them with my play." In fact, Holik's 54 points—his best output in four years—and his four goals in the Devils' playoff loss to Carolina were eloquent testimony to his clear-minded dedication. In the heat of July, his earlier estimate of a $7-million salary offer now looked very under market.

Lamoriello's final offer had matched the $8-million-per-year contract awarded the previous summer to Brodeur, but Gillis had concerns about the deferred portion of the salary. The great Mario Lemieux had been stung by taking deferred money in Pittsburgh, only to see the club slide into bankruptcy. Lemieux took ownership of the Penguins to save his millions. "Who's going to even own the Devils in ten years?" Gillis asked as he sipped a coffee. "What guarantees does that give Bobby?"

Holik agreed: "Lou was always trying to mask it, use deferred money. Mike kept telling him, 'What don't you get? He's not taking deferred money. It's got to be up front.'" Gillis's concerns would be reinforced in early 2003 when the bankruptcy of the Ottawa Senators and Buffalo Sabres would jeopardize the deferred money of former players and employees.

Gillis has changed into shorts and a golf shirt by the time Leafs assistant GM Bill Watters calls. A team without a Stanley Cup in thirty-five years (only Chicago has waited longer for another Cup win), the Leafs are under the microscope of a pitiless media and passionate fans. No team is scrutinized more closely, and after another frustrating playoff run ended in a semifinal loss to Carolina—and a healthy hike in ticket prices—Watters is under pressure to do some-thing, anything, to get his club over the hump. With Mats Sundin in his prime and Alex Mogilny matured into a playmaker as well as a sniper, Watters knows the clock is ticking to add a dominant element such as Holik to the mix.

The Leafs are widely regarded by agents as a soft touch in nego-tiations. The previous summer they'd showered $3 million a year to bring the laconic Robert Reichel back from Europe; after 21 goals in the regular season, Reichel scored exactly zero goals in the Leafs' eighteen 2002 playoff contests. They also paid indifferent defence-man Anders Eriksson $1.5 million to play barely half their games. Yet their fans are under the impression that the club is cheap and penny-pinching.

The latest Leafs soap opera involves star goalie Curtis Joseph, who has also decided to take the plunge into unrestricted free agency. Joseph turned down the Leafs' offer of $15 million over two years during the season (he wanted $17 million), and a nasty public-relations war (stirred up by Joseph's agent, Don Meehan) was fought in the media. There were allegations from Joseph's camp that Pat Quinn, the Toronto coach and GM, had left Joseph to rot on the bench during Canada's Olympic victory in Salt Lake City, and that the Leafs didn't appreciate their stalwart goalie. Then Joseph almost refused to shake Quinn's hand at a public ceremony honouring the Canadian Olympic hockey teams at the Air Canada Centre. After a shaky start in the 2002 post-season, Joseph's star turn in Toronto's playoff loss to Carolina preserved his value in the free-agent market. In the days leading up to July 1, it looked as if the two sides might be close to a deal to keep the Keswick, Ontario, native in blue and white. It never happened.

Now, as Joseph becomes a free agent, Watters knows he must make a splash on more than just the goalie front. He has targeted Holik as Toronto's top choice of free agents. Joseph can wait. (Watters's confidence in his ability to re-sign Joseph, combined with an undercutting offer from another free-agent goalie, Ed Belfour, will

cause a bitter Joseph to abandon a higher offer from Toronto to sign
with Detroit the next day.)

Watters, once the most prominent player agent after Eagleson, is
calling Gillis from his summer home in Orillia. After the obligatory
small talk, Gillis caresses an offer from the Leafs. "Uh-huh," he says,
scribbling in his legal notebook. "That's $38 million...five years.
Right. Any room for movement on that? What are we talking about
here? Okay...I told Bobby we'd gather these offers and I'll be talking to him soon."

Gillis hangs up. "Thirty-eight over five. There's a chance he can
bump it to forty. Now we're getting a little traction here."

The phone rings again. It's Tony Amonte, calling from his home in
Massachusetts. The Chicago captain is about to meet the Stars' travelling retinue and wants Gillis's counsel on how to handle the meeting.

Amonte is a rare commodity in the defensive-minded NHL, averaging 36 goals a year for the past seven seasons. He's also virtually
indestructible, having played 650 straight regular-season games, a
phenomenal streak given the physical pounding of the current game.
For Dallas, which failed to make the playoffs just three years after
winning the Stanley Cup, he seems a natural fit. But the Hawks'
soulless capitulation in the first round of the playoffs against St.
Louis (Amonte had just one assist in five games) is thought to reflect
badly on him. If holding one bad week against a player seems unfair,
welcome to the NHL, where "what have you done for me lately?" is
gospel. While Holik's value has soared in the past year, Amonte's has
levelled off. His seasonal statistics have declined in the past few
years. After torturous negotiations that included everyone from
Hawks GM Mike Smith through team president Bob Pulford right up
to owner Wirtz, Chicago's final offer to Amonte was $5.4 million a
year. Gillis estimates Amonte's free-agent value at $7.5 million.
Placing Amonte with Chicago's division rival Dallas would be sweet
revenge, but there have been hints that the Stars would prefer
Boston's 41-goal scorer Bill Guerin. Gillis's worst nightmare this day
is for Guerin to sign with the Stars at less than market value, drag-

ging down Holik's value and removing a bidder from the Amonte
sweepstakes.

Gillis leans back in his chair to counsel Amonte on strategy.
"Here's what you'll say, Tony. 'I care about winning. I've played 650
straight games. I can make your team better.' Don't be afraid of your
accomplishments. Let them know how you can make them win
again. You'll be awesome."

Amonte asks how things are going.

"A little quiet so far," says Gillis. "Maybe Gary [Bettman] has
been urging these guys to wait us out a little. Listen, New York and
Dallas say they may want to package you and Holik. I told them they
might have to pay a premium to do that. Don't worry. Call me."

Gillis hangs up, presses his voice-mail button. "You have five new
messages..." Reporters from Toronto and New York, and someone
from Detroit who hopes Gillis might squeeze in a televised interview.
As if.

While Amonte heads off to meet with the Stars in Massachusetts,
Canadiens GM André Savard calls from Montreal. He and Gillis discuss the many millions at play for Holik as if talking about the price
of lawn mowers. For the Habs, still trying to sign their star goalie
José Théodore and veteran centre Doug Gilmour, Holik is the type
of player who could push them to the top of the Eastern Conference.
Montreal's a small team that could use his bulk. But Holik's price tag
for any Canadian franchise outside Toronto is daunting. Gillis hangs
up. "Too rich for his blood," he says, crossing Montreal's name out
of his notebook.

Next up is GM Dean Lombardi of San Jose, who is also thought
to have some interest in Amonte. It's soon clear that the Sharks, who
must deal with Teemu Selanne first, are not about to make any firm
offers. So Gillis tries to massage the market for his guys. "I know
what Gary's saying about the league, but he's got to realize that
there's a different dynamic at work in each of the markets. He can't
be penalizing large markets who need to do what's good for them."
Lombardi makes reassuring noises, but it's clear the Sharks are not

players on this day. Gillis hangs up with a few choice words about the NHL commissioner and his efforts to restrain market forces.

Asked how the Rangers can justify the numbers it will take to sign Holik, Amonte, and Mike Richter (who's waiting for his wife to deliver their third child at any moment), Gillis points out that in the cable-TV market in Manhattan there can be as much as a $40-million swing in revenues for the Rangers if they win. In that context, $7 million or $8 million a year for a hockey player can be a worthwhile investment.

Though both his phones are jammed with callers by late morning, it's who's not calling that Gillis notes. Detroit, Atlanta, the Rangers, St. Louis—all thought to be active bidders on free-agent day—have yet to show their hands. "Sather's playing Twister with me," says Gillis. Rumour has it that Bettman has imposed a 1 p.m. moratorium on offers to free-agent players, and the scuttlebutt has some agents getting antsy. Of course, if rumours were wheels, everyone in the NHL would be a bus. The latest rumour has Washington signing centre Robert Lang at $5 million a year for five years to bolster the spirits of ex-Pittsburgh buddy Jaromir Jagr. Depending on whom you talk to, this is either pure fabrication or a done deal (it turns out to be the latter). Such a financial commitment to an 18-goal scorer seems like good news for all free agents.

Gillis heads down to the kitchen for a quick lunch. By the time he's back in his office, Amonte has returned from meeting the Dallas brass. Things went well with Hicks, Armstrong, and Carbonneau, who are now off to see Bill Guerin (he lives near Amonte in Massachusetts). Dallas GM Armstrong (son of former NHL linesman Neil Armstrong) will call back at one-thirty to present Dallas's offers for Holik and Amonte. It will be the pivotal point of the day, Gillis believes. "We have to get someone out of the box, someone to make an offer," he tells Amonte soothingly. "If they give you $7.5 for five, do you want it? Okay..."

Gillis heads downstairs to meet, finally, with Gilles Léger, who will outline the Rangers' offers for Holik, Amonte, and Richter. The two men know each other well, going back to Gillis's days in the Ontario Hockey League. Sather will be the closer on any deals, but Léger is the trusted emissary. Gillis knows that Sather wants Holik for several very local reasons: he craves Holik's Messier-like toughness for the Rangers (who now ironically include the aging Messier himself); he doesn't want his players facing Holik in a Devils uniform six times a season; and he'd score a public-relations coup against the tristate rivals from New Jersey.

Then there's the Dolan factor. Since Jim Dolan's firm Cablevision acquired the Rangers, the chief executive has become "very, very, very, very involved" in the running of the Rangers, says former general manager Neil Smith. "Cablevision believes if every company has one CEO, we should have ten." That philosophy extends to hockey players, too, says Smith. While he tried to rebuild an aging 1994 Stanley Cup team with younger players, Smith says, Dolan was obsessed with the latest veteran free agents, whether they fit the Rangers or not. When winger Theo Fleury—who'd already been in rehab for substance-abuse problems—became a free agent in the summer of 1999, Dolan insisted Smith fly west to get him. "He told me I had to come back with him," says Smith. "If I didn't, I was through." When Smith questioned the advisability of signing the emotionally volatile Fleury, Dolan replied, "It's my money." Fleury was signed, but subsequently checked into another rehab centre; Smith was fired and replaced by Sather. Clearly, Dolan has been telling Sather that he wants Holik on his team in 2002–03.

But Holik wants to play with a winning club. The Rangers, having missed the playoffs five years in a row before 2003, will have to pay a generous premium to persuade him to help Eric Lindros, Pavel Bure, and Brian Leetch revive their underachieving team. The Rangers will have to top offers from Toronto, New Jersey, Dallas, and perhaps other teams, by a considerable margin to land him.

At one-thirty, Dallas's Armstrong phones back as promised. Gillis's pen is poised above a legal notebook, ready for what he hopes will be benchmark offers from a team with deep pockets. He

can use the Dallas offers to lever the other Holik and Amonte bidders. No such luck. Dallas is offering Holik $6.5 million a year for
four years, Amonte $5.5 million for four. Their current teams have
already offered more.

Gillis's thick shoulders sag, but his voice doesn't betray disappointment. "I don't think that's going to get it done with either guy,"
Gillis tells Armstrong. Indeed, the Stars will sign Guerin much later
in the day for five years at $9 million per, and remain non-players in
bidding for both Holik and Amonte.

And so the stalemate drags on through the afternoon. Gillis's only
consolation, amid a steady stream of calls from reporters, friends, and
contacts, is that no one else is getting much business done either. By
dinnertime, Detroit—the big spender the previous summer, when it
signed or traded for Dominik Hasek, Brett Hull, Luc Robitaille, and
Fredrik Olausson—surfaces with its offer for Curtis Joseph. The
Wings want him to replace the retiring Hasek, but they appear to be
coming in below Toronto's offer. Gillis senses that something is happening behind the scenes in Toronto, but it won't become official till
the next day that the Leafs goaltending star has severed ties with the
club. (Insiders will say that the problems in the Joseph case lie in communication; they believe GM Pat Quinn, who's in Vancouver losing
weight and treating a heart arrhythmia, is not being told what's really
going on in the top-heavy Toronto organization.) The Kingston agent
can only speculate on whether this is good or bad for Holik.

Gillis phones Holik to brief him and wife Renee on the three
offers to date. Holik has a high-pitched voiced that belies his massive
frame, and the Middle European habit of talking from his tonsils.
His questions for Gillis are incisive and, though several clubs have
lowballed or made no offers whatsoever, he betrays no anxiety. "We
knew it was not a matter of yes or no," he will say later. "We knew
it was just, how good is it going to get? So I was calm."

Although Holik would prefer not to move from his home in New
Jersey, there's a feeling that the Leafs will bump their $40-million
offer, believing they'll become a Cup contender with him. Then there

are the Rangers. "Okay, I'll talk to you after I speak to Glen," says Gillis, winding up the call.

By six-fifteen, Gillis has Sather on the phone. The two men are friendly adversaries with a healthy mutual respect. There's no need for flattery; they both know what's at stake. Still, the heat of the day is only now breaking in Kingston, and an urgency has settled in the agent's office, a desire to get this done. This is a typical phase in negotiations, when emotions or fatigue can start to dictate a deal.

"Tell me a number, Glen, that I can take to my client." Sather's not prepared to be tied down, and they agree to speak again within the hour. Gillis calls Holik to tell him he thinks Sather will make an offer soon. "What's it going to take for you to play in New York?" he asks.

"I think $9 million across the board for five years would be good," says Holik matter-of-factly. The two men set to work designing a payment schedule: a $4-million signing bonus and $2-million payments to be made on July 1 each year throughout the life of the contract. They agree they will not ask for personal bonuses or a no-trade clause. Gillis—who has negotiated these sorts of deals for Pavel Bure (who makes $10 million a year)—reads back the figures. "Is that what you want?"

There's only the slightest pause. "Yes. I'll have no doubt about it if that's what they offer. That's what it will take."

While Gillis waits for Sather to call back, Gilles Léger pops his head in the door. He's on his way back to Toronto, his work done. There's a twinkle in his eye. At this moment in a long, trying day he may be the only one who believes a deal will get done to bring Holik across the river to Madison Square Garden.

As he says goodbye to Léger, Gillis fields a call from Mike Milbury about Amonte. On the surface, the Islanders look like a good fit for a speedy winger such as Amonte, who could play alongside either Alexei Yashin or Mike Peca. The Isles also look like a team on the upswing, with new owners and their first playoff appearance in eight seasons. The big question is whether, leveraged by the contracts of Yashin ($6.4 million plus bonuses), Peca ($3.25 million), and goalie Chris Osgood ($3.75 million)—they can find another $7 million per for Amonte. Gillis tells his former teammate, "Tony understands the importance of players twenty-three, twenty-four, twenty-five years old like you have, your centre-ice men, your coach [Peter Laviolette]. He likes your team." Milbury and Gillis continue their dance, but there is still no offer from Long Island when they hang up.

Gillis phones Amonte at his home. "Milbury thinks you're a perfect fit with the coach and the situation." He assures Amonte, who was disappointed by the Stars' offer, that there will be a market for him. "At the end of the day, the guys who don't sign Holik or Guerin are going to come looking for you. We're going to get traction on you soon." (In fact, it will take another week and a lot of traction before Amonte finds a home with the Phoenix Coyotes at $6 million a year for four years.)

It's almost eight-thirty, and with the first hint of nightfall, firecrackers bang outside Gillis's window to start the Canada Day celebrations. Inside, too, the fireworks are about to start. On the line is Sather. He outlines the Rangers' offer: $43.75 million for five years, with the signing-bonus schedule outlined by Gillis. That's $8.75 million a year, an epic contract for Holik.

"Bobby told me he wants $9 million," says Gillis, not missing a beat. "If you tell me you'll do that, I won't go back to any other teams. We'll have a deal." On the other end of the line, Sather is the one playing Twister now. The Rangers GM, a proponent of fiscal sanity when he managed Edmonton, a small market, is now fuelled by the Cablevision money that runs Madison Square Garden. He asks for a little time, knowing his window of opportunity could close quickly and allow other teams back into the bidding.

Gillis calls Holik again with the latest number. If the rugged centre is happy, you wouldn't know it from his voice.

"So what do you want to do?" asks Gillis.

"I want $9 million," Holik says.

"I think you're right," says Gillis. "I'll call him back."

"He definitely wants the $9 million," Gillis tells Sather. "He'll take the signing bonus as per your offer. No no-trade clause. If that's all right, you can have him right now." Sather asks for a moment. Gillis smiles as he cups his hand over the receiver. He has two dozen phone messages waiting, but this game is heating up. "Glen says Brian Leetch is telling people he's happy because he won't have to play against Bobby any more. Brian must not know how hard Bobby practises."

The phone rings: a reporter asking, "Any news?" Gillis fobs him off with a few cryptic comments. The wink while stringing along a media source tells bystanders that Gillis is in his element.

Sather rings back. It's a done deal: $45 million over five years; $4 million to sign; $2 million on July 1 in 2003, 2004, 2005, and 2006. The rest in salary. Just one wrinkle: Holik must purchase half a corporate box per game for charitable purposes.

"How much is that, Glen?" asks Gillis. Sather says he'll get a price on the charitable donation. Gillis wonders how they'll announce the deal. "Are you going to call Bobby? He wants to know how to handle the press." Sather says his staff will take care of the announcement.

It's nine o'clock. Gillis has been up since seven that morning, with only a pause for lunch. Downstairs there's some special wine for a small celebration with family and friends. Diane Gillis, once a world-ranked long-jumper for Canada, sticks her head in the office door. All day she has shepherded their three children to summer camps, friends' homes, and shopping, keeping the house quiet. She remembers when Mike was a struggling law student with a bum leg and a crooked agent. She's been friends with Bobby and Renee Holik for years, many of them spent in tough hockey towns, battling injury and disappointment. Perhaps no one besides her husband can better understand the joy, the relief of this day.

"Holik's done," Gillis tells her. "Nine million, five years."

Diane shakes her head in amazement, exhaling loudly.

"Now you can buy the curtains," he adds. Player representatives typically charge anywhere from 1.5 per cent for simple contract negotiations up to 10 per cent for a full package that includes financial management, promotion, and legal work. Whatever Gillis's take on the Holik deal, Diane will be able to afford new curtains.

An hour later, Bobby Holik's voice comes across the TV, discussing his new deal. There is the same level tone to Holik's voice. This is clearly a cool customer. Gillis sips a 1989 Château Clinet in his well-appointed kitchen. As he unwinds from the Holik deal, his ear is cocked to the sports news. Robert Lang is confirmed at $25 million in Washington. Curtis Joseph is undecided in Toronto. Bill Guerin looks like he'll land in Dallas for the $45 million also won by Holik. There's work to do tomorrow: Tony Amonte and Mike Richter are still unsigned. "It's a way different market this year," he'd told Richter earlier in the evening. "It's like pulling teeth. Glen's going to grind the snot out of us."

Sather does indeed grind Gillis and Richter for three days before the acrobatic goalie re-signs with the Rangers at $4 million a year for two years. The idea is that Richter will split the netminding duties with young phenom Dan Blackburn in order to rest his surgically repaired thirty-six-year-old knees. (Unfortunately, Richter will suffer a severe concussion in December and miss the rest of the season.) Amonte, a week later, will sign with Phoenix. The public will gasp that someone was willing to pay Bobby Holik $45 million at a time when Gary Bettman described the NHL as teetering on financial ruin. Toronto fans, angry not to have landed a marquee free agent, will batter the Leafs for not getting Holik, Guerin, Amonte, or defenceman Darius Kasparaitis (who signs for seven years at $2 million a year with the Rangers).

The disbelief at such rich contracts is all the more marked because the NHL had been the sport that traditionally kept a lid on salaries. While baseball, football, and basketball saw huge salary leaps in the

1960s, 1970s, and 1980s, NHL stars were compensated meagrely in comparison. As recently as 1990–91, the NHL's top salary was the $3 million doled out by Bruce McNall's Kings to Wayne Gretzky. Just ten other players, including Mario Lemieux and Brett Hull, made more than a million that season.

By Bobby Holik's final year in New Jersey, ninety-one players were making $3 million or better; 346 were paid a million or more. The league's player payroll had shot from $195.2 million in 1991–92 to $1.1 billion in 2001–02. And while team revenues had also soared, Bettman moaned to anyone who'd listen that they hadn't kept pace with salaries. How had this happened in the span of ten seasons? What caused a modest, anachronistic little business ("the Albania of pro sports," as one journalist called the NHL) to lose fiscal sanity?

Gary Bettman could be forgiven if, replying to that question, he borrowed a line from the Bard: "But I am fortune's fool."

3

Bread and Circuses

It is hockey's version of the Last Supper, a tableau instantly recognizable to any hockey fan. The date: August 9, 1988, eleven weeks after the Edmonton Oilers' fourth Stanley Cup triumph. The place: the Molson Room, at the brewery's Edmonton headquarters. Wayne Gretzky, tanned, newly married, greatest player of his generation, dramatically daubs the tears from his lean, angular face. He has just announced the unthinkable: the finest scorer ever, hero to a nation, he has been exiled to Los Angeles, where ice is found floating in poolside glasses and most people don't know a puck from a burrito. "I promised Mess [teammate Mark Messier] I wasn't going to do this," Gretzky sniffles, then bursts into a self-mocking laugh.

Behind Gretzky sit the men who have directed his career since he arrived in the Alberta capital from the Indianapolis Racers of the WHA in 1978: Oilers owner Peter Pocklington, a look of doomed resignation on his bearded face; Glen Sather, president, general manager, sometime coach of the Oilers since Gretzky's arrival, an ironic smirk on his lips; Mike Barnett, the former restaurateur (who, as Gretzky's agent, has guided the Great One's career), his mind already a thousand miles away in Los Angeles; and Messier, the bookend centre of the great Oilers team, looking like he's lost his best friend with the departure of Gretzky.

He's losing three friends, actually, for going to Los Angeles with Gretzky are his loyal bodyguard, Marty McSorley, and a gritty centre, Mike Krushelnyski. In return, the Oilers will receive centre Jimmy Carson, promising winger Martin Gélinas, a handful of draft picks, and, most important to the cash-strapped Pocklington, $15 million. For a number of reasons—all of them incomprehensible to fans—Pocklington has felt this was the best moment to move a twenty-seven-year-old who has rewritten the record books in the blue and orange of the Oilers. In a landmark deal he's swapped the greatest offensive player in history at the peak of his powers.

The hockey press will call it a grossly one-sided deal for Kings owner Bruce McNall; years later, even that assessment seems generous to Pocklington. Gretzky will continue to produce exceptional numbers in the Kings' black-and-silver uniform, though not at the mind-boggling rate he achieved in Edmonton. The players the Oilers receive in exchange will do little to fill the void left by Gretzky; and the $15 million is swallowed up within days. A mocking Pocklington will tell the local media that Gretzky's tears at the dais were just for show, a flourish played for the cameras. But history will record that it's the Oilers owner and his NHL partners who will shed real tears as a result of Gretzky's move south. Once a small six-team circuit wedged into the northeast of the continent, the NHL will see Gretzky open up the United States market in the new West, cities with no hockey tradition but plenty of disposable income.

At about the same time as Gretzky is drying his eyes, a drama of equal significance is playing out elsewhere in Edmonton. In his cramped office on the North Saskatchewan River, player agent Ritch Winter is talking by phone to fellow agent Ron Salcer in Los Angeles. The two are not concerned with the Gretzky shocker, however; they're agreeing that the NHL Players' Association must unburden itself of its executive director, Alan Eagleson, who has held the post for twenty-one years. The players' saviour has turned into their worst nightmare. A walking, talking affront to the men who hired him in 1967, Eagleson treats the players as a sideshow in his personal three-ring circus of sports, politics, and business. "We worked for him, not the other way round," says former player Jim Kyte. While the NHL and Eagleson appear to enjoy untold prosperity, the players languish far behind those in their sister team sports. Worse, Eagleson seemingly cannot be made to fight for improvements unless he has a personal stake in the action.

Eagleson's authority is absolute, his methods crudely effective. He calls players "frogs," "shitheads," and worse in tirades before their teammates in an effort to quash dissent. He seems impervious to the occasional challenges that have been mounted against his leadership over the years. Players feel impotent in the face of his power. "Looking back at Alan," says former defenceman Tom Laidlaw, now an agent, "we have to shoulder some of the blame. We hired him to do a job and we allowed him to just go ahead and do what he wanted to do and tell us what to do. And it should have been the other way around. With Alan, it was him going off with Mr. Wirtz and Mr. Ziegler on a yacht someplace and having fun and cutting a deal on the side."

"There was a lack of accountability," says player representative Don Baizley of that era. "Alan just would not answer for things he was doing."

Eagleson may appear unassailable to most players and agents in the summer of 1988, but Winter, an earnest lawyer from Drumheller, Alberta, and Salcer, a former financial consultant from New York, have been plotting strategy nonetheless. Frustrated in their attempts to have Eagleson answer for his dubious running of the Players' Association, they've decided to enlist a hired gun, former NFL Players Association director Ed Garvey. Pitting Garvey against Eagleson—two men of Irish descent—will produce a bare-knuckle brawl fought with nastiness and insults, but it will bear fruit. Within nine months of soliciting Garvey, Winter and Salcer set in motion a process for removing Eagleson from the director's chair at the NHLPA, a process accelerated by the interest of the FBI and the U.S. Justice Department in Eagleson. Eagleson's replacement, former agent Bob Goodenow, will revolutionize the business of the NHL.

"I remember thinking," says lawyer Bob Riley, who went to law school with Goodenow, "that the NHL folks didn't know who they were dealing with when Bob came in. I'd heard stories about Eagleson and how he ran things, and I knew Bob wasn't going to be that kind of guy. They didn't know what they were in for."

Though no one understands it this summer day in Edmonton, pro hockey players have reached their Anno Domini in 1988. The Gretzky trade and the unseating of Eagleson represent the start of a new dynamic, one that finds its origins in the Original Six, considered the most glorious era of NHL hockey—for everyone except the players. The billions that will be lavished on player salaries in the first years of the twenty-first century will be a sweet payback for the actions of the owners in earlier times.

It's the spring of 1955. Two wives of players from the Stanley Cup champion Detroit Red Wings huddle around the living-room radio, listening to the broadcast of a game featuring their husbands, superstar Gordie Howe and journeyman defenceman Benny Woit. Late in the game at the Olympia, Woit accidentally knocks the puck into his own net. His gaffe makes a loser of the Wings. Within seconds of hearing her husband's blunder, Julie Woit gets up and leaves Colleen Howe alone in the living room to listen to the rest of the game. Colleen calls, "Julie, where are you?" From the bedroom, Julie calls back, "I'm packing the baby, and I'm packing the bags. I know when he comes home we'll be gone."

Julie Woit understood the life of the hockey player in the era before unions and million-dollar contracts: if you played for the uncompromising Jack Adams in Detroit, mistakes were not tolerated. She knew her husband's days in a Red Wing uniform were over the instant he put the puck in his own net. Sure enough, Woit was soon dealt to the woeful Chicago Blackhawks in an eight-player trade.

In the NHL's Original Six era (1942–67), the prosperous management of the six teams (the Red Wings, the Blackhawks, the Montreal Canadiens, the Toronto Maple Leafs, the Boston Bruins, and the New York Rangers) ruled absolutely; players such as Benny Woit feared for their livelihoods every day. The psychic scars inflicted in those days were still felt forty years later. The mere mention of Jack Adams was enough to unify players who'd hated each other their entire playing careers. "We were taught to hate each other," said Ted Lindsay, "and we did a very good job of it."

Even Howe, the NHL's top drawing card from 1950 to 1970, felt vulnerable and unappreciated by the Red Wings. His struggles form a template for the times. There was the winter of 1954, when the Red Wings were driving for the first of two straight Stanley Cups and the Howes had their first baby. "Jack Adams told the doctor to keep Colleen and little Marty in the hospital, because they didn't want anything affecting my game," Howe recalled. Only after the game did he learn he'd become a father. Then there was the time Howe tore rib cartilage against the Bruins at Boston Garden. Doubled over in pain, he was told by Adams to get himself to the hospital. The pain-wracked Howe was ferried to hospital in a Boston cab while his team played on without him.

Finally, there was the notorious salary squeeze for the man who played twenty-five seasons in the red and white. Howe had been promised by Bruce Norris, the team's playboy owner, that he'd always be the best-paid player on the team. In 1968, Howe was stunned that teammate Bobby Baun knew his salary—$45,000. Baun further shocked Howe with the news that he himself was making $67,000. "But don't feel bad, Gord," commiserated Baun. "Carl Brewer's making more than both of us at $90,000." When Howe finally spoke up about his experiences after decades of being a good soldier, NHL president John Ziegler threatened him with a libel lawsuit. Said Howe, "I wish I had been smarter. I wouldn't have played so long."

In Toronto, Major Conn Smythe, the Maple Leafs owner, also kept players on a short leash for decades with a military regimen. In the wake of Bill Barilko's Stanley Cup–winning goal in 1951, Cal Gardner, who'd finished seventh in NHL scoring that year with 23 goals and 28 assists, was told he'd be fined an astronomical $1,000. Had he absconded with club funds? Thrown a game? No, at a time when $7,500 was a good salary, Gardner was being docked a grand for letting the lumbering Barilko score the Cup winner instead of potting the goal himself. "He showed me the film and said, 'Now why didn't you put the puck into the net?'" Gardner recalled years later. In the dark room with the film shuttling by, Gardner desperately tried to justify why he'd let Barilko score. Smythe eventually relented and withdrew the fine. "But that was Smythe," remembered Gardner. "No nonsense with him."

Babe Pratt, Smythe's fun-loving defenceman, discovered as much when he tried to explain how he'd allowed an overtime goal against Detroit. The goal had been scored when a Red Wings forward drove the puck between Pratt's legs. A screened Turk Broda, the Leafs goalie, never saw the shot. In the sepulchral dressing room afterwards, Smythe stood accusingly before Pratt's chair. "So what do you say?" Smythe demanded. "Major," the Hall of Fame defenceman replied, "I guess I should've kept my legs closed." Smythe paused a moment and hissed, "No, your mother should've."

Smythe would occasionally reward a favourite player with a cheque—he once sent Bobby Baun $2,800, the amount of the fine Baun had received for brawling with Reggie Fleming of Chicago. But mostly he was tight-fisted, brutal, and direct. In 1951, he traded John McCormack, who'd gotten his girlfriend pregnant; Smythe felt the player's mind would not be on the game with all the turmoil. In 1946, he accused Frank Selke of disloyalty, firing the man who'd kept Maple Leaf Gardens running profitably during Smythe's absence with the Canadian Army during the Second World War. (Selke's farewell note: "Lincoln freed the slaves; I quit.")

Selke left the Leafs for Montreal, where as GM he built eight Stanley Cup winners within fifteen years. The players did not have Selke's ability to start over in a new city of their choice, however. The reserve clause bound a player for life to the last team with whom he had a contract. Unless that player could convince his team to trade him, he was effectively serving a life sentence and could be demoted or recalled an unlimited number of times. Punch Imlach used this stick to punish "insubordinate" players such as Mike Walton, Jim Pappin, Pete Stemkowski, and Billy Harris in Toronto.

The flip side of the reserve clause was a team's right to trade a player anywhere, any time. Even senior players had no say in where they were dealt. Most clubs abused the trade threat, flipping players around like trading cards, sometimes during the Christmas season. Defenceman Larry Hillman played for eight different NHL clubs, five AHL teams, and three WHA teams during his 982-game pro career. Goalie Gary "Suitcase" Smith wore eight NHL jerseys, five AHL sweaters, and one WHA jersey in his 555-game pro career. "Broadway" Nick Mickoski played for four of the Original Six clubs in a ten-year span before embarking on a five-team minor-league career. Demotions and trades were the lot for any free spirit or player who asked too many pointed questions.

Doug Harvey of the Canadiens was one such questioner. During his term on the board of the players' pension fund the great defence-man spoke up often. "What the fellows are interested in," Harvey said at a 1957 meeting, "is if they went into a pension scheme on their own at twenty-two and paid $900 a year until thirty-two...is it true—as they come to me and say—their payments would be bet-ter?" Harvey's boss, Selke, bridled at the question. "How can an intelligent man say that if they put money into some other invest-ment he would have the same return in twenty years? Where can you get the services of men like these directors and Mr. [NHL presi-dent Clarence] Campbell for free?" (Harvey and his fellow players later discovered that, even gratis, the management of the players' pension fund had been no bargain.) The inquisitive Harvey was protected in Montreal by his great skill; when it waned, he was quickly traded away.

It's not entirely fair to condemn Smythe, Selke, or Adams, of course. It was a less forgiving age, populated by rough-hewn men forged by the hard times of the Depression and the cruel sacrifices of two world wars. Communism and unions were thought to be a real threat to the North American way of life. Labour conditions in other industries were appreciably worse than those in the NHL; there wasn't any residue of fame attached to going down in the mines or pulling a plough. When employees of Smythe's gravel pit tried to unionize, Smythe simply closed the business. Whatever the mitigating circumstances, however, the treatment of the NHL's star players by the likes of Adams and Smythe chafed and gnawed at the players' dignity well into the 1960s. Though feted as heroes, they weren't treated or paid that way.

In the Original Six era, when teams played to packed houses, a typical salary was about $8,000. "In New York in 1958, I made $7,500, and for that I had to check guys like Howe and [Eddie] Litzenberger every night," says Eddie Shack. "Of that money, $900 went to the pension plan [after taxes]. Living in New York on that money, I had to sell hats, whatever I could do to make ends meet." With many players maintaining two residences—one where they played, one where they worked in off-season jobs—their salaries paid for groceries, not Porsches. And if a player was injured in the playoffs and couldn't work in the summer—as happened in 1956 when Tod Sloan dislocated his shoulder and missed six weeks of work—there was no reimbursement. Even the introduction in 1947 of the long-awaited pension plan for NHL players was a burden. Most players shelled out an onerous 20 per cent of after-tax income as their contribution. In 1993, a court ruled they'd been grossly shortchanged on that sacrifice by the owners running the plan.

The owners' take from the regular season in the Original Six days may not have been impressive, but there was money to be made in the playoffs and in owning an arena where the NHL team was only one of many tenants. The addition of TV revenues in the 1950s also fattened the bottom line. Yet the NHL justified minuscule salaries and benefits by crying poverty. Smythe and fellow owners such as Jim Norris, the Chicago businessman who owned three of the American teams, portrayed themselves as sportsmen, maintaining their teams at a break-even level for the enjoyment of the fans. Norris liked to talk about a "gentleman's loss of $500,000" on one of his teams, as if describing a modest gambling debt. After Howe won the Hart Trophy, Art Ross Trophy, and Stanley Cup in 1951–52, he was faced with a tale of financial woe from Jack Adams when he came in for a new contract. Grimacing as if in physical pain, Adams grudgingly surrendered a $1,000 raise for one of the greatest seasons in NHL history. Howe actually felt guilty for causing "Jolly Jack" such distress.

In 1962, players got a glimpse of what a top player might be worth on the open market. After a night of heavy drinking at Toronto's Royal York Hotel, Chicago owner Jim Norris offered to pay the Leafs co-owner Harold Ballard a million dollars for the rights to scoring sensation Frank Mahovlich. Ballard, who never let common sense get in the way of a quick score, accepted Norris's cheque. The Toronto papers were full of the sensational transaction the next day. Ballard's partner Stafford Smythe—son of Conn—needed to call in many favours to undo Ballard's deal. Mahovlich stayed a Maple Leaf, and the man valued at a million by his owner had to battle his GM Imlach for a $500 bonus in his contract that season.

The NHL discouraged players from disclosing their salaries to each other, using agents, or socializing with opponents. "That's what management preyed on," said Bobby Hull, who entered the NHL in 1957. "Don't tell anyone what you're making, don't get together, don't be a group. Keep it a secret so everyone stays apart." Paul Henderson came up in the Detroit system and remembers the pressure of working in a business that had just six teams, 120 jobs, and many, many players waiting in reserve. "The competition was cutthroat. Management used this fear as leverage to get you to do what they wanted. The front office held all the cards and ruled a player's life completely." That sometimes included counselling players' wives on their sex lives. In 1957 Doreen Worsley, wife of Rangers goalie Gump Worsley, was called in by her husband's coach, Phil Watson. With the 1957 playoffs on, Watson was concerned that Gump needed his mind on the game, not on nights of wild abandon. Doreen Worsley listened to Watson's lecture in amazement: she was seven months' pregnant at the time.

Contract negotiations were a theatre of the absurd, remembers Hall of Fame goalie Glenn Hall. "Tommy Ivan, the general manager, used to keep all the contracts in his desk drawer. You'd be talking to him and he'd rattle these papers that you couldn't see. One time, my teammate Glen Skov was talking contract and Mr. Ivan, he was rattling away with his papers. Ivan said, 'I see you got a raise last year, Glen.' *Rattle, rattle.* 'And a raise the year before that.' *Rattle, rattle.* 'Why should I give you another raise?' And Glen said, 'Because I spent all that money, Tommy.' And that was the end of that negotiation."

Decades of arbitrary trades, capricious demotions, and extreme frugality from owners were a corrosive force in players' lives. While most players were appalled by the notion of trade unionism and strikes in hockey, they had an overwhelming desire for representation and protection from the whims of their bosses. Led by Montreal's Doug Harvey and Detroit's Ted Lindsay—bitter rivals on the ice—players on the six clubs secretly banded together in the fall of 1956 to form the first group to advocate and protect the players' interests. (The birth and death of the first NHL Players' Association is told in detail in David Cruise and Alison Griffiths's book *Net Worth*.)

When Smythe and Adams got wind of the plan, they squeezed the fledgling organization. Stories were planted in friendly media detailing the sweet life enjoyed by Lindsay and his highly paid teammates. Moles on each team were encouraged to stir up dissent among the rank and file. By the summer of 1957, most of the instigators—Lindsay, Jimmy Thomson, Tod Sloan, Dollard St. Laurent—had been traded to Chicago, the Siberia of the NHL. "In a sense, we isolated the Association," wrote Smythe years later, "and it was ten years before it became effective." Within a year of its founding, the first NHL Players' Association was finished, dissent was stifled, and an ineffectual player-owner committee to discuss issues of concern was eventually disbanded. The owners enjoyed another decade of free rein over their humbled workforce, the most profitable period in league history.

By the time Alan Eagleson came on the scene in the mid-1960s, the NHL was flush with cash from booming attendance, a longer schedule, and escalating TV deals. While a lid had been welded shut on salaries through this period (the players' share of gross revenues actually declined amidst the plenty), team revenues jumped from $892,000 a team in 1960 to more than $2.2 million in 1968. In 1967, the two Canadian teams were sharing in an unprecedented $330,000 TV and radio deal. It took no genius to see that the contracts for televising Major League Baseball ($12.35 million), the AFL ($35 million), and the NFL ($28 million) meant that the half-dozen owners of the National Hockey League would own a goldmine if TV broadcast their sport across the continent via expansion. The addition of the six new teams would also deliver an estimated $18.5 million in expansion fees to the band of brothers known as the NHL Board of Governors.

For the players, however, nothing much changed. Whether the issue was pay for training camp, per diems on the road, moving expenses, leave for the birth of kids, or even laundering of equipment, the players found themselves locked in a time warp. Over beers or on the golf course, grievances were exchanged. All agreed: a new players' association was needed. But after years under the boot of Campbell and Co., they needed a David to slay the NHL Goliath. In the pugnacious, ambitious Eagleson, they felt they had found their man.

The NHL had an embarrassment of riches as it expanded to twelve teams (new franchises being established in Philadelphia, Pittsburgh, St. Louis, Minnesota, Oakland, and Los Angeles). With the union-hating Jack Adams now out of the picture, the owners seemed amenable to allowing its players some representation—just so long as they didn't go all pinko. If the league could limit payroll to 25 to 30 per cent of revenues, it could tolerate this peripatetic character named Eagleson. Besides, the forbidding Teamsters Union was sniffing around, looking to organize NHL players, and league president Campbell understood that Eagleson would be the lesser of these two labour evils. Even Conn Smythe approved. "I don't like unions, but I'm glad it's Eagleson at the head of the Players' Association rather than someone else."

Eagleson had been hanging around the edges of the league for much of the 1960s. Originally a real-estate lawyer from Rexdale, Ontario, a Toronto suburb, he had built up a clientele of players on the formidable Leafs teams of the 1960s, acting as a liaison for Bob Pulford, Carl Brewer, and Billy Harris, among others, in their negotiations for the scraps offered by Punch Imlach. He also introduced the players to local businessmen, organizing real-estate ventures between star-struck business types and green hockey players. Though he made limited inroads with the flinty boss of the Leafs, Eagleson became known around the NHL as a man who could solve your problems. (In a celebrated 1967 incident, he claimed to have ended a strike by players of the AHL's Springfield Indians against their overbearing boss Eddie Shore. Whether he solved the strike is hotly debated, but he made sure the press corps believed he had bested the tyrannical Shore.) His reputation was assured in 1966 when he became the agent—and apparent best friend—of the NHL's next wunderkind, Bobby Orr. After winning the precocious defenceman a landmark first contract ($25,000 to sign, $25,000 the first year, $30,000 the second), Eagleson was rarely out of his young client's company—or out of the newspaper headlines.

Thanks to Orr, Eagleson had access to dressing rooms around the league and soon revived the dream of a players' association. First, he had to unite the fractious players, who resented each other and harboured grudges from battles on and off the ice. Using his prize catch Orr and his pals on the Leafs as salesmen, Eagleson finally brought together the great egos of the NHL. "They all wanted to be the boss cow," remembers Bob Baun. "Boom Boom Geoffrion, Dickie Moore—there had to be a catalyst like Eagleson who could smack them down with his mouth. Then they'd all be quiet and listen." Smack them down he did with a vocabulary that made even veteran players blush. After a whirlwind recruiting drive in the winter of 1966–67, Eagleson enlisted every active NHL player to the cause of a players' association. To his later regret, Bobby Hull was soon singing the praises of "The Eagle."

Better yet, Eagleson signed up an estimated 250 NHL and minor-league players as clients of his own sports agency, making him the dominant agent as well. This meant he was now being paid twice by much of the league's workforce. Key reporters in each city became his de facto PR agents (prominent Montreal reporter Red Fisher was even cut in for a piece of Bobby Orr Enterprises as a reward for loyal reportage). The Orr and Shore episodes cemented Eagleson's modus operandi for the next twenty-five years: talk loudly, carry a big stick, and make sure the reporters write it your way.

While media tales of Eagleson's prowess abounded in those early days, the first executive director of the NHLPA scored few significant concessions in his first negotiations with the league. He won pay for exhibition games and expenses on the road, and the league agreed to increase the minimum salary to $10,000 from $8,000. Eagleson touted these gains as groundbreaking; he was silent on the fact that the NHL was also tacking on four more regular-season games and an extra playoff round to the schedule in exchange for the concessions. A short time later, he also allowed the NHL to take complete control of the players' pension fund, a move that let the NHL redirect surplus moneys to itself.

For all the public bravado, Eagleson was shortchanging players. Though NHL gross revenues jumped 15.9 per cent from 1969 to

1971, salaries and benefits advanced just 9 per cent. The first collective bargaining agreement with the NHL wasn't signed until 1975. And while the baseball union—begun by Marvin Miller the same year Eagleson started the NHLPA—was quietly moving towards its first free agency and millions for its players, Eagleson had yet to make a dent in the reserve clause in the basic player's contract or the artificial restraint on salaries enjoyed by the owners. Though expansion and the new TV deal had left the NHL vulnerable to work stoppages, Eagleson never said a word about this leverage in efforts to win real concessions. Reporters, in turn, never said a critical word about Eagleson's achievements.

The apparent lack of bargaining progress was helpfully masked by Eagleson's role in the famous 1972 Canada–U.S.S.R. hockey showdown. Eagleson, as usual, was highly visible and adversarial, battling hand to hand with the KGB, displacing Bunny Ahearne as boss of international hockey, lecturing Canadian fans on their lack of loyalty, and flipping the bird to the Moscow hockey crowd during game eight. "He is what Canada is," blared Chris Lang, a pal with Hockey Canada. "Trudeau isn't, Eagleson is." Behind the scenes, however, he was increasingly accommodating the league's owners. For the 1972 series, the NHLPA director allowed the NHL to bar Bobby Hull, J.C. Tremblay, Gerry Cheevers, and others who had jumped to the newly formed rival World Hockey Association.

Eagleson's involvement in the Hockey Cold War had a deleterious effect on the NHLPA as well. He would later claim that he did what was right at the time. But the record shows that he was often too busy with other issues to better the association's status. While he flitted about the globe, part promoter and part sports executive, hobnobbing with everyone but his membership, baseball's union director, Marvin Miller, was travelling from team to team, building his union's treasure chest, and educating his members. While Eagleson was building up his own player agency, his position in international hockey, and his political career as president of the Ontario Progressive Conservative party, Miller was preparing his members to use their leverage for free agency, pension benefits, and a stake in the upcoming television revolution. The NHLPA office in Toronto was run by people who worked on Players' Association business when they had a break from Eagleson's thriving legal and business empire. Miller staffed the baseball union with dedicated labour lawyers and marketing specialists whose only loyalty was to the MLBPA.

To compensate for his lack of thoroughness, Eagleson adopted a buccaneer style that became infamous. Former player and coach Terry Crisp remembers asking Eagleson for help negotiating a new contract in St. Louis. "I'd made $8,000 the year before and wanted a raise. So he went off, and then later he called me and said, 'I got you $10,000.' I was really excited and told one of my teammates about how Eagleson had gotten me more money. And this guy said, 'They just raised the minimum NHL salary to $10,000. You didn't get anything.' I couldn't believe it. Three weeks later, I got a legal bill from Eagleson for $720 for negotiating the contract. So now I was making less than the NHL minimum. That was Eagle."

The birth of the World Hockey Association in 1972 was a godsend for players—and for the Eagle. It instantly created the first seller's market for hockey players and it masked the real lack of progress made by the NHLPA director since coming on board. The WHA was the brainchild of American promoter Gary Murphy, but served as a vehicle for Canadian cities that had been overlooked for NHL expansion. With the NHL charging $6 million for a new franchise, the WHA asked just $500,000 for membership, which left lots of money for stealing players from the NHL. And the WHA spread money around liberally, picking up some great stars: Winnipeg shocked the hockey public by awarding Bobby Hull a million dollars to leave Chicago to play for five years in Winnipeg. He was joined by many other marquee players, including Derek Sanderson, Bernie Parent, J.C. Tremblay, Marc Tardif, Johnny McKenzie, Rick Ley, Jim

Dorey, and Gerry Cheevers. Before the league finally disappeared, it would also attract Gordie Howe and his sons Mark and Marty, Frank Mahovlich, Dave Keon, and two young phenoms named Gretzky and Messier.

The NHL was unprepared for this challenge to its domination. "I was the first player publicly signed," recalls Blues GM Larry Pleau, a Montreal farmhand in the summer of 1972. "I called Sam Pollock [his GM in Montreal] and said, 'I'm going to sign with the WHA tomorrow. I'm not going to play here. But I'd like to stay in the NHL. Just trade me to one of the expansion teams like the Islanders or the Canucks. I just want to play. If you can tell me you'll trade me to a team that would play me, I'd stay'. And he said, 'Larry, I'm not going to trade you, and there's never going to be a WHA.' I spent seven seasons with the New England Whalers in a league that wasn't supposed to exist. There wouldn't have been the growth in hockey without the WHA. That was a big step in getting salaries up."

Diehards such as Wirtz in Chicago and Ballard in Toronto simply pretended the competitor didn't exist—and lost many of their top stars by refusing to match salary offers. Other owners, such as the Flyers' Ed Snider and the Rangers' Bill Jennings, recognized that a new day had dawned and paid market value to keep players such as Rod Gilbert, Vic Hadfield, and Bobby Clarke under contract. "[Clarence] Campbell ridiculed Snider before the other governors at their next meeting [after re-signing Clarke]," remembered Flyers counsel Gil Stein, later president of the NHL. "He said he had information that the league would fold before its maiden season. When that did not happen, he said they would definitely not last beyond Christmas. At the December 1972 Board of Governors meeting, he said they would never finish the season. The more his predictions of the WHA's demise proved to be wrong, the more insistent he became that collapse was imminent." By heeding Campbell, Chicago, Detroit, and Toronto became laughingstocks during the WHA years; the Flyers, in contrast, retained their best players and won two Stanley Cup titles in the next five years.

Boston GM Harry Sinden remembers the impact of the WHA. "When I got home from the '72 Canada–U.S.S.R. series, the team had promised the players who stayed big raises because of the WHA. In those days it was $10,000 or $20,000. I got that handed to me, and we had to live up to it." Hockey players, meanwhile, moved from fourth to second in compensation among pro team athletes in North America; in 1977, their $96,000 average salary dwarfed the NFL's $55,000 and baseball's $76,000. The eighteen NHL clubs and twelve WHA teams bid up the price of hockey players who had, in many cases, been languishing in the minors the season before.

The players were also aided by the U.S. Justice Department, which looked into the NHL for possible restraint-of-trade and antitrust violations. As a result of a federal investigation and a lawsuit from the WHA, the NHL replaced the reserve clause in 1974 with a pale form of free agency under which players could move to other teams at the end of their contracts. The catch was that their old clubs were to be compensated with players or draft choices of equal value. If a deal couldn't be brokered, the NHL president would decide the appropriate compensation. "Essentially, the current system protects teams in smaller markets," said the *New York Times* of NHL free agency in the late 1970s. "A hockey player would rather give his front two teeth—if he hasn't surrendered them already—than play in Winnipeg or Quebec. These are teams with losing traditions, in outposts with the highest taxation rates in the country." Naturally, few "free agents" switched teams over the next fifteen years.

As union leader, Eagleson might have sought to establish the WHA as a credible alternative; he might have worked to establish the Players' Association as a real force in bargaining. Instead he focused on becoming the power-broker of international hockey. Of the many hats he wore, global deal-maker seemed to flatter him most. Travel, high-level politics, and big money were more stimulating than waiver claims and grievances over moving expenses. Starting in 1972, running Hockey Canada, meeting with foreign politicians, and schmoozing business leaders became his real passion. Eventually the self-made lawyer from humble beginnings came to have more in common with the high-powered businessmen who gathered at the Breakers in Palm Beach than with sweaty, inarticulate hockey players from Flin Flon and Sarnia.

"He used to say we could call him up any time," recalls Pat Verbeek, who scored more than 500 goals in his NHL career. "I phoned him up when I was coming off my 46-goal season in New Jersey. That was probably 1988, before salary disclosure. I remember asking him how much I should ask for from the Devils. This was at a time when Dave Taylor was making $1.3 million or so from the Kings. He says to me, '$200,000.' I said, That's all? And he said, 'When you become an owner you can pay yourself more than that.' I just looked at my wife and shook my head. He was our guy." Former Montreal Canadien Murray Wilson felt "the love" of Eagleson when trying to collect on an injury arbitration case in the 1980s. "I called him for help, and he said, 'Go get your own fucking agent to help you.' I hadn't had an agent for three years, but that didn't matter to Al."

As time went by, Eagleson found international hockey gave him an easy ride in collective bargaining. He could trade off meaningful free agency and independent arbitration during collective bargaining in exchange for contributions to the players' pension fund generated by profits from his international events. It cost NHL management virtually nothing to fund the pension, because the players were earning the premiums with their patriotic labours at Canada Cups, Soviet Tours, and other events. In effect, the players were playing international hockey to pay themselves.

From the first CBA in 1975, virtually all major NHLPA negotiations took place in the run-up to a large international event stage-managed by Eagleson. He'd bluster about winning the free agency and higher salaries enjoyed by baseball and NBA players, but he always gave in on the significant issues in return for future benefits to the players' pension. Any pension expert could see that the players' funding of their own pension amounted to a sellout, but the Eagleson-run NHLPA had no pension experts.

The demise of the WHA perfectly illustrated Eagleson's style. The league was faltering in 1979, and the NHL had been badly mauled by fighting the upstart league. A merger was imminent, but with U.S. Justice officials watching for antitrust violations the NHL needed approval from the Players' Association to effect the deal (and collect $24 million from the four WHA teams absorbed into the NHL). When the National Basketball Association had sought to merge with the American Basketball Association in 1976—a similar situation—NBA players had won free agency and a range of benefits from desperate owners. With the NHL over a barrel in 1979, Eagleson had the chance to win real concessions. Instead of pressing the advantage, as NBA players had done when the ABA folded, Eagleson disappeared into the shadows, letting his partners in international hockey bully players such as NHLPA president Phil Esposito into paltry pension benefits for his members but no meaningful free agency. Espo—Eagleson's mighty hero in the '72 series—subsequently admitted that he was manipulated into the one-sided deal by owners while Eagleson stood aside. Years later, Edmonton GM Glen Sather admitted that the players could have had almost anything they wanted had they fought for it. But there was suddenly no fight in the scrappy lawyer from Toronto.

Some on the players' side understood what they had sacrificed. "When the NHL decided to free all the Europeans on its negotiation lists in the final days of the WHA, we saw what free-agent players such as Anders Hedberg and Ulf Nilsson of Winnipeg were worth," recalls sports lawyer Don Baizley, who began his career representing players in the rival league. Baizley got them both free-agent deals worth an unheard-of $750,000 signing bonus and $225,000 a year guaranteed from the Rangers. Today, Baizley can only shake his head. "The NHL saw what free agents were worth on the open market. That's why they were in such a hurry to get the [merger] deal with the players."

With no WHA to use as a bargaining tool after 1979, Eagleson soon allowed NHL players to become the lowest paid and most vulnerable athletes of the big four pro team sports, and the only ones without meaningful free agency. Players hoping for an advocate to voice their concerns about diminishing returns discovered only silence. "Deep down, there's a resentment," says Dennis Polonich, a crowd favourite at Detroit's Olympia in the 1970s. "The building was full, and I can remember them yelling my name, 'Polo! Polo!' I was making, what, $65,000 or $70,000, and leaving my blood on the ice. How much were they making? I felt cheated after. I just didn't know any better."

The league, meanwhile, was boasting a business turnaround. NHL president John Ziegler claimed that a $100-million accumulated operating loss in 1978 had become, by 1989, a $60-million profit. "From a business standpoint, we are proud of that turnaround." When they heard such talk, players such as Mike Milbury and agents such as Brian Burke and Pierre Lacroix wondered why their man Eagleson was shooting blanks at the bargaining table. But they could never create enough support to get past angry words and raised voices. Eagleson was careful to keep the top players of the day—Orr, Esposito, Gretzky, Mario Lemieux—pacified. Without the initiative of a superstar, no movement to oust the Eagle had a chance in the tribal hierarchy of NHL players.

The NHL left little doubt that Eagleson had crossed over to their side. On one occasion, Ziegler openly extolled the virtues of "my friend Alan Eagleson" before Toronto's Empire Club. "One of the things I'm proud of—and I know Alan Eagleson is, too—is that we have taken the owner-player relationship and used it as a means to solve problems. We do not go out of our way to confront or compete." Which led one critic to observe, "With the lowest average salary in team sports, lowest minimum wage, lowest percentage of gross revenues going to players, and worst collective bargaining agreement, Ziegler should be friends with Alan."

On another occasion, the NHLPA director was instrumental in solving a feud in the ranks of supposed adversaries. In the late 1970s, Ziegler told the authors of *Net Worth*, he and the NHLPA director decided—for the "good of the game"—to heal the bitter rift in the owners' ranks between Chicago's Bill Wirtz and Philadelphia's Ed Snider. "So Alan and I worked very hard bringing the two together. And Alan played a very important part." Soon, thanks to the union leader's mediation efforts, the reunified owners were again taking the players to the woodshed in negotiations.

The spoon-fed media rarely pointed any of this out, of course, preferring to deify the man who'd always been good for a bottle of Scotch at Christmas and a scoop on mundane hockey matters. Mostly they produced fawning, wink-wink coverage of the irascible, unstoppable Eagle, the lovable rogue who seemed to be everywhere. When players such as Milbury or agents such as Winter or Salcer complained about the slipshod operations of the association, Eagleson unleashed a torrent of profane abuse. "He embarrassed me," admitted Phil Esposito. "If I asked a question he'd say, 'For Christ's sakes, don't be so stupid!' in front of everybody. Al's smart. He knows if he does that to me or to a Bobby Clarke, the other guy is going to say, 'Holy shit, I'm not opening my mouth.'" Jim Kyte was a young defenceman with Winnipeg in 1984 when he witnessed an Eagle assault. "We had a meeting and Robert Picard asked a question about something. And Al just went after him. 'Where do you get off making comments, you fucking frog? You haven't done anything in this league.' I couldn't believe it. I just put my head down and didn't say a thing."

Eagleson also mused aloud about switching sides to become the commissioner of the NHL. "They need a benevolent dictator like we have in the Players' Association," he once told reporters without the slightest hint of modesty or irony. Another guerrilla tactic to quash opposition was the flash resignation. In 1986, Eagleson threatened to quit the association on the eve of negotiations for a new CBA unless he got a lucrative new contract. The players acquiesced. "We couldn't tell him to stuff it," says Pat Verbeek, then with the Devils. "There was talk about him becoming commissioner of the NHL if he didn't get the raise. We didn't want to be facing him across the table the next day."

Years later, NHL president Gil Stein (who'd served on the Pennsylvania Labor Relations Board) marvelled at Eagleson's handling of the NHL players. "I have never seen anything like what passed for collective bargaining in the NHL....Putting it mildly Eagleson was enmeshed in serious conflicts of interest, but there appeared to be full disclosure...and none of his clients seemed disturbed by them....To us in the league office, it appeared that the executive and player reps were absolutely in awe of Eagleson...they respected, trusted and feared him at the same time."

Stein, the NHL's counsel for the final half of the Eagleson years, observed that the Eagle and his drinking pals, NHL president Ziegler and board chairman Wirtz, effectively orchestrated the business of the league amongst themselves. "The course of hockey may have been set and re-set during many a late night—and early morning— revel aboard the magnificent Wirtz yacht....It does not take a great stretch of imagination to believe that when Eagleson, Ziegler and Wirtz led their respective troops into collective bargaining negotiations, the results might have been pre-ordained...."

In his book *Power Plays*, Stein describes a typical "staged" negotiating session, which ended with a settlement that had actually been agreed to days earlier. Stein writes, "[T]he differences between the two sides were whittled down and a final agreement reached, usually reasonably close to Ziegler's original prediction. Owners, players, and players' wives then celebrated at a posh dinner party hosted by the owners. Everyone would attest to how difficult the negotiations had been, and how fruitful the hard-fought gains for both sides. To us, it appeared the players never suspected the scenario might have been scripted in advance. As Roman lawyer and satirist Decimus Junius Juvenalis observed in his Satires in the year A.D. 125, bread and circuses kept the Roman citizenry pacified."

By the time Gretzky was traded to Los Angeles and Ritch Winter and Ron Salcer made their call to Ed Garvey, many NHL players were no longer pacified by bread and circuses. "I felt the association was a disgrace for a long time," Garvey said later. "But

I told them I would only do it if the players wanted me." Two hundred and twenty-five $100 cheques from NHL players told Garvey they wanted him to bell the cat they'd hired to represent them. Garvey soon articulated the players' dissatisfaction with Eagleson, ripping holes in the "Czar of Hockey" through a series of meetings and newsletters. They pointed out the obvious conflicts, of course: the Mad Hatter routine of "Now I'm an agent; now I'm a union leader; now I'm an international hockey promoter." Eagleson had always justified this charade by saying that his myriad conflicts were declared and no one had complained. But the Garvey-Winter-Salcer truth squad turned up many undeclared conflicts, such as Eagleson's secret ownership of the building that housed the union's offices, his lending of NHLPA money to friends at favourable rates, and his charging his own clients and members (Mike Gillis included) unjust fees to collect their NHLPA disability insurance.

They also made the first critical analysis of the NHL's collective bargaining. The free-agency-for-pension-benefits strategy employed by Eagleson left players with the lowest percentage of revenues, lowest average salary, least free-agent mobility, and worst licensing deals of the major team sports. The founding director of the NHLPA was responsible for his members having the least movement of established free-agent players while at the same time restricting the options of entry-level players via a twelve-round draft that bound every prospect to a single team. Even when loopholes were created in 1985 that permitted undrafted U.S. college players such as Adam Oates to be free agents, Eagleson allowed the NHL to amend the rules so that there would be no recurrence—without getting anything in return. His stock reply to criticism was to say, "We did what we thought best at the time, and there's nothing more you can do." Even when the failure of his strategy was revealed later, he clung to his outdated claim of doing "what's best for the game."

"The thing that really upset me the most is that we were talking free agency at one point in negotiations," Verbeek recalled of the 1986 CBA talks. "Within an hour, Alan had talked to Ziegler and suddenly we were talking about this four-hundred-game pension package instead of free agency. How could we change our position so quickly? It didn't seem like we were serious about fighting for free agency."

"You have to remember that it was a different world," recalls goalie Mike Liut, an executive board member who supported Eagleson at the time. "The emphasis was on benefits for the average guy, not salaries for the stars. The issue was raised by some of the biggest names that there should be a fundamental shift in direction under Al. But the players collectively, innocently, unwittingly—whatever word you choose—chose the path of least resistance. So the stars underwrote the employment of medium- and lower-range players by forgoing high salaries through free agency. You can say it wasn't necessary, but it was a different world."

Even when Eagleson won a concession that might have helped the stars—guaranteed contracts, salary arbitration—there was no attempt to exploit it. For instance, winning salary arbitration without getting salary disclosure—something Eagleson resisted—was a token achievement. Even more damning was the evidence of malfeasance that emerged from the books of the NHLPA: chummy below-market loans of players' money to Eagleson's business partners and friends; non-existent accounting of expenses; overcharging of fees to his law office—the Garvey-Winter-Salcer faction laid it all out. What the players had feared about the man in whom they'd placed their trust was now exposed. It was a devastating campaign that led, at the annual general meeting in June 1989, to a vote on whether to keep Eagleson.

"Jimmy Fox was our rep in Los Angeles," remembers former Kings goalie Kelly Hrudey. "It was exciting, because we were told how everything was going to change. How the other unions worked. We were getting a lot of pressure from management not to change things. I remember many times hearing through the grapevine that they were really happy with Eagleson, and we'd be really stupid to get rid of him."

Eagleson didn't get to the top of the heap without being a fighter. Just ask the Soviet officials who worked with him on the Canada Cups. He'd often claimed his resignation letter was on file at NHLPA headquarters, but now he rallied his loyal executive board (whom he'd personally appointed), chosen current and retired players, his personal lawyer, and his family to West Palm Beach to fight back. (Wayne Gretzky, who could have swayed the vote, chose to absent himself.) Eagleson played for sympathy in the media, claiming he was being ambushed by an anti-Canadian sector of the Players' Association, that back problems were crippling him—anything to distract attention from his dismal record on behalf of his members.

It was a bruising, charged weekend that threatened to rip the NHLPA apart. Whole teams supported one side or the other; other clubs were split between those who supported Eagleson and those who thought he should be boiled in oil. Charges, countercharges, and profanity flew. At one point it was revealed that the $250,000 pension award for players with ten years' seniority—a perk that helped seal the 1986 collective bargaining process—was funded not by the owners but by a surplus in the pension fund created by the contributions of retired NHL greats.

"You mean to tell me," said an incredulous Garth Butcher of Vancouver, "that the money contributed by Bobby Hull, Bobby Orr, Gordie Howe, and all those players is being used to pay current players' benefits? Well, that sucks!"

Worse, it was clear that the spare operation of the Players' Association—it officially consisted of three people, claimed Eagleson—and the democratic procedures of the union were a shambles. When Eagleson's loans of NHLPA funds to friends and business partners was revealed, PA president Bryan Trottier could not remember if he or the executive board had ever heard of these multimillion-dollar transactions, let alone approved them. Garvey attacked every gap in Eagleson's credibility. At one point, Eagleson's personal lawyer, Edgar Sexton, interrupted a Garvey onslaught with an objection. "Garvey asked him what he was doing at a meeting of hockey players," recalls Ritch Winter. "Sexton said he was there because I'd threatened to sue Eagleson. Garvey said there was no suit, and again asked who Sexton was representing in a union meeting of hockey players. Sexton tried to turn it back on Garvey. 'Who do you represent?' he says. In the blink of an eye, all these hands go up around the room." Sexton had made the elemental lawyer's gaffe: asking a question to which he didn't know the answer.

"The most interesting moment to me," recalls Brad McCrimmon, a defenceman with Calgary at the time, "came when I reminded him that he'd said he'd quit if the players didn't want him any more. His resignation letter was on file at his office. But there he was, with all these guys opposed to him, and he refused to quit. That told me a lot."

When the dust settled, Eagleson had barely escaped with his job, and then only by the votes of his hand-picked executive-board members. (The audio tape of the proceedings mysteriously disappeared.) As part of a humiliating settlement suggested by agent Herb Pinder to end the infighting, Eagleson agreed that a search committee should find his replacement.

He would linger at the helm of the NHLPA for another two and a half years, issuing brazen claims of triumph at having eluded his tormentors. "My attitude was, 'Boys, you won't get the chance again.' And they never will," he told CBC TV in 1991. His optimism was misplaced; by early 1992, his legal troubles with the FBI had forced his reluctant resignation from the NHLPA. At his farewell party, despite the efforts of old loyalists in the media to deflect the topic, he was badgered with questions about police investigations, not the good old days. Suddenly it was Uncle Sam and the Mounties looking at the balance sheet, not timorous hockey players.

For the shell-shocked players, who'd been reduced to purging their own representative from the union, the Eagleson years were an object lesson in labour law and politics. There was now no excuse for standing aloof and allowing the NHLPA to take care of itself. Duelling with a man who deserted them had left players with an indelible commitment: "We won't get fooled again."

Ironically, a new NHL owner—Bruce McNall of the Kings—proved a greater emancipator of players in two years than Eagleson had been in twenty-five years. McNall's acquisition of Gretzky in 1988 opened the eyes of the game's top players to their real value. While fellow owners howled in protest, the coin speculator dragged Eagleson's reluctant serfs into the modern age. His message in the Gretzky trade was pure showbiz: everything—and everyone—in the NHL had a worth that could be measured in cash. McNall felt you had to pay a star like a star. The more he gets, the greater his aura. The Gretzky deal was his blueprint.

Jerry Buss—a minority owner in the Kings and owner of the NBA Lakers—had convinced Peter Pocklington that he should realize the equity he held in Gretzky before injuries and time reduced the Great One to the status of mere mortal. While Gretzky was valued at a million dollars on his standard player's contract, he was worth many times that in the open market, Buss told the Oilers owner. To Pocklington, desperate for capital to prop up his failing businesses, this was music to his ears. Meanwhile, McNall needed a big star to vault his sad-sack Kings into prominence in Hollywood. He was willing to take Pocklington's asset off his hands at a rich price.

So even as Gretzky was leading the Oilers to their fourth Cup in 1988, then marrying Janet Jones in a summer wedding, Pocklington was quietly letting it be known that he might trade him. "Wayne had complete allegiance to the Oilers and Peter Pocklington," recalls Gretzky's agent, Mike Barnett, "only to find that, unbeknownst to him, Pocklington was offering him around the league. So we called Glen [Sather] and said, 'We know you're trying to trade him, so if we're going to work together, here's the two teams you need to work on...Detroit and L.A.'" While rumours of the deal started to trickle out, Sather went to work on making the trade. It soon became clear that McNall and the Kings were going to win the competition by sheer force of will. "I had heard that Vancouver and the Rangers might be in the picture," McNall told the *Sporting News* in 1989. "And that made me want the deal even more. I get that way. When

I get something in my head, it consumes me. I get frustrated along the way and I get obsessive. This was not a casual thing I could walk away from...in this case, it was an obsession with Gretzky."

What made the Gretzky deal a landmark was the contract McNall offered him and the cash he sent to Edmonton: $2.5 million a year for seven years to Gretzky, and the $15 million to the Oilers. The numbers were astonishing in a business that so recently had treated players as chattels. "There's no doubt the Gretzky deal catapulted the salary structure," said Bob Goodenow at the time. "There is an ability to pay that's been unlocked."

That concept, says Barnett, took some time to sink in with the modest Gretzky. "Wayne was so relieved to be out of Edmonton that when Bruce was saying, 'I think we need to give you $3 million a year. What do you think of that? Three or four million,' Wayne was going, 'Not right now, Bruce. Let's get our feet under us. Let's spend some money on other players so we get a better team.' I could have kicked him under the table. But that was Wayne."

"We were negotiating in reverse," McNall told the authors of *Net Worth*. "I was trying to pull him up. He was trying to keep it down...that was before he ever knew his value to the franchise. He could have said, '$10 million a year is what I want.'" Brought up in the high-stakes world of coin speculation and Hollywood glitz, McNall was unlike anything the NHL had ever seen. "Even when the purchase price was $15 million and he had to come up with it up front to pay Peter, he shared with us how he was doing it," says Barnett. "He immediately went to Prime Ticket [cable-TV network] and said, 'I've got the greatest hockey player in the world, you guys have broadcast rights, how much are you prepared to increase the rights fee to be a part of this?' Prime Ticket went up to $15 million; then Bruce had his people talk to his platinum sponsors. He covered off at least two-thirds of the $15 million by letting the other sponsors know what they were going to be able to earn with 99 on the ice." McNall changed the Kings uniform from gaudy purple and gold to a sleek new black-and-silver design that quickly became a best-seller in pro-sports paraphernalia—returning even greater financial dividends.

McNall's spending spree hit the NHL like a thunderbolt. After years of Clarence Campbell talking poormouth, here was an unlikely American saying there was money to be made in hockey—lots of it. In the two years after the Gretzky deal, the Kings' revenues soared. After losing $4 million in 1987–88, the team made $13 million in 1989–90. The franchise itself increased in value from $25 million in Gretzky's first year to $125 million in 1992–93. The value of all NHL franchises zoomed as a result. By 1992, the Disney and Blockbuster corporations were buying into the league at $100 million. ABC and ESPN were restoring the NHL to prime-time status on American TV with a $125-million deal over five years. The Kings had a luxurious plane, and Hollywood was flocking to the hottest game in town. Tom Cruise, Goldie Hawn, Kurt Russell, Charlton Heston, Michael J. Fox, John Candy, and even former president Ronald Reagan showed up at the Great Western Forum to see the Kings.

Naturally, players and agents adored McNall's extravagant approach. "I was negotiating what turned out to be my last contract," recalls Tom Laidlaw. "Rogie Vachon, the GM, wasn't going to give me what I wanted. So I talked to Bruce and he said, 'Come up to my office.' He had a nice office overlooking the Hollywood Hills. He said, 'What do you think is fair?' I said, 'I think $300,000 is fair.' 'How many years do you want?' Again I said, 'I think this is fair.' And he said, 'Okay, let's get this thing done.' That was how negotiations went."

"He changed the hockey universe," says Mike Barnett.

Management figures put it less charitably. "The guy who created this whole mess was Bruce McNall," says Neil Smith, the Rangers' former GM. "And it was proven later that it wasn't even his own money. How do you pay for this? Where's the return on the investment these people are making? I blame McNall for that." Glen Sather, too, is no fan. "I think in Wayne's case, whatever you pay the guy he was worth it. He filled every building he went to. He was the guy. But it wasn't McNall's money, we found out. He was giving away something that wasn't his."

Lou Lamoriello of the Devils joins the chorus. "No doubt it had a major impact. It started a trend. Gretzky was a case where ownership spent money they didn't have to spend. And we all had to pay the price for that. Every mistake like that is a burden for everyone around the league."

As Lamoriello observed, Gretzky's transfer to the second-largest media market in the United States, coupled with salary disclosure in the next eighteen months, propelled players into the modern age of salaries. Mario Lemieux, who by this time rivalled Gretzky as the game's top player, renegotiated with Pittsburgh for $2 million a year. Bob Goodenow then hitched the value of Brett Hull, a great scorer with defensive liabilities, to Gretzky and Lemieux, getting him $7 million for four years.

After the Hull precedent, every team with a superstar was obliged to rewrite contracts. By the 1990–91 season, Detroit's Steve Yzerman had nudged up to $1.3 million a year; Patrick Roy of Montreal got $1.2 million; Boston's Ray Bourque signed for $1.194 million; Paul Coffey, freed from Sather's iron grip in Edmonton, chalked up $1.150 million in Pittsburgh; Chicago's leader Chris Chelios got $1.1 million; and Scott Stevens jumped as a free agent to St. Louis for $1.217 million—the first significant signing in the open market since Gretzky was dangled by the Indianapolis Racers of the WHA back in 1979.

"The major one to me was Scott Stevens," Boston Bruins president Harry Sinden says ruefully. "I was in the middle of negotiations with Ray Bourque and Cam Neely at the time. When he got that deal [as a free agent signing with St. Louis], I figure it cost me about $1.5 million between those two players. It doesn't seem like a lot today, but it was plenty back then." Ten players in all cracked the millionaire club by the start of the 1990s. For a league that had survived mainly on gate revenues since the demise of the WHA, the volatility of salaries exposed just how lax the NHL had been in exploiting new revenue opportunities.

While the NFL, NBA, and Major League Baseball had been growing their ancillary revenues from TV, merchandising, and concessions during the 1980s, the NHL—with its cozy house union—had made only half-hearted efforts to do so. A visit to the decrepit Maple Leaf Gardens was ample evidence of the torpor that had enveloped one of the most profitable franchises and the NHL itself. Paint was slapped rudely over cracks in the walls, concession stands stocked the barest of foods and supplies, rats scurried through visiting dressing rooms. (In dingy corners of the furnace room, arena staff were also systematically abusing young boys.) And the hockey team drifted from disaster to disaster, an empty husk of the great clubs of the 1940s, 1950s, and 1960s. Yet still the money poured in in amounts sufficient to pay the players and sock away a tidy profit.

The trade of Gretzky to an American team and Bruce McNall's bold contract were warning shots to a dying Harold Ballard and the other NHL owners that the days of a captive workforce were over. It was going to take money—plenty of it—to compete in the 1990s. And to raise that money, the league turned to a proven milk cow in times of financial strife: expansion.

4

If Bullshit Were Music

The palatial Breakers Hotel in Palm Beach, Florida, designed in 1896 and favoured lodging for railway tycoons such as Henry Flagler and financiers such as John D. Rockefeller, was dressed up for the 1990 Christmas season. The ornate lobby sparkled with flashing lights on a huge tree. The smell of pine boughs and old money wafted through the 560-room masterpiece on Florida's Atlantic coast as uniformed bellmen pushed bulging suitcases through the lobby. Long a holiday spot of the Pulitzers and Vanderbilts, the Breakers is on a first-name basis with establishment America, including the princes who run professional sport.

On this day, in early December, the NHL's Board of Governors and their entourage frolicked amid royal palms and across immaculately groomed lawns, eager for a spot of fun and a chance to welcome some new—what was the word...friends? partners? investors?—into the lodge. Sixty team governors and alternates had arrived this year, a much larger gathering than usual for the annual meeting. But there was easy money in the air, always guaranteed to attract plenty of action in the NHL.

On Wednesday, December 5, after a breakfast of Florida orange juice and strong coffee, NHL president John Ziegler called the team representatives together in the Breakers' splendid meeting room. Impeccably tailored as always, Ziegler sported his omnipresent tan, a glow that belied his position at the head of a sport played in the depths of winter. His GQ look reflected a man seemingly at the peak of his power. As he surveyed the representatives of the twenty-one clubs, the fifty-six-year-old Ziegler took satisfaction in the careful balancing act he'd performed since being named president of the league in 1977. Considered a lightweight by some ("an office clerk...a know-nothing shrimp"—Harold Ballard), the former Red Wings counsel had found a fractious, divided league struggling to cope with the rival WHA. Elected by his Detroit boss, Bruce Norris, and the NHL's conservative wing, Ziegler had inherited from Clarence Campbell a business hemorrhaging money, a league without a proper TV deal in the United States, and an operation being scrutinized by the U.S. Justice Department for antitrust violations.

Fourteen years later, as Ziegler prepared to convene the first annual winter meeting of the 1990s, things were rosier. The NHL was flush from a decade of controlled labour costs and expanding revenues, and in no small measure the prosperity was his doing. He'd healed the rifts amongst factions within the league, tamed and manipulated NHLPA director Alan Eagleson, and stymied the antitrust inquiries of the feds. He'd also overseen the greening of America's sunbelt as a hockey hotbed; with Wayne Gretzky now packing them in at the Forum in Los Angeles, the frozen game was catching on in cities that relied on air conditioning. And Ziegler felt he had made the best of the NHL's low profile on American network TV, getting a $51-million deal from SportsChannel. It reached just 10 per cent of all U.S. homes with tvs, but so what if no one actually saw the games? Regional interest was strong enough to get a new network when the contract expired in 1991.

The room before Ziegler on this December morning had been reconfigured from its usual long conference tables to a three-tiered forum. Men such as Little Caesar's founder Mike Ilitch, billionaire Gordon Gund, Jeremy Jacobs of the powerful Delaware North

Corp., industrialist Bill Wirtz, and Paramount CEO Stanley Jaffe sat in neat rows facing him. Ziegler knew where the bodies were buried in the NHL and how to use them to get his way. But he also knew that he was here at the sufferance of these men, that a president's fortunes could shift quickly in the volatile world of pro hockey.

As a measure of the league's popularity, Ziegler could point to the prospective candidates for NHL membership milling about outside the hotel, clamouring for Ottawa or Hamilton or Miami to be allowed in, or to the media army that had descended on south Florida to see which cities would gain franchises. These same press people had tried to make an issue of Ziegler's unexplained absence during the referees' revolt in the 1988 playoffs, triggered after New Jersey coach Jim Schoenfeld called referee Don Koharski a "fat pig" and suggested he "go eat another donut." But on this warm Florida morning, where were the visible signs of a league in trouble? Not within the zip code of the Breakers, apparently.

It was time to call for the first order of business. A hush fell over the room. Expansion? TV deals? New rules of play? No, purred Ziegler, there would be chauffeur-driven limos for the cocktail party that night at Jeremy Jacobs's mansion. The next day, NHL luminaries were invited to golf, tennis, or the traditional croquet tournament held on the lawn of the Breakers each December. According to Chicago's Wirtz, the dean of NHL owners, there would be a string quartet to accompany the croquet, along with shrimp and cham- pagne served by hotel staff. Remember to wear your whites, gentlemen. The entire bacchanal would conclude with an intimate party aboard the seventy-five-foot Wirtz yacht, the *Blackhawk*, moored nearby. Questions?

If all this seems bizarre—croquet in the tropical sun—then you have some measure of the gulf that divides the people who own pro hockey and the people who buy tickets to watch it. As Gil Stein observed, "Do not be misled by public utterances during collective bargaining negotiations. There are no poor owners in the NHL." Stein, who left the NHL in 1993 after twenty-one years of service as team counsel, league counsel, and finally NHL president, divided the owners at the Breakers that day into two categories: the Haves and the Have Mores. Nine of the Have Mores in the late 1980s and early 1990s had personal fortunes worth half a billion dollars or more. (In 2002, seven of the richest four hundred people in America owned NHL teams.) The wealth of the Have Mores made them immune to sudden downturns in the economy. The Haves were slightly less well-heeled, most getting by on personal fortunes in the low nine or high eight figures.

Many of the NHL owners that day were self-made. For every Bill Wirtz, who inherited his money from his father, Arthur, there were two or three, such as Mike Ilitch, Peter Pocklington, Abe Pollin, or Harley Hotchkiss, who had amassed their wealth through hard work and sheer force of will. While they may have aped the manners of the rich at the Breakers, they had first-hand experience of what it took to claw their way to the top. "I picked tobacco back on the farm in Tillsonburg, Ontario," says oil executive Hotchkiss, whose offices now look out over Calgary's booming skyline. "So it really annoys me to be referred to as a 'millionaire owner.'"

While they succeeded in business by adhering to the bottom line, that frugality often disappears when a tycoon writes a cheque to buy a sports team. "There are relatively few franchises," says Pittsburgh sports lawyer Chuck Greenberg. "As a result, they become trophy properties and people want them and are willing to pay a price for membership in the club of professional sports owners that might exceed what someone would pay for a factory."

"It isn't just ego," says Smith College economist Andrew Zimbalist. "Sometimes people just feel gratified in a variety of ways from having a team. Sometimes, it's just enjoyment if you buy a yacht, you know... you don't do that necessarily because of an ego thing, you do it because it's a consumption product."

Ken Dryden knows hockey owners well from his thirty-five years around the NHL—as a player, a lawyer, a writer, and now as president of the Maple Leafs. The Ivy League–educated Dryden tried to explain the peculiar psyche of the sports owner one day as he drove through a torrential Florida downpour, looking for the Florida Panthers' arena. "Yes, they are all successful business people in their own fields of endeavour. And they are extremely competitive by nature. But they're also people in the community. At the golf club, at the church, wherever. And when people say, 'Why are we losing, what are you going to do about it?' it bothers them. They want to be well-thought-of. So when the chance comes to sign a star player, they are looking at a number of conditions, and that includes, 'If I sign player X, will it make me more popular in the community?' That's not always the best basis on which to build a hockey team."

Former Rangers GM Neil Smith was more blunt about sports owners as he talked over breakfast one morning on New York's Upper West Side. "After my first two years, there was nobody above me at Madison Square Garden who had one clue about the CBA in the NHL," he said passionately. "I'm talking about the bosses above me—the president of MSG and the owners at Cablevision. But they were always coming up with ideas of what we've got to do. These are guys who don't care about hockey, who didn't grow up in Don Mills, Ontario, watching the Leafs and Johnny Bower and Frank Mahovlich and Allan Stanley. They think it's great that everyone at the country club is going to think it's great that they have so-and-so on their team this year, and they're going to win."

The motto of most owners is best summed up by the sign on the wall of one team's offices: "1. The Boss is always right. 2. When in doubt, consult rule No. 1." The grandiose title of the NHL's 1990 Plan of the Sixth Expansion at the Breakers was typical of this autocratic approach. Observers were unable to explain how the 1979 merger with the WHA could be called the Plan of the Fifth Expansion when there had never been a Plan of the Fourth Expansion. "Only in the NHL," sighed Gil Stein, before donning his whites for croquet.

Owners of NHL clubs can indulge without irony in precious activities such as polo or croquet that would get you run out of a good hockey town like Kenora, Ontario, or Ladysmith, B.C. "Having grown up in a working-class environment," observed Stein years later, "I had never experienced anything like the sybaritic lifestyle of the NHL's governors." And there is a certitude about how to get things done when the world is your oyster. For all that had changed in the previous seventy-five years, one constant remained from the start of the NHL in 1917: the unbending, uncompromising will of the owners to control the players. "The players are like actors," said former St. Louis owner Harry Ornest. "You have to have them or you don't have anything. But there is an endless supply of them."

Such an approach to labour relations had worked when there was no players' union, and when the NHLPA was run by the accommodating Mr. Eagleson. To the owners, the dynamic between them and their players seemed more idyllic. "We were closer to the players then," recalled former Flames and Stars owner Norm Green, a real-estate developer in Calgary. "I remember I helped set up Joe Nieuwendyk's home for him. And there was the time Cliff Fletcher called in Lanny McDonald for his contract. I think it was $350,000 at the time, and Cliff said that wasn't enough for a player like Lanny. He increased his salary. There was a sense then that we were playing for a common goal."

After Eagleson was roughed up by his union membership and Wayne Gretzky was traded to Los Angeles, a new strategy was called for in dealing with the suddenly empowered players. Yet as they considered the NHL's Plan of the Sixth Expansion that morning in 1990 at the Breakers, the owners, presidents, and officials of the twenty-one teams were oblivious to the growing storm clouds. Not one believed that they were soon to lose control of their business to boys from Trois-Rivières with cracked teeth and fellows from Sverdlovsk with unconventional business acquaintances.

The previous year, Ziegler had submitted his business plan for the next decade, "A Vision of the '90s," to the Board of Governors. In it he called for expansion to a twenty-four-team NHL—"should all teams be healthy." At the 1989 meeting, there had been a sense that the NBA had erred charging its new expansion teams "only" $32 million. "We should remember that the NBA undervalued their expansion franchises," cautioned Jim Lites, then the son-in-law of Detroit owner Mike Ilitch. "We must learn from prior mistakes and from the success of the NBA," intoned Bill Wirtz of Chicago. While suggestions for expansion fees ranged from $40 million (New York Rangers) to $65 million (Pittsburgh), Ziegler had proposed a fee in the vicinity of $50 million for the newest NHL clubs. Expansion was partly a cash grab, but it was also an attempt to keep money-losing NHL owners from grabbing these ripe markets for themselves at no benefit to the league. Across North America, cities looking to boost their profile were writing sweetheart deals to attract clubs. Debt-free arenas, guarantees of profit, concession and parking moneys—all were used to make a Dallas or an Anaheim or a Tampa into a "major-league" market. Given a free market in open cities, the NHL could see as many as a dozen teams shift their operations to new locations. "I caution everyone," said Boston owner Jeremy Jacobs in 1989, "that potential transfer by present owners becomes a stalking horse for municipalities seeking an NHL franchise." In other words, keep your franchise where it is and cash expansion cheques instead.

Almost all the teams had enthusiastically greeted the possibility of fresh capital with which to combat the rising player salaries since the Gretzky trade. Bruce McNall, always bullish on growth, had summed up the prevailing sentiment: "We'd like to see expansion. We'd like to see new cities." "We must get cash up front," noted Chicago's Wirtz. "We should let them know the qualifications are going to be fair—but steep," added Islanders owner John Pickett.

And yet there had been warnings in the 1989 meeting. Gordon Gund, who owned Minnesota with his brother George, looked at the $300,000 average NHL salary and played skeptic on expansion. "Salary levels have been going up at an accelerated rate," warned the billionaire owner of the North Stars and the NBA's Cleveland Cavaliers. "Any slide down the scale of free agency is going to create salary problems for all of us. Player costs will be our largest cost. We don't have the luxury of NBC and Turner Network deals, which will provide each NBA club with $9 million per year. The difference in revenues between big-market teams and small-market teams must be addressed. A meaningful way has to be found to share these revenue sources."

Most teams had immediately dismissed Gund's caution at the 1989 meeting, claiming he just wanted to pluck the prime San Francisco/San Jose market before it could go to Howard Baldwin in an expansion. Others asked where the Stars got off being so high and mighty when their financial troubles were due to high administrative overhead. The trouble, hinted Washington's Abe Pollin, was "in the way some people run their franchises. When the proper time comes for expansion, it is a mistake not to expand. The time is now." That prompted Quebec's Marcel Aubut—always starved for cash—to gush, "I'm 100 per cent for expansion." Aubut then tipped his hand. "[But] first choice of sites should be given to existing franchises who wish to move"—which Aubut would do, from Quebec City to Colorado, in 1996.

The chorus was almost unanimous for a cash grab. "It would be foolish to hold back," ventured John Pickett of the Islanders. "Three teams in '92, four or so more in the '90s," chorused Edmonton's Peter Pocklington. Their enthusiasm was only slightly tempered by the remarks of Calgary's Cliff Fletcher, always among the NHL's most prescient administrators. The man who'd built Calgary into a power had noted Bob Goodenow's impending assumption of the leadership of the NHLPA and summed up the issue: "The attractiveness of an NHL franchise has never been greater. It will not be as good after the next CBA."

The teams had voted 19–0 (with two abstentions) at their 1989 meeting at the Breakers to invite applications, stressing that they would be asking for a healthy $50-million entry fee—up front. Gil Stein felt the league was inviting trouble by setting the price so high. "I got the impression none of those monetary realities really mattered to the governors. They seemed concerned only with how much money they could get from the expansion applicant, not whether the franchise would be financially viable."

As the day for applications—John Ziegler's day of reckoning—arrived a year later at the Breakers, there remained considerable doubt that any of the nine applicants who'd travelled to South Florida would even agree to pay the $50-million price tag. Rumour had it that most were going to barter for a team, or merely secure a concession for a new arena in their market. And none of the applicants was going to threaten the Forbes 400 with their wealth. One—the Tampa group headed by Phil Esposito—had lost its principal funding only that week. What of the league's prestige if it drew a blank after such a public process? How would a shutout reflect on Ziegler? The scenario had disaster written all over it. Thankfully for Ziegler, he had already engineered the Gunds' long-rumoured move into San Jose in the intervening year (with Calgary co-owner Norm Green taking over the North Stars), a move that put $20 million in the pockets of fellow owners. Without this sleight of hand, Ziegler's whole expansion gambit might be a bust.

The candidates presented themselves to the NHL Board of Governors in their boardroom. Sure enough, seven of the nine groups either couldn't or wouldn't meet the NHL's principal terms for expansion, namely $50 million on the barrelhead. The two Seattle applicants withdrew their applications before departing the boardroom. Others brazenly ignored the order for upfront money and tried to negotiate new terms. Detroit computer entrepreneur Peter Karmanos, whom Wirtz had heavily touted, asked for a conditional franchise for Tampa and seven years to pay off the expansion fee. (It was later discovered that Karmanos had engaged none other than Alan Eagleson to aid his efforts in getting a team, for a possible $1-million fee.) Ron Joyce's Hamilton group also refused to pay the $50 million, asking for a $25-million entrance fee and extended terms on the balance. Only two parties declared the ambitious $50-million price tag to be no problem: Esposito's reconfigured Tampa group (which the NHL wanted) and the Ottawa group headed by real-estate speculator Bruce Firestone (about which the NHL was ambivalent). In all, the checkered applicants left the NHL owners dismayed, and Ziegler vulnerable to attack for the quality of those he'd rounded up.

"I don't understand applicants coming in here and trying to negotiate with us," huffed Washington's Abe Pollin afterwards. "I think that's bullshit." "I would say that the [expansion] committee had the obligation to filter the applications for you," sniffed Boston's Jeremy Jacobs. "You should not have had to listen to that stuff." Hartford governor, and former NHLer, Emile Francis summed up the feelings of the owners in terms a hockey player could understand: "If bullshit were music, we had a couple of brass bands march through here." Despite the disappointing quality of applicants, Edmonton's Peter Pocklington said the NHL had gone too far to back down. "If we do not grant franchises to Hamilton and Ottawa, we'll look like complete idiots." Montreal's Ronald Corey ventured that perhaps the target for expansion had been misguided: "We should answer the question whether the $50 million is our first priority, or is it just getting the right cities for TV?"

Faced with the prospect of an easy $100 million from Ottawa and Tampa, the owners quickly recovered their equilibrium. "They've got the money, let's go with them," said Pollin of the Capitals. "I'm taking on face value what Ottawa and Tampa say," added Pickett of the Islanders. "We have two real good applications here," chimed in Washington's Dick Patrick. By that afternoon, the applicants, with their respective boosters in tow, were officially the twenty-second and twenty-third members of the NHL, to begin play in the 1992–93 season. Never mind that the Senators and Lightning would fail to meet many of the NHL's stated payment schedules over the following months (Firestone had to recruit computer executive Rod Bryden and others to pay the $50-million entrance fee), or that their vaunted arena projects both collapsed within the year (Ottawa's new arena opened in 1996 at double the budgeted price; Tampa needed four years to open its new building).

Ziegler tried to wax eloquent about his expansion master stroke, but he was drowned out by Karmanos, who unburdened himself to the *Toronto Star*: "They asked for a net worth of $100 million, and neither bid has that," he said. "They said no partnerships, and both are partnerships. The owner in Tampa isn't the same owner who applied for the franchise in the first place. They said they didn't want anything to do with real estate deals, and that's what they've got. They wanted money paid in a specific time frame with specific terms and conditions and neither lived up to that....I could go on all day....It makes me sick." The NHL, said Karmanos, is "as poorly run a professional league as there is."

The Sporting News likewise was not fooled by fancy notions of growing the game: "At $50 million a pop—the fee was set so high because hockey simply needs the money—the risk for the new teams will be great." Indeed, the expansion windfall was used by many owners to cover rising player costs. This short-term gain for long-term pain came as no surprise to anyone closely following the NHL. "We created our problems," reflects Lou Lamoriello of the Devils. "The temporary dollars of expansion caused teams to spend beyond their means. The expansion was a one-time number—roughly $15 million each club—put in one year. But the players bought with that money had to be paid the year after. And the year after that. We didn't do a good job of managing our business."

The boom in new arena construction was another example of the NHL's buy-now-pay-later economy. Most clubs were either construct-ing or planning large new buildings with many luxury boxes to maximize revenues and to pay their big stars. Getting your own new rink became the thing to do. But the debt loads on many of those buildings—particularly the four built in Canada—would soon prove as much of a drag on revenues as player salaries were. As Gordon Gund prophesied, something had to give if both the salary spiral and the debts were to be absorbed. Yet most owners shrugged it off, planning to address the salary issue when they confronted the play-ers in collective bargaining in 1991.

The owners failed to recognize that a labour crisis, in the person of Bob Goodenow, lay down the road, a crisis that would shake the foundations of the seventy-three-year-old operation. Business as usual had been good enough before; surely it would be good enough again. Or as Ziegler himself was fond of saying, "If it ain't broke, why fix it?"

There has always been an air of detachment about the people who run the NHL, a sense that hockey was merely an excuse to play croquet, hold grand parties, and compete ferociously amongst themselves. The legendary Detroit owner Jim Norris, Sr., who'd grown rich in the grain exchange in Chicago, set the tone for intramural competition in the 1920s. (Norris came from tough Canadian stock: his great-grandfather amputated his own leg after a logging accident left him pinned beneath a tree.) The hard-nosed Norris grew irritated when Blackhawks owner Major Frederic McLaughlin would not sell him the club (to add to the Red Wings). First Norris tried to locate a second NHL club in Chicago. When that request was denied, he started a rival league and placed a team, the Shamrocks, in Chicago. When McLaughlin (who was married to dancer Irene Castle) didn't budge, Norris purchased the Chicago Stadium—where the Major's men played—and immediately raised McLaughlin's rent by 50 per cent (this was during the Depression). Still, McLaughlin laughed at Norris, winning the Cup twice in the 1930s. Only after the Major's death in 1944 was Norris able to quietly purchase the team. Including the Red Wings and the New York Rangers, which he controlled through third parties, Norris now owned half the NHL; he also put Boston in his pocket after making emergency loans to aid Bruins owner Charles Adams through a financial crunch.

The three-team Norris domination prompted Toronto owner Conn Smythe to protest. For years, the irascible Smythe, who desperately wanted to be the NHL's lead dog, tried to get the league to admit that the Norris family and its many corporations controlled more than one club, contrary to NHL bylaws. At one point, Smythe tried to flush out the owners by accusing Chicago of deliberately running down the team so someone else could "step in and buy it at a bargain." He was censured for his comments. When NHL president Clarence Campbell refused to divulge the true owners of the Blackhawks, Smythe sent Campbell a list of the president's own expenses and salary since 1946, a reminder of who was boss. Finally, on the death of Jim Norris, Sr., in 1952, the family acknowledged Norris's ownership of the Chicago team and split the clubs among his children. Jimmy got the Hawks; Bruce received the Red Wings; daughter Marguerite—whom many considered the most able Norris offspring—was pushed into the background.

Another acrimonious clash pitted current Chicago owner Bill Wirtz against Philadelphia's Ed Snider; it reached a crescendo over who would succeed Clarence Campbell as NHL president in 1977. Wirtz and his ally, Detroit owner Bruce Norris, were worried that Snider would gain control of the NHL when Campbell stepped aside. They worried Snider was too liberal, too flashy (and, to Norris at least, too Jewish), and had been in the league for too short a time— only nine years. When Wirtz became chairman of the Board of Governors, he saw to it that Snider was kicked off the prestigious finance committee. Wirtz then convinced Campbell to stand aside as president in favour of his man John Ziegler, with the promise that the elderly Campbell would then be selected chairman of the Board of Governors. When Wirtz announced his plans to reward the loyal Campbell, Montreal's wily GM Sam Pollock turned to his neighbour at the table and said, "My name is Tucker, not Sucker!" A war of words developed over which faction would get their man—Ziegler or Snider—elected. The debate was finally settled with the election of Ziegler by a narrow 9–8 margin (Campbell was rejected for the chairmanship in favour of Wirtz). It was a divisive battle and it took several years before the rift between Wirtz and Snider was healed, by Ziegler and Alan Eagleson.

While the politics of the owners have always been Byzantine, their business practices have always been grounded in bricks and mortar. Jim Norris, Sr., quickly understood that the running of his beloved Red Wings was merely a nice sideline; there was more serious money to be made in owning and managing the buildings they played in. While he kept up the public posture of being a benevolent supporter of sport, he invested in a string of arenas and auditoriums around the United States. He bought circuses, ice shows, vaudeville troupes, wild-west shows, and boxing stables to fill the dark days between hockey games. He also purchased booking agencies and promoters to keep a steady flow of attractions for the Chicago Stadium, the Detroit Olympia, Madison Square Garden, the St. Louis Arena, and many other venues.

Later, his son Jimmy parlayed this impressive roster of buildings into control of the boxing business through his International Boxing Commission. Using regional arenas, he could develop fighters and then present the cream of the crop at the Garden in New York, for decades the de facto home of pro boxing. It was a cradle-to-grave system that gave Norris input at every level of the boxing business and discouraged competitors from moving in. (Just in case someone did try to use a little muscle, the younger Norris kept a few of Al Capone's old button men like Frankie Carbone and Sammy "Golf Bag" Hunt around to handle "security.")

Norris Sr. also perfected the art of maintaining balance sheets for the many businesses attached to his hockey teams. He could hide the real profitability of a team by having his arena charge exorbitant rents. A second way to decrease the team's profitability—while boosting the profits of his arenas—was to charge executive salaries and expenses from his related companies back to the hockey club. Another dodge was to keep the lucrative parking, concession, and souvenir sales in separate companies. When TV became a burgeoning source of revenues, these same techniques—overcharging for rights, siphoning profits into ancillary companies—were employed to make it look like the club was in trouble. And when all the subtleties were dispensed with, there was the simple scam of under-reporting the seats sold. In a famous example cited in *Net Worth*, the Rangers claimed attendance of 235,000 in 1954–55 when the true count was closer to 310,000.

In Toronto, Conn Smythe was emulating Norris's financial fan dance, but in reverse. The feisty war hero worked hard at keeping the profitability of Maple Leaf Gardens low by dumping the team's expenses on the arena, a gambit that depressed the stock price and allowed him to buy up stock in the building at bargain prices. Among Smythe's more enterprising accounting tactics was maintaining the cost of the team and the players on the books at $101,001 every year from 1931 to 1957. The downtown Toronto property upon which the Gardens stood was worth over $5 million by the late 1950s, yet Smythe was listing it as being worth just $467,138. Player salaries and expenses were padded and securities held by the Gardens in stock such as Massey Ferguson, Noranda, and International Nickel were listed at their original purchase price of $254,800, even when their real value was almost twice that.

Such accounting legerdemain allowed Smythe, Norris, and their general managers to tell players and the press that their clubs were far less profitable than they really were. It was a simple, brilliant strategy so long as you weren't caught by Revenue Canada or, in the U.S., by the Internal Revenue Service or the FBI. With friends in the right places at city hall or Congress, that was unlikely to happen. (The tactic of hiding profitability looked less clever decades later when Bob Goodenow went after the "hidden" profitability of clubs during the strike of 1992 and the lockout of 1994–95, demanding owners open their true books if they wanted to prove financial hardship. The clubs demurred.)

The Norris template has been the NHL's model ever since, with the most creative playing the arena shell game to perfection. When Harold Ballard assumed the running of Maple Leaf Gardens from the Smythe family in 1971, the venerable building was quickly dubbed the "Carlton Street Cashbox" for its ability to produce revenue from a dizzying parade of events other than hockey. And yet Ballard pleaded with his fans that the Leafs couldn't afford to meet the contract challenges of the WHA.

St. Louis was awarded an expansion franchise in 1967 despite the fact that no one from the Missouri city was applying for a team. The secret of St. Louis's appeal? Jimmy Norris and Arthur Wirtz (father of Bill) owned the antiquated St. Louis Arena and needed a tenant. So St. Louis—with no hockey tradition or team—got one of the six new franchises, while more established hockey cities such as Buffalo, Vancouver, and Baltimore were stiffed in the first wave of expansion. But perhaps the great modern exponent of real-estate power was Flyers owner Ed Snider, who purchased the old Philadelphia Spectrum from bankruptcy, established an arena-management company called Spectacor that ran numerous buildings (including the Ottawa Senators' rink), then built the new First Union Center. Snider has parlayed his success on the real-estate balance sheet into power at the NHL governors' level.

Those who failed to heed Norris's lessons on real estate were usually gone in short order. The Oakland Seals, Atlanta Flames, Kansas City Scouts, Colorado Rockies, Quebec Nordiques, and Winnipeg Jets were all arena-poor. They expired when they couldn't generate sufficient revenue from rinks they did not own or control or paid for in depressed Canadian dollars. Despite winning two Stanley Cups with Mario Lemieux in the 1990s, Pittsburgh has been a faltering franchise since 1967, because undercapitalized owners have never been able to use the Civic Center/Igloo/Mellon Center as a profit maker. They have been in and out of bankruptcy three times since 1967. After buying the club from the latest bankruptcy in 1998, Lemieux is now the Pens' playing owner; but even Mario the Magnificent has been unable to produce the new building that will guarantee the club stays in Pittsburgh.

The Minnesota North Stars had the most hockey-crazy market in America, with a long tradition of high-school and state hockey. But in 1993 they moved to Dallas, again due to real-estate woes. The various owners of the club, including the Gunds and Norm Green, did not own the Met Center and were unable to finance a new arena that would let them compete with larger NHL markets. Despite growing gate receipts, no property taxes, and a share of all events held at the Met Center, Green said in 1993 he had lost $24 million on the franchise. Using as a threat the prospect of moving the North Stars to Anaheim or Dallas, he lobbied local politicians for even more concessions or a new arena. He was given the cold shoulder. So the man who'd said in 1990, "Can you imagine saying, 'Buy tickets or we're going to move the team'?...that's the worst possible approach you could have. You can't blackmail people," pulled up stakes in the Twin Cities. When Bruce McNall told Green that Anaheim was being promised to others (namely Disney, which paid McNall a $25-million indemnification fee), the NHL salved his pride by offering him the Dallas market without an expansion fee.

Green—a Calgary real-estate developer who lost much of his fortune in the NHL—still seethes that Minnesota politicians later granted conditions to the expansion Wild that they did not give him. "We wanted to use a clause in our contract that allowed us to borrow against the lease to make improvements to the building," he recalls. "But the government wouldn't help. So we had to move. Six years later they gave the new people exactly the same thing. Why do governments always do that, paying after the fact?" Green's old club, the Flames, and their Alberta counterparts from Edmonton have both led a perilous financial existence since coming into the NHL in 1979 because they cannot use their home buildings to drive revenues, in the fashion of Detroit or Toronto.

While slick accounting was crucial to a successful NHL operation, so was knowing how to work the political levers to finance a new rink. According to critics of public financing for sports facilities, they found many politicians only too willing to listen. "They get free tickets, invitations to sit in the owner's skybox, and the chance to meet star athletes," says Ron Utt of the Heritage Foundation, a conservative Canadian think-tank. "Their boyish enthusiasm takes over."

Says St. Paul, Minnesota, mayor Randy Kelly: "Sometimes you'll get political leaders who are drooling to promote themselves into higher office, and you'll find they're willing to make short-term decisions that might create some excitement but don't look good for the communities." Pittsburgh city controller Tom Flaherty has seen how sports teams can spin the market. "You throw in baseball and apple pie, and it's the kids and the dreams of the kids—they've just got all the B.S. covered. You can't beat them."

In the early days of the NHL, arenas such as Maple Leaf Gardens and Chicago Stadium had been private projects with no direct government input. That dynamic changed in 1957 when Major League Baseball's Brooklyn Dodgers and New York Giants—both frustrated in attempts to build new ballparks—abandoned their long-time supporters for new homes in Los Angeles and San Francisco, respectively. The political nature of the moves (Robert Moses, head of urban development for the New York area, rejected the plans of Dodgers owner Walter O'Malley for a new stadium in downtown Brooklyn) infuriated jilted Dodgers and Giants fans, who took out their rage on politicians as well as O'Malley. From that time forward, no American or Canadian politician wanted to have a popular sports franchise skip town on his or her watch. Thus the concept of civic responsibility for a private business entered pro sports.

Politicians were soon falling over themselves to keep their teams and fans happy. New York officials, embarrassed by the Dodgers-Giants fiasco, lobbied for a new team in their area (they received the Mets in 1962). Baseball was happy to grant the request, adding the Houston Colt .45s (later Astros), Los Angeles Angels, and a new Washington franchise in a two-year span. Major League Baseball owners were even happier to see civic, state, and federal governments assist in building new stadia for the Mets and the Astros. Helping expedite construction of these sporting palaces was an American policy that exempted from federal taxes the interest paid to purchasers of bonds issued by state and local governments to finance objectives. The public borrowing for sports facilities soon became routine, prompting a rash of new stadia and arenas around the United States.

As Canadian-born Harvard law professor Paul Weiler points out in his book *Leveling the Playing Field*, these bonds were costly for governments: on a thirty-year bond for $300,000, public losses on tax-free interest can amount to as much as $120 million. Despite these losses, politicians were unwilling to say no to owners who used the threat of relocation. When a 1986 federal bill attempting to curtail this practice of tax-free bonds was enacted in Congress, team owners simply forced local politicians to rewrite the leases on the stadia to skirt the bill's impact. As a result, American cities, counties, and states committed or spent about $11 billion to build sixty-five new facilities in the 1990s.

In Canada, politicians such as Jean Drapeau and Paul Godfrey fell into line as well, pushing for the grotesquely over-budget Montreal Olympic Stadium and Toronto SkyDome respectively. Olympic Stadium has cost Montreal taxpayers well over a billion dollars since it was built in 1976, while the SkyDome has swallowed about $300 million in public money since 1989. Those boondoggles hardened Canadian attitudes about public funding of sports facilities. All four new arena initiatives for NHL clubs in Canada since then have been privately funded and, in some cases, heavily taxed. Montreal paid more in civic taxes on the new Bell Centre (which replaced the Forum) in 2002 than all the American NHL clubs combined paid on their arenas. The Ottawa Senators were obliged to spend $25 million on a highway interchange for their new arena when the Ontario government refused to fund the project. This attitude—coupled with the exchange differential on the Canadian dollar—has created several fiscal disadvantages for Canadian NHL teams. Yet when then–industry minister John Manley suggested a federal scheme to offset some of these handicaps to Canadian teams, he was quickly shouted down by angry citizens' groups and the media.

In the U.S., the pattern has been different. When the NHL finally released the pent-up demand for new franchises in the late 1960s (adding twelve clubs in seven years), teams did not need to use the relocation threat to get politicians onside. Glowing estimates of spin-off economic activity from teams and their playing facilities were

touted as justification for investing public money. But few economists support the spinoff theory. Andrew Zimbalist of Smith College
points out that for the seventy-two stadia and arenas built or
planned in the U.S. since 1990, almost two-thirds of the funding has
come from the public. Yet the financial impact has been short-term
and negligible. "If you want to inject money into the local economy,"
says University of Chicago economist Allen Sanderson, "it would be
better to drop it from a helicopter than invest in a new ballpark."

Still, civic and state officials were happy to help build luxurious
arenas with all the amenities in many of the expansion cities to host
NHL and NBA franchises. "It used to be the lords of industry had to
build their own railroads," Pittsburgh lawyer Kevin Forsythe told
the *New York Daily News*. "Now when you come to the major
league sports, putting Internet access into a luxury box suddenly
becomes a public cost. How did that happen?" But, went the idea, a
happy owner with a comfortable lease and concession deal in your
district made for a happy electorate. And with leagues operating as
de facto monopolies, it was incumbent on politicians to appease
their local owners—particularly after U.S. courts upheld the right of
a team to move even when the league does not approve (in the 1982
NFL v. Raiders case).

In locations such as Indianapolis and San Diego, the city is
obliged to pay the NFL teams when attendance falls short of pre-
scribed levels. In St. Petersburg, Florida, the city gets a small amount
for each ticket sold to the perpetually awful Devil Rays but has to
pay property taxes for the team. "The whole contract is an exercise
in stupidity," says Professor Darryl Paulson of the University of
South Florida.

When the NHL owners convened to welcome Ottawa and Tampa
into the fold in 1990, they were on the verge of a building boom that
would see twenty-three new facilities constructed in the next dozen
years. Just four would be built exclusively with private money. Many
of the teams occupying those buildings would receive advantageous
lease arrangements from local politicians.

So Washington's Abe Pollin was simply singing from the NHL's real-estate hymn book when, at the 1990 meetings, he pushed his colleagues for a $50-million price tag on new franchises. "We're awarding not just the right to play in the league," said the man who also owned the NBA's Washington Bullets at the time, "but real-estate opportunities and other business tie-ins." As Pollin had guessed, the value of both winning bids was predicated on developing the new arenas and adjoining real estate. Several of the unsuccessful bidders stated that they weren't that interested in hockey per se, but planned to build arenas that needed tenants.

As John Ziegler left the Breakers for New York that December day in 1990, he felt more relaxed than he had in weeks. He'd delivered the expansion booty he'd promised the owners—even if the applicants were less than sterling—and the board had approved further expansion for later in the decade. His patron, Bill Wirtz, was still onside, and there was the pleasing prospect of taking Bob Goodenow to the cleaners in collective bargaining the next year. As the excited shouts of the successful Ottawa group rose into the warm air of a balmy Florida evening, it seemed a great time to be John Augustus Ziegler, Jr.

5

Disclosure

It was the summer of 1991, and agent Rick Curran had a problem. Glen Sather, the Edmonton president and GM, was on the phone, and he was hot. Sather, who has a cutting wit and the vocabulary of tow-truck driver, is not a man to be crossed in the hockey world. The High River, Alberta, native built the small-market Oilers into five-time Stanley Cup champions with guile and swagger and by speaking his mind. One agent suggests taking a cut man with you for a frank exchange with the one-time NHL agitator, who had a ten-year on-ice career. Curran's ear burned against the receiver as Sather implied that the agent had been less than forthcoming in negotiations to re-sign the young Oilers centre Adam Graves.

"I told you you wouldn't get it, and you didn't."

"Didn't get what?" replied Curran, who has worked alongside Alan Eagleson, Bill Watters, and Bobby Orr in his lengthy career.

"You told me you were getting $500,000 for Graves," said Sather.

"I did."

"No, you didn't. I've got the contract right here in front of me."

"Have you got the face of the contract?"

"Yeah, I'm reading it right now."

"Read pages 8, 9, and 10, because that's where the rest of the money is. He got the $500,000. He got every cent. And more, just like I said he would."

Sather thumbed through the contract and found that Curran was right; the New York Rangers were paying the twenty-three-year-old Graves $500,000 a year to leave Edmonton. Sather could only shake his head in exasperation: he had lost his rising star to a big-city team, because his owner, Peter Pocklington, would not—or could not—match the Rangers' offer for the young free agent. As Sather hung up the phone, he realized that the inmates were suddenly running the hockey asylum.

Give-and-take between a miffed general manager and a determined agent is the lifeblood of the hockey business. Leverage, ego, anger, and strategic bursts of profanity all have their place in sealing a deal. "It can become difficult in the heat of a negotiation," allows Mike Gillis. "Especially when people are trying to enter the business as agents or general managers, it can be extremely difficult for them." But most agents and GMs can count on the fingers of one hand the times they've actually lost their cool; anger and abuse are not conducive to long-term survival in this world.

Before the 1990s, NHL management controlled the negotiating dynamic. Free agency was tightly controlled by a punitive compensation system. Players had little knowledge of what even their closest friends made, and management kept them in the dark. General managers could consult with the management of other clubs for advice on negotiating strategies. While athletes in other team sports had made quantum leaps in pay and mobility, the NHLPA under Alan Eagleson had always been a toothless tiger, rarely challenging the owners' domination.

Longtime Boston GM Harry Sinden remembers a typical exchange in the mid-1970s. "We had a player named Gregg Sheppard, made $65,000 or $70,000 a year. He was a 30-goal scorer that year. His agent came in and said, 'We want a five-year deal at $230,000 a year.' I remember I was looking down at a pad on my desk. I never looked up. I said, 'You've got thirty seconds to tell me you're kidding or get out of here.' And after a pause, he says, 'Well, what have you got in mind?' And we got a deal done. That kind of nonsense wouldn't fly today. Sheppard would go out and get his $230,000 somewhere else."

As a promising young centre in 1971, Larry Pleau, now the Blues GM, tried to wheedle money from the redoubtable Sam Pollock in Montreal. "I was injured most of the year, I came back at the end of the year, and we won the Stanley Cup. I was making $10,000. I didn't have an agent, so I went in to talk to Mr. Pollock myself. He always had a white handkerchief in his hand, and he was chewing on it as he talked to you. I said I deserved to make $20,000. He looked at me and said, 'What do you base that on?' And I said salaries have gone up since Orr came into the league, the cost of living, everything had gone up, so I think I deserve that much. And he said, 'You were a benchwarmer all year. I'll tell you what: you go home, reassess what you think your abilities are, and come back tomorrow.'

"So the next day I went back and he said, 'Have you thought about it?' I said, 'Yes, I still think I'm worth $20,000.' So he said, 'I'll give you a choice. You can have a one-way contract for $15,000 or you can have a two-way deal for $14,000 in the minors and $16,000 in the NHL.' I said, 'I'll take the one-way for $15,000 in the NHL.' That's a true story. That's what it was like."

The legendary Montreal goalie Ken Dryden, now president of the Maple Leafs, also recalls Pollock's handkerchief treatment. "He had this pained expression the whole time. You had a feeling you were physically hurting him when you asked for more money. For a moment you'd think, 'What am I doing, inflicting pain on this poor man?' And then you'd come to your senses."

As an Islanders forward, Pat Flatley tried negotiating on his own with GM Bill Torrey. Flatley arrived at Torrey's office for yet another meeting. "You may have noticed that the last few times we talked, I was holding a pencil," said Torrey. "This time, I'm holding a pen. That means I am not changing my number." Flatley signed for

Torrey's figure. So did defenceman Dave Lewis, now coach of Detroit, when he matched wits with the Isles GM and president. "Torrey told me that a team is like a pie," laughs Lewis. "There's a slice for Mike Bossy, a slice for Denis Potvin, a slice for Bryan Trottier...and so on through the lineup. Then he got to me. But for Dave Lewis, he said, there are only crumbs."

There were good reasons why the players found it hard to squeeze decent salaries out of the teams. "In the Eagleson era," recalls Devils GM Lou Lamoriello, "you didn't have those big TV and other revenues. When I came to New Jersey in 1987, the top contract on the Devils was for $300,000. We were going back and forth over hundreds of dollars. Now we're talking hundreds of thousands of dollars to make a deal happen. Maybe it was too one-sided then, but it's gone the other way to the point where we have a CBA we're all scared of."

Kirk Muller has been on both sides of the salary divide in his long career. "My first year in the NHL, I was making $105,000 in New Jersey," recalls Muller, who marked his nineteenth NHL season in 2003. "I missed the first day of training camp in 1984, because we were fighting over a $5,000 bonus. It took me until my thirteenth or fourteenth year in the league—when I went to Florida, where I signed a deal for $1.7 million—before I got to the big numbers."

Indeed, when Glen Sather called the Philadelphia-area home of Rick Curran in 1991 to gripe about Adam Graves jumping to the Rangers, the two men were functioning in new territory, the changing economy of the NHL. Eagleson was in a slow retreat from running the NHLPA, and new opportunities were opening up for creative agents. Owners, meanwhile, were preoccupied with grabbing easy money from expansion and dreaming of the blockbuster American TV deal. While they had trusted Eagleson's evaluation that his successor, Goodenow, would be a pushover, they were getting a rude shock from the man who looks like an Irish bouncer but negotiates like a Wall Street banker. "There are those who call the 1980s a golden era of hockey," Goodenow told ESPN in 2000. "But there was a sense of complacency then. The owners had it good. They sat around and got fat and lazy during the 1980s."

The owners had been aided in this lethargy, of course, by the indifferent running of the Players' Association. "In a sense, the NHL held all the cards until 1991," says IMG agent J.P. Barry, who worked for the NHLPA in the mid-1990s. Whenever an agent or player had a question about the working of the CBA, the questions were referred by the PA to the NHL for a ruling. "Sam Simpson was the conduit for the PA at the time. He would just write these letters to Gil Stein [then–NHL legal counsel] saying here's a series of status questions about the players and the CBA. And the NHL would look at these letters from their own standpoint and say, 'We'll tell him no, this is the rule and you can't go.' The answers always came back favourable to the NHL. And the Players' Association would never appeal the rulings. They accepted Gil Stein's word and that would be the position from that time on. These rulings still come up in grievance arbitrations to this day, and when they do, the commissioner is usually the arbitrator." The permanent control of NHL rights to drafted Europeans is an example of Eagleson's unchallenged acceptance of such a league ruling; it haunts European players to this day.

But the lax operation of Eagleson's PA also lulled ownership into loosening its grip on the wheel. A typical example of Eagleson helping out management—his supposed adversaries—came when the short-lived Cleveland Barons were in their death throes in 1978. The Barons—who had begun life as the Oakland Seals—were in last place in the Adams Division and out of money to finish the season. The NHL owners shrugged their shoulders when asked for money to keep Cleveland alive to the end of the year. Eagleson, however, leapt in, lending the team $750,000 from NHLPA funds, enough to get them through the year. With friends like the Eagle in management, it was easy to become complacent. Without Eagleson to help owners avoid their own excesses in the 1990s, hockey-men-turned-GMs such as Rogie Vachon, Ed Johnston, and Tony and Phil Esposito were thrust onto a high-stakes tightrope with no net. Men unschooled in salary negotiation found themselves up against a motivated force of lawyers and businessmen who combed the small print of the CBA, and a Players' Association that would back them to the last comma.

"They didn't have the background to deal with many of the new legal issues," says J.P. Barry, who went from NHLPA legal counsel to running IMG Hockey in 2001. "A lot of them had no technical expertise at all. They just looked at a guy and said, 'What do you think he's worth?' They didn't want to get into anything more than that. I don't think they were prepared for a well-armed agent force."

Adding to the problems was a GM's expanding job description. "On a day-to-day basis," says Neil Smith, "the GM is worrying about the farm team, call-ups, injuries, the coach's gripes, the media—all these things. Along comes an agent who's only analyzing one thing: how to get the most money for his client. You'd have maybe an hour a day to devote to the agent for, say, Mike Gartner. The agent could spend all day thinking about Gartner's contract. So when the agent came back the next day, you couldn't compete with what he had to say."

Mike Barnett concurs: "In the early stages, the responsibility was falling in the GM's lap. He had so many things to deal with that the time was not there to prepare and be as sophisticated as he wanted to be." Dealing with men whose primary job skill was evaluating talent, agents such as Curran used the new policy of salary disclosure and novel interpretations of the standard contract to rip holes in the traditional relationship between teams and players. "The biggest issue facing the NHL is managerial competence," says one NHL management source, who requested anonymity, "but they refuse to face up to it. You see the same old faces making the same old mistakes year after year, and the league does nothing about it."

Another former management figure paints a stark image. "It's like having a guy who simply carries a gun up against a guy who uses a gun for a living," says former Calgary Flames president Ron Bremner to describe the gap between the players' advocates and management.

Bremner's club was a perfect example of a franchise being out-gunned. The Flames had flourished under Cliff Fletcher, one of the best general mangers in NHL history, first in Atlanta, then in Calgary. He'd built a team from scratch that competed on even terms with the great Edmonton teams of the 1980s, reaching the finals in 1986 and winning a Stanley Cup in 1989. When Fletcher fled to Toronto in 1991, the Flames had a team loaded with stars established (Al MacInnis, Doug Gilmour) and emerging (Joe Nieuwendyk, Gary Roberts, Theoren Fleury). They also had one of the highest payrolls in the NHL.

The Flames, near the top of the standings and with a seemingly inexhaustible talent pipeline, felt they could forestall the strategies of the agents and a re-energized NHLPA. So they handed Fletcher's job to an untested Doug Risebrough. A former journeyman centre with Montreal and Calgary, Risebrough was soon out of his depth. After an acrimonious salary arbitration with Gilmour, he made the disastrous Gilmour–for–Gary Leeman trade with his old mentor Fletcher, then running the Maple Leafs. MacInnis was peddled to St. Louis, where he has remained a superstar; the man he got in return, Phil Housley, flopped in Calgary. Gary Suter was dispatched to Hartford. After almost four seasons of declining results and poor drafts, Risebrough was let go in 1996 (the last year Calgary made the playoffs).

Once again the Flames entrusted their GM's job to a first-timer. Al Coates, who'd started as the team's public-relations man, set out to learn on the job in the new business climate. But Coates now had one of the league's lowest payrolls, and he did no better than Risebrough. Nieuwendyk, Roberts, and Fleury were jettisoned for financial reasons, and the team began a string of seven consecutive years out of the playoffs. The high draft picks produced by those low finishes should have revived the franchise, but Coates's personnel man, Nick Polano, drafted poorly. Instead of stars such as Marian Hossa, Nik Antropov, and Sergei Samsonov, the Flames instead picked Daniel Tkaczuk and Rico Fata, who never lived up to their lofty draft status.

When the flickering Flames replaced Coates in 2000, you might have thought they'd have learned the lesson about untested executives. Progressive teams were hiring managers with a broad range of hockey and business skills. They also surrounded them with financial experts to manage the payrolls. But Calgary hired Craig Button, a personnel man from Dallas with no GM experience. Further, the Flames rejected Button's request for a contract specialist to handle the payroll. Button then handed out big contracts to underproductive players such as Mike Vernon, Rob Niedermayer, and Igor Kravchuk, while letting go such valuable ones as Jean-Sebastien Giguere, Filip Kuba, and Martin St. Louis. The losing seasons followed one after another, and in the summer of 2003 Button, too, was let go amid concerns that the Flames would flee Calgary.

Finally, was an experienced manager hired? No. Once again, the Flames chose a first-time NHL general manager, promoting veteran coach Darryl Sutter into the dual roles of coach and GM. All the while, as Calgary stumbled with an inexperienced front office, co-owner Harley Hotchkiss led the cry for a new, workable CBA—one that would save teams such as the Flames from their own mistakes. Author Michael Lewis used Oakland A's GM Billy Beane to illustrate the new managerial competencies in his book *Moneyball*. Beane, says Lewis, has looked past the accepted clichés that hamstring baseball. He goes outside the tight circle of conventional thinkers to employ Ivy League grads to chart probabilities and help him make personnel evaluations. The same data-crunching is used to peg the values of players to the A's' contract offers. Using this new, sleek paradigm, Beane has outfoxed many teams whose payroll exceeds Oakland's— the third-lowest in baseball in 2002. Since Beane adopted his sophisticated approach of looking outside his sport for answers, the A's have been the one small-market club to consistently make the playoffs. Rather than exploring the possibilities of Beane's tactics by going outside the lodge of old friends and former teammates to be more competitive, NHL teams continue their fruitless attempts at breaking the NHLPA as a solution to their chronic problems.

As they haggled over Adam Graves in the summer of 1991, neither Glen Sather nor Rick Curran could have foreseen a future of $10-million players. Salaries were bound to be pushed up by expansion and salary disclosure, but nobody imagined that hockey would emulate the lordly salaries of baseball or basketball. After all, owners reasoned, the collective bargaining agreement signed in 1986 had been a bulwark this long. Without major changes in that contract, went the reasoning, salaries ought to have remained fairly stable.

But the voluble Curran wasn't simply creating holes in the standard player's contract; he was forging a whole new deal between players and clubs. Curran's prize client that summer, Eric Lindros, was in limbo. Drafted first overall by the inept Quebec Nordiques in June 1991, the massive Oshawa Generals junior was refusing to sign with them. Lindros was a rare combination of size and skill, the prototype NHL player of the 1990s. He also knew his market value and was prepared to obtain it. The Nordiques and their top pick were now engaged in a waiting game. The Lindros standoff inflamed nationalist sentiment in Quebec, enraged the NHL establishment, and made Lindros a media whipping boy for the modern, selfish athlete. Marcel Aubut, the Nordiques owner, had two options: he could trade his rights to a team of Lindros's liking, or let Curran convince an ambitious NHL club to sign the prodigy and test the NHL bylaws about free agency.

Curran, Lindros, and Lindros's family were undaunted by the hostility their stand had generated. They knew there was no shortage of bidders; in an open market, every team would have gladly bid a fortune for the services of this bull with soft hands. But custom and the CBA prevented teams from talking to Lindros unless they dealt with Aubut first. A vain, competitive man, Aubut was not going to let his prize catch get away for less than a king's ransom. The Lindros saga was to be a revolutionary exercise in brinksmanship that would change the hockey business. But it would take a full year to resolve.

With Lindros on hold, Curran was also exploring the market values of his other young clients, such as Graves and Brendan Shanahan, who had played out their current contracts. The summer before, Curran knew, twenty-six-year-old defenceman Scott Stevens of Washington had signed as a Group One free agent with St. Louis. A prized young rearguard who played for Canada in the 1991 Canada Cup, Stevens had cost the Blues five first-round draft picks in compensation. But the Blues had been willing to pay the hefty price and suffer the wrath of fellow owners for breaking the gentleman's agreement on signing each other's free agents. That wrath came swiftly. "The Blues' aggressive spending in free-agent hockey players for huge salaries and bonuses made the club a pariah to other owners," noted Gil Stein years later.

Curran decided to exploit the same provision in the CBA. In essence, any Group One player—someone under the age of twenty-four when a season began—could play out the option year of his contract and become a free agent. The team signing the player would then have to compensate his original club with draft picks or a player of equal value. Both his new team and his old team put forward the names of players on the roster of the latter they believed were fair compensation. If the clubs couldn't agree on the player to be sent in compensation, the matter went to an independent arbitrator. There were many unknowns in the process, and while the free-agent gamble had been available since the 1970s, it had rarely been tested. In a famous example, Detroit had tried to sign Kings star goalie Rogie Vachon as a free agent in 1978; the case went to arbitration when Detroit was asked to give up their young centre Dale McCourt as compensation. After a drawn-out process, McCourt and Vachon stayed with Detroit, but the Wings surrendered two first-round picks to Los Angeles. To many, signing someone else's free agent seemed a risk not worth taking if it meant losing top stars of the future.

Since then, only Ron Caron, St. Louis's iconoclastic GM, had seemed willing to try his luck before an arbitrator who may or may not have hockey smarts. "Everybody talked about it," says Curran today, "but nobody had the balls to do it." Using the precedent set by Stevens in 1990, Curran decided to act. He selected Shanahan of New Jersey as his Trojan Horse for Group Ones. A top-three draft pick of the Devils in 1987, Shanahan had tallied 88 goals in his first four seasons with New Jersey, but with the tight-fisted Lamoriello guiding the Devils there was little hope of more than a marginal raise from his $130,000 salary.

Curran approached Ron Caron, the pepper-pot Blues GM. Despite having signed Stevens and amassing 105 points the previous season, the club had folded in the playoffs. Caron felt that Shanahan just might put them over the top. The Blues agreed to sign him to a $625,000 deal for one year and offered Rod Brind'Amour and Curtis Joseph in compensation. The Devils requested star defence-man Stevens—the same Stevens who'd signed as a Group One free agent in St. Louis the summer before. When the clubs could not agree, an arbitrator found for New Jersey; Stevens reluctantly went to Lamoriello's Devils (where he would win three Stanley Cups in the next fifteen years), while Shanahan became a Blue.

The steep compensation for Shanahan seemed to confirm every general manager's fears about signing other team's free agents: they could cost you dearly. "Shame on the Blues for being so naive," scolded *The Sporting News*. "Double whammy on them for daring to be so different." While most teams were frightened by the risks of free agency, the players were clearly impressed by the financial impact of changing teams. When Shanahan (who had 33 goals in his first year in St. Louis) re-signed with the Blues for $1 million a year in the summer of 1992—a 700 per cent raise in two seasons—it underscored how lucrative free agency could be, by taking a player from a team that doesn't pay (New Jersey) to a team that does (St. Louis).

Curran went to work finding a buyer for Graves. Though he'd scored just 23 goals in the previous three years in Edmonton, the Windsor Spitfires graduate was highly prized as a rugged player who'd helped the Oilers win the Stanley Cup in 1990. He'd made just $145,000 in his last season with Edmonton, but after the signings of Shanahan in St. Louis and Mark Recchi in Pittsburgh that summer, he was due a big raise as a free agent. Except that Sather, like Lamoriello, was a renowned hard-ass saddled with a tight budget and an owner pointed towards bankruptcy.

After weeks of discussions, Curran and Sather reached a tentative agreement to pay Graves $485,000 the following season—pending approval by Sather's financially strapped owner, Peter Pocklington. "Slats was pissed because there was no way he wanted to pay a young player that kind of money," says Curran. "Adam was going to become one of his top-paid players. But I told him, 'Glen, as God is my witness, if you don't give it to me, I have $500,000 from someone else, and I'm going.'" Sather snorted in disbelief that anyone would give the Oilers third-line forward $500,000 a year.

Sure enough, Pocklington (still draining the Oilers to support other money-losing ventures) passed on giving Graves the raise. Perhaps the Oilers owner—who never missed an opportunity to miss an opportunity—felt the $500,000 figure was a bluff; perhaps he simply didn't have the money. In any event, Curran knew that Neil Smith, the new GM of the Rangers, had scouted and signed Graves while working for Detroit. He loved the young power forward and thought his character was just what the Rangers needed to win their first Stanley Cup since 1940. And Smith's club had big money. Smith agreed to bring Graves to New York (where he would indeed help take the Rangers to the Cup three years later and score 52 goals in the 1993–94 season). The cherry on the sundae for both Curran and Smith was the arbitrator's decision on compensation: Edmonton received journeyman Troy Mallette for Graves; Mallette lasted just half a season with the Oilers.

"When we talked to Smith, our biggest conversation was not to negotiate the numbers," says Curran, who worked with Bill Watters after they split from Eagleson. "The biggest part of the conversation revolved around, 'Who do you think you're going to lose in the arbitration?' If you could build a case that you were not going to lose something significant, then it was worth going out to sign a guy.

Now it hurt when Shanahan went and the Blues lost Scottie Stevens, but what really pushed it over the top was when Neil Smith stood up and grabbed Adam Graves, because he only lost Troy Mallette. And the other teams said, 'Holy shit, that's a hell of a deal.' The beneficiaries were the kids who were already with their teams—Craig Patrick in Pittsburgh said, 'I can't afford to lose Mark Recchi,' and the Bruins said, 'We can't afford to lose Glen Wesley.'"

Curran saw almost everything he touched that summer come up gold. When St. Louis signed another Group One free agent from Boston, the Bruins decided to retaliate. Assistant GM Mike Milbury called Curran to inquire about another client. "What are you doing with Glen Featherstone in St. Louis?" asked the former Bruins tough guy. Curran said he didn't know yet. "Fuck it, we're going to sign him this afternoon," snapped Milbury. So Featherstone, who'd scored just 5 goals with 205 penalty minutes in St. Louis the year before, moved to Boston and saw his salary quadruple in the process.

The Stevens, Shanahan, and Graves contracts cracked open the door to a free market in players, one that had been sealed shut for seventy-five years. Based on the Blues' willingness to explore new ways of building their team (the dreaded "thinking outside the box" of M.B.A. schools), agents could now shop their eligible players in ways thought impossible a few years earlier. Finally, an agent could play one club off another. Creating these markets for a player is often the most important thing an agent can do for his client. Sometimes it's as simple as answering the phone; other times it means saying to management, "Gary Bettman won't get fired if you don't sign my client, but you might." While agents are not allowed to discuss clients under contract with competing clubs, there's nothing to say that you can't make suggestions to a willing GM. "You can talk about their team, what they have, what they lack," says Mike Gillis. "You paint a picture of what you see as their needs and you let them put it together. You never have to mention any of your players."

While they were highly competitive amongst each other, owners had generally opted for the NHL's "greater good" over their own local imperatives until the 1990s. They were wary of starting a salary spiral and angering their fellow governors (as the Blues learned when they signed Stevens). So the big-money clubs in New York, Boston, Chicago, and Philadelphia acted like small markets, agreeing not to cannibalize their smaller compatriots, while pocketing a healthy profit in return from the depressed payrolls. It helped that, until the 1990s, most teams were also still owned by a single figure or family who could be held accountable by the other owners. This was a massive disincentive to "free agents" changing teams.

Large corporations, though, were coming to see that owning a sports team was a great way to create synergies with other businesses and with clients. Operating a hockey team as a loss leader for other businesses became a fashionable corporate strategy. The concept of buying naming rights to an arena also crept into the mix, showering more money on hockey owners. The Board of Governors was no longer peopled exclusively by sportsmen, as in the good old days; some of the governors were CEOs of large corporations.

To Dave Checketts, president of Madison Square Garden—including the Rangers and the Knicks—from 1994 to 2000, this corporate influx was bad news for sports leagues. "My very strong feeling is that big companies should not own teams," he told *Newsday*. "It's a different business than they're used to, and there's no way they can appreciate the culture and chemistry that has to be part of a team to succeed." But the corporate wave continues to dominate in the NHL—and other leagues.

There were other reasons why the NHL resisted an open market in free agents. The conventional wisdom said that hockey in the United States could never compete evenly with the big three team sports in North America: the NFL, NBA, and Major League Baseball. Until Gretzky's move into Southern California in 1988, the NHL's popularity remained confined to those areas of the country where ice was readily available. Beyond a few *Slap Shot* locales, hockey was a non-factor south of the Mason-Dixon line. Baseball, basketball, and football were played throughout the U.S., and their appeal dwarfed that of hockey.

Some of this inferiority complex was self-imposed. In the 1950s, when Walter Brown ran both the Boston Bruins and the Boston Celtics, it was the basketball club—winners of seven straight NBA titles—that would accommodate hockey games. There are stories of the Celtics playing games at midnight in the Garden or slopping across a parquet floor left damp by the ice beneath. And as the authors of *Net Worth* pointed out, CBS TV had been willing to pay $210,000 to show NHL games nationally in the 1957–58 season, when pro basketball couldn't get a sniff of network time. By the time Curran was doing his shopping, however, the NBA held the upper hand in the rivalry between the two sports. The proof was in the TV ratings: where the NHL playoff games on ABC in 2002 drew a 3.3 rating (3.3-million U.S. TV households), the NBA championship series garnered a 10. And for those who say that basketball has always been more popular than hockey, it's important to remember the strides made by the NBA since the 1970s, when the NBA championship final series was shown on tape delay at 11:30 p.m.

Despite the presence of media-based owners such as Ed Snider—who'd made millions from his cable-TV business—the NHL had typically let its network opportunities pass, convinced that it was a marginal enterprise in the U.S. Chicago owner Bill Wirtz still refuses to televise the team's home games in the belief that it hurts the gate. "My question is," said Skip Prince, the NHL's vice-president of television in 1992, "are there hockey fans [in the U.S.] or team fans? Would national exposure to a game in which there is not a current interest on a national basis be anything more than putting on a long and expensive infomercial?" Using this reasoning, the NHL signed with small cable outfits such as Cablevision and remained a regional sport in the United States for many years.

This lack of broad appeal in America and the NHL's ultra-conservative approach to television naturally produced puny national TV contracts. This intransigence is best illustrated by the now-famous tale of an owner in the 1960s asked to move a few seats in his arena to make room for TV cameras. "No way," he is reported to have said.

"I'm in the business of selling seats, not helping out TV." The NHL's first deal with CBS, in 1967, was for $2 million; the NFL's deal was then worth $14 million and rising fast (a 1:7 ratio that is now 1:13.5). After the initial interest from U.S. networks in the 1960s and early 1970s, the NHL was not seen nationally on an American network from 1974 till 1992. The greatest years of Guy Lafleur and Wayne Gretzky passed far from the gaze of U.S. network-TV viewers. Instead, the league concentrated on local and regional deals. "I now believe that it is no longer in our best interest to continue trying to get some sort of game-of-the-week package on national U.S. television," said John Ziegler in explaining the league's strategy.

TV executive Ralph Mellanby, once the executive producer for *Hockey Night in Canada*, discovered that while the league felt it wasn't up to prime time, it wasn't about to adjust the style of play to attract new viewers either. "We put together a six-person committee for John Ziegler in the early 1980s to make the game more attractive on TV," recalled the veteran broadcaster, who headed up the 1988 Calgary Winter Olympic Games telecasts. "We had Danny Gallivan, Scotty Connell [who started ESPN], myself.... We came up with a series of eight changes to speed the flow of the game for TV. There were twelve-minute intermissions, goalies not allowed behind the net to play the puck, line changes only on the fly, free faceoffs if the player was thrown out of the circle...eight in total. And they rejected them all. They were against changing the game, and they still are. It's the same dinosaurs running the game as back then."

Even the five-year, $125-million deal with ESPN and ABC in 1992 was seen as an exploratory thrust into the market, concentrated mostly on the fledgling espn2, a secondary carrier of the sports cable giant. John Pickett, the Islanders governor, summed up the NHL's media timidity in the early 1990s: "TV is important and will be some-day, but maybe not in our lifetime."

In the same period, NASCAR transformed itself from a regional Southern outfit populated by rednecks and daredevils to a sleek national TV and promotional powerhouse that generated billions for itself and its sponsors. If the ugly duckling of NASCAR could market itself into billions, why couldn't the NHL? "It may be unfair to compare the NHL to NASCAR or the NFL," David Carter, a sports-marketing consultant in Los Angeles, told the *Globe and Mail*. "But [the NFL and NASCAR have] gone past getting the hard-core fan to really embracing the casual viewer. And it's those casual viewers and broader audiences that the advertisers are really looking for. Hockey's had a hard time getting past that anemic TV rating."

By the time Rick Curran marketed his young free agents in the summer of 1991, NHL people led by McNall started suggesting that TV money might be the panacea for maintaining competitive balance between the markets in Canada and the United States. Noted Gil Stein, the NHL's president in 1992–93: "The discrepancy in local revenues between our small-market and large-market teams was getting so great that the small-market teams would be unable to compete in the marketplace for star free agents. A significant leap in shared league revenue from U.S. network rights could be the key to the ultimate survival of the league."

Revenue-sharing worked perfectly in the NFL, where big national TV contracts created a pool of wealth that allowed Green Bay, a city of a hundred thousand, to compete against New York, Philadelphia, and Chicago. In the 2002 season, each NFL club received an even share of $77.34 million from these national TV contracts—enough to fund their salary-capped payrolls and have plenty left over.

This enlightened sharing approach had been developed in 1961 by NFL commissioner Pete Rozelle, back when national TV revenues were tiny and the NFL was still considered subordinate to college football in most markets. Rozelle had persuaded Congress to allow the NFL to bargain for TV rights as one entity, not as fourteen separate clubs. (As a result, NFL teams now cannot sell local TV rights for their games, except in the pre-season.) Owners in the early 1960s gave little thought to their small shares at the time ($400,000 each), concentrating instead on gate receipts—as the NHL does to this day. But thanks to Rozelle's skilful marketing and the technological explosion, those paltry early cheques from TV turned into the current eight-year, $18-billion deal with ABC/ESPN/Fox/CBS. Rozelle pioneered the NFL's push into prime time with *Monday Night Football* in 1970, which increased TV revenues exponentially. While the NFL model is today the envy of other sports, it's unlikely that today's commissioner, Paul Tagliabue, could get mercenary NFL owners such as Jerry Jones of the Cowboys and Al Davis of the Raiders to think so selflessly had Rozelle not paved the way through his lobbying of Congress and obtaining even shares of the TV pool in the 1960s.

Baseball and the NBA, too, developed large national TV contracts while hockey slept. The NBA now gets $4.6 billion from ABC, ESPN, and TNT; baseball gets about $3 billion from Fox and ESPN. These healthy contracts enabled the leagues to fund salary escalations while maintaining some balance between small and large markets—a balance that finally broke down in the late 1990s with the advent of gargantuan regional TV contracts like the Yankees' ten-year, $500-million local cable-TV contract with Cablevision (which has also owned the New York Rangers and Knicks since 1994).

Hockey's national TV money, meanwhile, crept along at a pathetic pace, shackled by diminished expectations and pedestrian marketing. When NHL president John Ziegler resigned in 1992, the league's current TV deal with SportsChannel America brought in a modest $51 million over three years. (The NBA's national deals at the time were worth $275 million a year.) Today, Gary Bettman has boosted that to about $850 million from ABC, ESPN, and the Canadian carriers CBC and TSN. That's $5.7 million per club (compared to $12.66 million per club in the NBA).

"The biggest difference with the other three sports is TV," notes Blues GM Larry Pleau, who must compete in St. Louis with the legendary baseball Cardinals, the Rams, and college sports. "When the Board of Governors in the NFL sit down, they've all got that same big amount in their left pocket. That's TV. What's in their right pocket is what they make for themselves. All the other sports are like that. In the NHL, though, when we sit down, there's just a little in the left pocket. What really counts is what's in the right pocket, what you can come up with at the gate."

"The league gets so little central TV money," agrees sports economist and author Andrew Zimbalist. "And there has been little formal revenue-sharing amongst clubs beyond the TV money and licensing revenues. So you have the potential in the NHL for not just economic disparity but competitive disparity, too. That has been—and remains—the big challenge that hockey faces."

Until the early 1990s, NHL owners and general managers had balanced that challenge and were reluctant to get into a spending frenzy, with the aid of a compliant NHLPA. But Curran understood that, with the eclipse of Eagleson and Ziegler, the hockey world was in flux. He could see it in Lindros, a man who knew his worth and who was not willing to submit to the accepted rules for the rank and file. He could see it in the trend away from individual ownership in the league and towards corporate bosses using the sport as a loss leader for their cable- or satellite-TV enterprises or other entertainment-related businesses.

Most of all, he could see the changes brought about by salary disclosure—the publication of players' salaries and bonuses for comparative purposes in negotiations—a shift so radical that the NHL has not yet recovered. "It was a huge development," says agent Don Baizley. "I don't think any of us who were proponents saw how inflationary the effect was going to be. It was just like what happened to CEOs in the 1990s when their compensation became public. They started to leapfrog each other, higher and higher. 'He got this, I need more'—that sort of mentality."

The NHL had prospered for decades by hiding their employees' salaries. When Eddie Shack was traded to Boston from Toronto in 1967 for Murray Oliver and cash, Shack tried to find out how much money had changed hands. Punch Imlach told him the figure was $30,000. The true figure, Imlach revealed in his autobiography, was

$100,000. "If Shack had known he'd been sold for $100,000 U.S. and Murray Oliver, he would have been down to see Milt Schmidt with a lawyer, demanding $50,000 a year. I couldn't do that to Uncle Miltie after what I'd already done."

The players' own man was no help, either. The late Billy Harris recalled Eagleson phoning him to ask what amount he was seeking in contract talks with Oakland. Eagleson told Harris he was trying to help Bob Baun get a grasp of what number he should request from the Seals. Harris asked Eagleson what he should ask from Oakland GM Bert Olmstead. "Twenty-five thousand," replied Eagleson. Of course, Eagleson never told Harris that Baun was asking $70,000— which he received. Had Harris known, he would have asked for much more than the $25,000 he settled for. Harris learned thirty years later that Eagleson was in fact calling on behalf of Olmstead, not Baun, and that his old Leafs teammate had made $45,000 more than he did in Oakland. As a kicker, Eagleson billed Harris $750 for the legal "advice."

Former Hab Gilles Lupien, now an agent, recalls the negotiating process before salary disclosure: "My agent didn't know what other guys were making. I remember he walked into the room and asked the other defencemen how much money they were making so he could do negotiations. As soon as they opened the salaries and told everybody what they're making, everything started to budge."

The veteran Bruins GM Harry Sinden understood the value of keeping salaries secret. "An agent would come in, and I'd know he didn't have the information. He'd say, 'Wait a minute, in Chicago they're paying that much to a guy who got 20 goals. My guy got 25.' And I'd say, 'No, I talked to Chicago and they're not paying him that.' He'd usually bullshit you a bit, but I could always say, 'No, you're wrong.' So you'd negotiate from that position of knowledge." Occasionally, a salary was made public. When Dave Taylor inked a seven-year, $1.7-million deal with the Kings, agents seeking information grabbed it like a drowning man grabs a life preserver. But these opportunities were few. Glen Sather agrees that management was firmly in the driver's seat. "The information wasn't as readily available to everybody, and we kind of had things more in control. They were being paid well, but they weren't being paid as well as they could have been."

Says agent J.P. Barry, who took over IMG Hockey when Mike Barnett accepted the GM's job in Phoenix, "People didn't know the rules, they weren't handed out. Salary disclosure was a huge step, because the agents knew exactly what was going on with the bare bones of different contracts." Salary disclosure is such an obvious negotiation tool that one wonders why it was not adopted years earlier, as in the other major team sports. Eagleson claims he couldn't get the players to approve. "I've been for salary disclosure, gentlemen, for years," he said, "and you guys have been against it."

The players tell a different story. "It wasn't high on Al's agenda," recalls Mike Gartner, an executive-board member who now works for the NHLPA. "He did bring it up to the guys on one occasion, and a lot of players wanted it to happen. But some had reservations about their salary being public: 'We're going to get hammered in the paper, your teammates are going to be jealous, people are going to be saying you're making this or that.' And it's true…every point. But it was a negative, short-sighted view of the consequences. What Al didn't convey was the benefits, and those benefits are enormous. It was the biggest factor in escalating salaries, I think."

Former player rep Pat Verbeek says he tried to convince his fellow members of the NHLPA's board to vote for salary disclosure. "I said, 'Look what it's doing for baseball. They're getting rich. How can you not vote for it?' But Al was always selling the negative side of the issue, so guys like Bobby Smith would vote against it, because they didn't like the idea of people knowing what they made. When it finally did come, salary disclosure was the thing that broke it open on salaries." Says former defenceman Tom Laidlaw, now an agent. "Looking back, if Eagleson really had our best interests at heart, it would have been done long before 1990." Harry Sinden knew exactly what was at stake. "The history in other sports, especially baseball and basketball, was that their salaries increased 35 per cent as soon as they got salary disclosure. A few clubs were really against giving it to Eagleson in 1990."

Opinions vary on why Eagleson resisted salary disclosure. Some say he was kowtowing to his pals Ziegler and Wirtz. But Curran, who worked in Eagleson's office, points out, "Sports Management Ltd., of which he was president, represented more players in the NHL than anyone else. Part of the value in representing all those players was his knowledge of what they made. It wasn't disclosed. We knew what they all made, though, because we had most of the players. That was an element of our company that we used to our advantage when we recruited young players. Why would he put on his PA hat and screw with a system that worked so well when he had his agent hat on?"

The effect of salary disclosure soon became obvious. Agents began using it as a hammer on unsuspecting GMs. "The way we used to do the contracts," says Sather, "you would compare players throughout the league to the top scorer, not to the top scorer on every team. Pretty soon, the trend was set by the agents and the Players' Association that every team had a top scorer, every team had a top player who was getting more minutes. As the system evolved you had twenty-one top scorers, twenty-one best defenceman, twenty-one tough guys or twenty-one goaltenders. That created the spiral of salaries."

Employing previously undisclosed salaries and Group One free agency in 1991, Curran not only moved Brendan Shanahan to St. Louis, Adam Graves to the Rangers, and journeyman Glen Featherstone to Boston; he also got his clients Mark Recchi (Pittsburgh) and Glen Wesley (Boston) re-signed with their clubs at greatly increased salaries. "What that summer told me," says Curran, who now works with his old friend Bobby Orr, "was that there were ways for clubs to improve themselves. But teams had been reluctant to do so up to that point, because nobody else had done it. Once a team did it, others were less reluctant to jump in and grab a kid who had been drafted a couple of years earlier in the top number-two, -three, -four draft picks." It also demonstrated that unrestricted free agents of even marginal quality would command as rich a salary in the NHL as they had done in baseball and the NBA.

The players—now led by Bob Goodenow—saw this escalation and cheered. Management, of course, vowed to crush it in the next round of collective bargaining, slated for the 1991–92 season. The stage was set for the NHL's first off-ice showdown.

6

Hired Gun

If the dressing room is a hockey player's home, then a beer joint is his sanctuary. Dressing rooms are for media sound bites, weary clichés, and coach's speeches. It's the last place a player wants to bare his soul. To get honesty from players, you need to put them at a battered corner table filled with beer glasses. It was in pubs and taverns that a players' association was spawned in 1956 and again in 1967. The aroma of stale beer is a player's truth serum, the flickering TV high above the bar his firewall against the pressures of fans, owners, media, wives, and agents.

As a man with hockey in his blood, Bob Goodenow knew this as well as anyone. When the rookie director of the NHLPA needed a secluded spot for an economics lesson in 1992, he found it in the dank atmosphere of a pub in the Leaside area of Toronto. Just four months into the executive director's job, he sketched his theory on the economics of the NHL on a bar napkin.

Goodenow put the rich clubs, such as the New York Rangers and Toronto, at the top of the napkin. The poorer clubs, such as Pittsburgh and Minnesota, he scribbled at the bottom. In the middle of the beer-stained napkin were teams such as Los Angeles and St. Louis, the NHL's middle class. "Here's where you find the fair market value of a player in today's economy," he said, jabbing the pen into the words "Kings" and "Blues" on the napkin. "Not up here with the Rangers and Leafs. In the middle. But the NHL wants them to be paid down here." He jabbed derisively at the words "Penguins" and "Stars" on the lower portion on his napkin. "And we're not going to get a settlement till we establish this"—he points to the middle-rank teams once more—"with the league." The pen clattered on the wooden tabletop, and Goodenow sipped his beer.

Over the previous few months, Goodenow had used this message in dressing rooms, pubs, and airports to unite hockey players as never before. As details of Alan Eagleson's corrupt handling of the Players' Association surfaced in police reports and the media, Goodenow's star rose; he had become the saviour players longed for twenty-five years earlier at the advent of the NHLPA.

Others do not have such a warm appreciation of square, sandy-haired Goodenow. Harry Sinden, who has run the Boston Bruins for over thirty years, lowers his voice and looks into the questioner's eye when asked about the NHLPA executive director. "This is my opinion only. Alan Eagleson had a genuine concern for the good of hockey. I don't think Bob Goodenow does. If you could show Eagleson that the game was in trouble, he'd try and help you out of it. If you show Goodenow you're in trouble, he says, 'I don't believe you' or 'I don't care.' That's how he comes across to me."

There are almost as many views of Goodenow as there are people in the hockey business. He's a pariah, a saviour, a bragging bully, a protector of the weak; he's a pitiless exploiter; he's an emancipator on the order of John L. Lewis. He inspires fear, awe, and loathing—sometimes all at the same time. Rick Curran says, "Bob has his own challenges, his own agenda to deal with, and that's fine. But...having been a part of the early days, sitting here twenty-five years later, [I think] he's done a hell of a job. Has he made some mistakes? He'd be the first to admit it. Is he always right? Not necessarily. From a player's standpoint, every player today is better educated than he was in the old days. They're better off for it, and I think that's a positive."

"I remember I had a player held out at training camp," says player agent Tom Laidlaw. "The contract finally got done and Bob called up and said, 'What are the numbers?' I told him. I think I got $1.5 million in the first year and $1.8 million in the second, something like that. Bob automatically says, 'Well, I think you should have got 1.7 and 2.' If I told him we got 2 and 2.5, he would have said 2.2 and 2.7. At first it kind of takes you aback and you think, 'What a jerk this guy is.' But you know what? Bob always wants everybody to be doing their best for the players. For that I admire him."

Whatever your opinion of Goodenow, his impact on the hockey business can't be disputed: in ten years, the inscrutable Harvard-educated lawyer turned the NHL Players' Association from a house union into one of the most effective employee associations in North America. While maintaining many of the legal rights of a union— such as protection from owners' collusion—he has also protected the players' individual right to negotiate independently with management. Without him, it's doubtful that players would make half the money they do today. How you feel about that last statement probably determines whether you see him as a hero or a villain.

"That guy helped everybody," says agent Gilles Lupien, a former Montreal defenceman. "Even the teams—I think he helped them, too, because the value of a franchise was $50 million, now it's $150 million for many."

"I think Goodenow's done a great job if your only concern is making money," says former Rangers GM Neil Smith. "I think the NHLPA is killing the golden goose. To me, they've got their foot on its throat, stomping it to death. I don't understand that. He's got to take the long view. You can't just pound the shit out of everybody."

A Detroit native, Bob Goodenow is a product of the same minor hockey system in which NHL owners Mike Ilitch and Peter Karmanos once sponsored teams. (Ilitch was reportedly miffed when the young man he'd known from minor hockey later led Ilitch's Red Wings out on strike in 1992.) For a time he played on the same Junior Red Wings teams as Mark and Marty Howe, who went on to enjoy NHL and WHA careers. Described by friends as "modestly talented but massively motivated," Goodenow went on to captain the varsity hockey team at Harvard and play on the U.S. national team in 1974–75. He then played two seasons with Flint of the International Hockey League, scoring 25 goals and 65 points in 108 games. "I could see I wasn't going to be an NHL player," Goodenow says, "and I wanted to finish my education."

After retiring from pro hockey, Goodenow went to University of Detroit law school to study labour law. There he met a fellow student named Bob Riley. "Bob's as competitive a man as I've ever met," says Riley, who works as counsel for the NHLPA in addition to his practice in Detroit. "Whether it was tennis or law school or business, he was a burning competitor. If you played cards with him, you definitely wanted him on your side." Upon graduation, Goodenow went to work for Unisys in Pittsburgh, then returned to Michigan and practised labour law.

Through his hockey contacts, he began helping players with their contracts. His most celebrated negotiation was on behalf of Brett Hull in St. Louis in 1990. Like his father Bobby, Brett was a deadly scorer but not stellar at the defensive side of the game. Hard-liners called him lazy, and Calgary had found him wanting enough to send him to the Blues, where he racked up 205 goals in three-plus seasons. In the wake of Gretzky's precedent-setting deal in Los Angeles, Goodenow was able to peg Hull's value to that of Gretzky. Coming off a 72-goal season in 1989–90, Hull was the most dangerous sniper in the NHL and a box-office draw—yet he made just $125,000 a year. Goodenow extracted a three-year, $7.3-million contract from GM Ron Caron of the Blues. Goodenow's skilful linking of Hull to Gretzky marked the genuine beginning of the salary spiral.

But the real epiphany for Goodenow came not with Hull but with journeyman winger Paul Fenton, whom he helped with an arbitration case in the late 1980s. Looking for help from the Players' Association in Fenton's case, Goodenow was instead confronted with a disjointed, haphazard NHLPA head office that could offer little beyond wishes of good luck to agents seeking help—that's if you got a reply at all. Analysis of contract data was practically impossible to come by. The executive director—who bragged about the thriftiness of his "three-man" operation—was typically preoccupied with international hockey or his agency work. Unless he could find an angle for himself, Eagleson was typically unresponsive or even abusive to rival agents. Any improvements in the bargaining process during the years of Eagleson's leadership were made by individual agents. "You were operating in a vacuum for the most part," recalls Mike Barnett, "in terms of what other players on the team, or in the league, were getting. It was a very loose group when Alan was running the PA. Agents used to talk to agents, but the common denominator was seldom Alan."

The frustration of trying to represent Fenton without help from the PA convinced Goodenow that if hockey players were to share in the riches enjoyed by baseball and NBA players, it would take a modern, committed operation ruled by computer programs and bright young lawyers. He only had to look at how baseball players had been led by Marvin Miller and Don Fehr to sense what could happen in the NHL. If he hadn't been convinced before that players needed to take back their union, he was converted by the mess he found on Maitland Street in Toronto when he sought help for Fenton. But with Eagleson doggedly hanging on to his job in the midst of a firestorm of dissent, Goodenow never harboured illusions of running the NHLPA. "My practice was building, I liked my clients, my family was happy in Detroit. I wasn't really interested in the job," he recalled. Even when a search committee was formed to find a successor to Eagleson, Goodenow played the reluctant candidate, suggesting other names but resisting any efforts to draft him for the post.

After the divisive 1989 NHLPA showdown between Eagleson and Garvey in West Palm Beach, finding an ideal candidate proved tricky amid hockey's fractured union politics. Most of the names proposed were perceived as either pro-Eagleson or pro-Salcer/Winter. Others were not interested in trading in the profitable business of representing players for the headaches of modernizing the NHLPA. In this void, Goodenow's name kept reappearing. Even though many of his clients had been ringleaders in the move to unseat Eagleson, he was not generally believed to have had a particular bias. Still, there was subtle pressure for "Goody" to take the Eagle's perch. Finally, with the Hull deal concluded, Goodenow stopped playing hard-to-get and signed on as the deputy executive director of the NHLPA in the summer of 1990. It was agreed that he would move to Toronto, drop his agent business, and work with Eagleson on an orderly transition of authority.

The idea was that, by 1992, Eagleson would retire as executive director but stay on as the international hockey promoter. Then, at a to-be-determined date, Eagleson would depart and leave Goodenow with the reins of the NHLPA. Most crucially, Goodenow would be responsible for preparing the association for collective bargaining, which was to start the following year. Eagleson would consult on the talks, but would concentrate on the 1991 Canada Cup tournament.

To anyone who knew Eagleson, a consulting role seemed laughable; almost everyone in the NHL head office assumed that, when the owners got tough with the new man, Eagleson would return in triumph to orchestrate a deal, as he had always done with his pals Ziegler and Wirtz. Eagleson himself had sketched out such a scenario for the NHL president and chairman of the Board of Governors. "The problem with this surreal daydream," wrote Gil Stein, "was that Eagleson really believed it—and so did Ziegler and Wirtz. They had been told by Eagleson that it would happen, and he had also assured them the players would never strike."

Eagleson belittled Goodenow in private, which is not surprising, considering the threat Goodenow posed to him. Of the 1989 meeting in Florida, Eagleson later wrote, "I saw the whole operation then, and still do, as an attempted U.S. takeover of a Canadian union." (His anti-U.S. sentiment didn't extend to his own salary and pension, which he thoughtfully squirrelled away in American currency at banks in North America and Europe.)

Eagleson welcomed Goodenow to NHLPA headquarters by installing him in a cramped back office where visitors were obliged to duck under a low ceiling. His barely disguised contempt showed itself in many ways: he insisted Goodenow get his own passes for the 1990 World Championships from Team U.S.A.; he hid documents; he offered minimal staff help. "Eagleson had no respect for Goodenow," observed NHL vice-president Gil Stein, "and resented his presence at the NHLPA. He felt Goodenow was his intellectual inferior and would stumble badly in his first foray into collective bargaining."

Unfortunately for the NHL, the owners trusted Eagleson's appraisal. They were soon to find out what a mistake that was. Says Bob Riley, "The term 'advocate' is overused these days, but in Bob's case it's appropriate here. He was the first true advocate many NHL players ever had."

Goodenow conveyed that he was nobody's patsy during his initial encounters with the league. After seeing him at a holiday resort in Massachusetts in the summer of 1990, one NHL insider described the former Harvard captain as "introverted, sullen, and humourless." Of course, next to the crass, garrulous, noisy Alan Eagleson, even Jerry Lewis might come across as an introvert. If the dramatic change in style hadn't hit the owners, Goodenow's comments a week later at a sports-agents' symposium certainly did. Asked about the progress of talks towards a new CBA, Goodenow noted that the league had proposed meetings in the winter of 1990–91. "Had they asked me," Goodenow told the gathering, "I would have told them not to bother, since 98 per cent of a collective bargaining agreement is negotiated at the eleventh hour, the day before the old agreement is to expire." If they hadn't already nicknamed him, the NHL might have slapped the moniker "Eleventh-Hour" on Goodenow. (Ziegler and crew had already applied the sobriquet "Jingle Nuts" to their adversary.)

"Eleventh-hour" aptly described Goodenow's bargaining strategy for the 1991 CBA talks. Eagleson would probably have spent the winter in his Toronto office issuing veiled threats and lofty promises through the media—all to be recanted at crunch time during negotiations. But Goodenow spent the time visiting players, setting up lines of communication, fostering an understanding of the issues and the need for a real strike threat. Much of his work involved dealing with the fears and apprehensions of his conservative membership. "Most players are Canadian," the late Carl Brewer once explained. "We're polite to a fault. We don't want to tip the boat. So we let a guy like Eagleson play with our fears until we don't know what's right or wrong any more."

"Guys are just afraid," agreed Ed Olczyk, then with the Leafs. "You're only in this league for so long and you don't want to piss the wrong guy off." For Danny Gare, who played in Buffalo and Detroit, it came down to trust. "The NHL, Alan Eagleson, they were great names when you were a young player, and you felt like everything was supposed to be done the right way. Then you find out that it hasn't been done the right way."

Goodenow was able to translate those fears and anxieties into a brotherhood with a common cause, something that had not existed during Eagleson's quarter-century in power. "One advantage Bob had," says Riley, "coming from the hockey background he did, he understood what a team was, the dynamics of the dressing room, the response to good leadership. He was a guy you could have a beer with. That's a huge advantage. He understood where the players were coming from."

Goodenow set about making over Eagleson's haphazard, indifferent management style. Out went untrained office administrators such as Sam Simpson and Eagleson's accountant Marvin Goldblatt, who'd handled much of the PA's clerical work. After extensive consultations with Don Fehr and the Major League Baseball Players Association ("the Cadillac of sports unions," Goodenow calls it), Goodenow hired trained economists, lawyers, and marketers as permanent NHLPA staff members. And he considered the knowledge and experience of players in the association for the first time in a quarter-century.

"Bob was surrounded by some very good people in the early years," says Riley. "Andy Moog, Kelly Miller, Mike Gartner, Mike Liut, Steve Yzerman, Joe Nieuwendyk, Doug Wilson—solid team guys to the core. And Ken Baumgartner was so underrated. To hear this tough guy in a meeting, articulating goals and objectives, you wouldn't be surprised now that he's become a Harvard Business School graduate."

Goodenow recognized that the NHLPA was in no financial position to endure a long strike after years of being funded by dues alone. He encouraged players to save money from each paycheque as a strike war chest for 1992, and he set about finding new pools of revenue. One income source was group licensing—in particular money from trading cards, a previously ignored cache that was becoming a gold mine in other sports. When Goodenow joined the PA, the players had the right to sell their likeness for trading cards, but they had to pay 50 per cent of the money to the NHL for use of its logos and uniforms. A concerted effort in this area, Goodenow believed, could produce millions for a strike fund.

"I remember him coming to my office in Los Angeles," says Mike Barnett, "and saying, 'One of the first things we're going to need is to increase the revenue stream from our group-licensing programs.' He wanted me to roll Brett and Wayne and several other star players into the group-licensing program. To that point I'd held them out, because 40 per cent off the top is going to the Licensing Group of America. I just didn't feel that was an appropriate amount. So I said, 'Bob, if you can get out of the LGA relationship and take it in-house, then you'll get my guys.' They did that, and the thing ended up in litigation. But they got it finally, and we rolled our players in, and over a period of years that ended up rolling millions more dollars than the PA had ever got its hands on. Those are the kind of things Bob did—very hands-on."

Goodenow also showed players that the NHL had left itself vulner-able to a labour action at playoff time. Under NHL contracts, salaries are paid over the course of the regular season; the only money made by players in the playoffs are the bonuses based on how far a club advances. Thanks to Eagleson's neglect, these bonuses were minus-cule. In 1992, a Stanley Cup-winning player could expect $25,000 for six weeks of the hardest, most dangerous play of the year. Losers could expect just $10,000 for a possible twenty-eight games.

The owners, by contrast, found the playoffs highly profitable. According to the NHL's own Unified Report of Operations (which reported in mixed Canadian and U.S. dollars), the league made a $29-million profit in the 1990–91 playoffs and $24 million in the post-season of 1991–92. These figures did not include revenues from luxury suites, souvenir sales, and rink-board signage—other signifi-cant money-makers. Nor did they show the profits made by ancillary companies for parking, concessions, or other revenue generators. Goodenow convinced players that if the undercapitalized NHLPA were ever to exercise its strike threat, the eve of the playoffs would be the ideal time.

Eagleson had never bothered to educate the players in the culture of labour negotiations. He preferred them to rubber-stamp a deal he'd made on the Wirtz yacht or with Ziegler in a hotel room.

"In the old days," says Rick Curran, "if a guy had a question, he didn't feel comfortable standing up and asking, because Al probably would yell at him and tell him to sit down. Now, I know that all my clients feel very comfortable to go to a meeting. They are not hesi-tant, intimidated, or afraid to ask a question. To his credit, Bob has encouraged all of us to make sure our clients not only feel comfort-able enough to ask a question, he put the onus on us to encourage them to participate. He's recognized the value in educating the play-ers so they have a role to play. That's the single most critical factor: that a player knows what he's doing and why he's doing it."

Against that background, Goodenow had a large job convincing players to do it for themselves. "Players didn't relate to the timing and nuance of a labour organization," says former goalie Mike Liut, who was on the executive of the NHLPA at the time. "I always remember what a businessman said to me. 'Business does not stop and start in sixty-minute intervals.' It can take days and weeks in a labour negotiation and sometimes you come up with nothing. Players are used to playing games with outcomes every night. Bob was excellent at developing an understanding of issues and timing, and communicating them."

Goodenow's education of the players paid dividends when negotiations came to a crunch in the spring of 1992. "The main issue was to take away our names and our faces—the trading-card issue," says Mike Gartner. "There was more to it than that, but they felt because you put on a jersey they had full control over who you were, your name and face and how it got marketed. To me it was such an easy issue to explain and hang tough on that there wasn't a lot of debate on it."

While Eagleson and his NHL cadre believed that Goodenow wouldn't last, there were signs that his education process was having an effect. Having discovered that their patriotic efforts in prior international tournaments had merely relieved the NHL of its obligations to the pension fund, many players balked at Eagleson's efforts to recruit them for the 1991 Canada Cup. He had to beg Wayne Gretzky to participate for Canada, hoping other reluctant players would follow. Even so, Ray Bourque and several other stars took a pass on the tournament.

Elsewhere, players were going public with their concerns about the shambles at the NHLPA. First, *Net Worth* uncovered the real business history of the NHL; then exposés by Russ Conway in the Lawrence (Mass.) *Eagle-Tribune* (and later in the book *Game Misconduct*), and television investigations on CBC TV, tore away Eagleson's veneer. These pieces used brave testimony from players such as Andy Moog, Pat Verbeek, Marty McSorley, and Jim Korn, as well as a host of retired players led by Carl Brewer. Clearly, the disclosures of Eagleson's wrongdoing had an effect outside the arena. By Christmas week of 1991, the U.S. Justice Department and the FBI announced that they were investigating Eagleson's running of the PA, international hockey, and his agency business. NHL and NHLPA offices were raided for documents by the FBI, while a grand jury was soon convened in Boston to hear evidence of possible crimes. It was a revelation for many players to see the man who'd intimidated them now running scared at the prospect of racketeering charges.

While Eagleson began a six-year fight to stay out of jail, the NHL took its first licks at Goodenow. The new NHLPA leader was savvy enough to understand the implications of what was happening to Eagleson. "The man Goodenow is," notes former Flames president Ron Bremner, "is because of the man he followed. He knew he had to be radically different from Eagleson. And we paid the price for that."

In the summer of 1991, Goodenow fired his first shot, notifying the league that the PA was giving 120 days' notice of termination of the current CBA on September 15, 1991. The NHL fired back. On June 13, 1991, Ziegler claimed that the notice was invalid because it failed to include a series of proposed changes to the contract. NHL lawyers contended that a notice of termination had to include those changes to be legal. If the NHL was right, the CBA would be automatically extended for another year, robbing Goodenow of the opportunity to negotiate and humiliating him in front of his members. The league also presented players with a weighty tome on the bargaining issues, a document they called the "silver bullet." It was laden with the usual NHL chestnuts, including the "peaceful" NHL labour-management climate as compared with other sports. "Problems have been solved quietly—through give-and-take," it read. "As a result, players, owners and the game of hockey have all been winners—there have been no losers."

But on the next page, the "silver bullet" seemed to suggest that there were indeed plenty of losers in the NHL: the booklet contained forbidding statistics that suggested hockey Armageddon was waiting by the Zamboni because of payroll demands. Player compensation in the previous six years, it said, had risen 130 per cent, while revenues had increased only 78 per cent. Player compensation had risen from 49 per cent of club revenues in 1985–86 to 63 per cent in 1991–92. If the current escalation continued, it warned, player compensation in five years would reach 173 per cent of revenues.

Two more proposals in the NHL presentation were aimed squarely at Goodenow's heart. First, the NHL wanted to amend the pay schedule for players so that they are paid semi-monthly for the entire calendar year. In other words, the league wanted to remove its vulnerability to strike action in April by spreading out its payments over twelve months, not the seven months dictated by the current CBA. Second, the NHL wanted trading-card rights to be negotiable. If Goodenow and the NHLPA wanted to fund their organization from card moneys, they were going to have to fight for the right in collective bargaining. This was war.

The NHL delighted in its strategy: "Goodenow was shaken," cackled Stein. "He was red-faced, figuratively and literally. The Ziegler-Wirtz plan to embarrass him had worked to perfection." Stein soon realized that the league had miscalculated. Not for the final time, it misjudged the mood of the players. The full-frontal assault meant to humiliate Goodenow only served to underline the us-versus-them attitude he'd been drilling home with players on his visits. While congratulating itself on the legal sophistry of its arguments, the NHL had unwittingly reinforced Goodenow's portrait of owners as bullying, adversarial foes. Had the players needed a flag to rally round, they got it in Ziegler's legal attack. The scorched-earth tactic also effectively removed the return of Ziegler's friend Eagleson to the negotiations as well.

Goodenow turned the attack back upon the owners, using their own puffed-up sales pitch to expansion applicants against them. Goodenow announced he was not going to negotiate "take-aways" in a time when the league was raking in $125 million for expansion fees and John Ziegler was trumpeting its $50-million TV deal with

SportsChannel in the U.S. at the Empire Club of Toronto. The players wanted better playoff money, increased free agency, a neutral arbitrator to interpret NHL bylaws and the constitution, plus a shortening of the NHL amateur draft each June. This negotiation was going to be about players getting a larger, fairer slice of the pie.

This approach—and Eagleson's unhelpful contention that Goodenow was in over his head—produced a deadlock. The NHLPA refused to meet with the owners again until the legal challenge to the termination notice was withdrawn. The NHL huffed and puffed in the face of this insubordination for a while, but as the start of the 1991–92 season dawned and the resolve of the players hardened, the league relented on its clever strategy. In giving up on the termination notice, the NHL handed Goodenow his first victory.

The two sides agreed to start playing the 1991–92 schedule without a CBA, and to negotiate the new contract during the season. Ziegler—still trying to sway public opinion—assured Goodenow there would be no lockout of players by the owners. In spite of what they'd seen of Goodenow thus far, the owners were still counting on the players to cave at the crucial moment of a strike. The promise of no lockout was meant to ratchet the pressure on Goodenow. By the following March, however, there was still no agreement on a new CBA. The NHL was still holding a hard line on the trading-card rights, independent arbitration, and other contentious issues. Players—unswayed by Ziegler's tactics—felt that the NHL was daring them to strike in the hope that their solidarity would crack under public pressure. "The owners did not feel it was something that could or would happen," says Mike Gartner. "Otherwise they never would have allowed the season to start without a contract."

Washington goalie Mike Liut, tormented by a ruptured disc, remembers one last-ditch negotiating session in the hotel gymnasium in Toronto that tumultuous March. "I was sitting around the workout equipment, trying to stretch my back, at four a.m. with the smallest of groups from both sides. I thought we had the deal done that night. I left there and thought it was a deal. I went back to my room, showered, and got on the plane to Washington. When I got back home, I found out there was no deal."

As the final weeks of the 1991–92 season slipped away, it became clear the players were facing a baptism of labour fire: jeopardize the playoffs—even the Stanley Cup—or settle and confirm the owners' suspicion that they couldn't stand together? Debates raged around dressing rooms about the first labour disruption since the old Hamilton Tigers walked out in the 1930s over unpaid salaries. For traditionalists such as Gretzky, it was a heart-rending decision to forget the "good of the game" in favour of the "good of the players." For Mike Gartner, it was a more emotional decision. "And that was because the Stanley Cup playoffs were involved. Obviously it was a great leverage point from the players' point, but we were also horrified because we could miss the Stanley Cup playoffs."

"Bob made his point very clear from the start," recalls former Kings goalie Kelly Hrudey, now a broadcaster, "how difficult this was going to be. He said ownership wasn't going to cave in. So it was a really scary time. He gave us examples from other sports. He made it clear he didn't expect the strike to last long, but the next opportunity the owners got we're going to be locked out, and we have to be prepared for that both financially and mentally. This is all wonderful, we'll make our strike and make our point. But the real fight is down the road. If we're not willing to prepare for that, we shouldn't strike this time."

Liut, a member of the executive board, says the doubts went right to the top of the NHLPA. "We had to make the decision forty-eight hours in advance to let everyone know in time. I remember sitting around in a group of the executive having discussions at the Marriott Eaton Centre in Toronto. It was late. They were vacuuming under our chairs. And we were all asking each other, 'What do you think?' It was not an easy decision. We had our days of trepidation. The players participated a lot more than the public thinks. It was a players' decision. Bob had a great influence, but it was the players dictating how far they wanted to go."

On April Fool's Day in 1992, the NHL players voted massively (560–4) in favour of a job action. (One player, Michel Petit, told his teammates he was broke and had to vote against his brethren.) The next day, the unthinkable happened: for the first time, all NHL players walked away from rinks and dressing rooms across North America in a strike. From millionaires like Wayne Gretzky and Mario Lemieux down to André Racicot and Tom Tilley (fringe performers earning the minimum wage), the players bore silent homage to the rebels of 1957 by stowing their skates and sticks. For all their determination, they were about to learn some keen lessons about sticking together and the public mood.

The moment the players headed home, the playoffs—a lucrative $75-million broadcast staple on CBC TV as well as a treasured tradition—were in jeopardy of being cancelled. While the idea of breaking seventy-five years of Stanley Cup tradition scared many players, hawkish owners such as Bill Wirtz of Chicago and John McMullen of New Jersey felt losing the 1992 Cup playdowns entirely was a small price to pay to crush the emerging union solidarity. They had Ziegler inform the PA that no negotiations would take place until the players returned to the ice. But moderate owners such as Buffalo's Seymour Knox, and those with new buildings to pay for, urged Ziegler to find a compromise.

In Minnesota, GM Bobby Clarke—a former president of the NHLPA—summed up the quandary facing ownership. "It won't be the poor owners who decide to give up," Clarke told the staff of the North Stars. "It'll be the rich owners who want to get back to playing. They can still make money. The poor owners can stay out forever, because they have nothing to lose." The schism between rich and poor owners threatened the solidarity of the Board of Governors and required Ziegler to do some of his best behind-the-scenes work to conceal the split from players and fans.

In public, Ziegler—coached by his spin doctor, former broadcaster Fraser Kelly—mounted press conferences that portrayed the NHL as a business on the verge of insolvency due to rising player costs. Gone were the boastful days when he told a crowd, "Now if it sounds like I'm a little proud [of selling 87 per cent of our seats], you bet your bippy I'm proud." Using graphs, pie charts, and occasional tears, Ziegler said that player demands would land the league $150 million in debt within two years. He claimed playoff revenues represented only 8 per cent—$8.8 million—of total revenues. He said the average salary was $379,000 (it was actually $239,000). In one memorable press performance, the dapper, fussy president was reduced to tears at the prospect of an end to *Hockey Night in Canada*'s playoff tradition. "I don't know if our fans will ever forgive us," he sniffled. "I have difficulty understanding why players want to ruin or irrevocably scar this great season." What was never explained was how the $450-million business that Ziegler had extolled in glowing terms to expansion applicants in 1990 was now on the brink of insolvency. Or where the $150 million in expansion fees had gone.

In his first foray into labour conflict, Goodenow appeared stiff in public next to the emotional outbursts of Ziegler. The NHLPA director made little effort to reach over the heads of reporters to reassure fans, as Eagleson might have done. His efforts at media spin were conducted in private. But his tight-lipped performance was in keeping with his philosophy: he represented players' interests, not the mythical "good of the game" that Eagleson loved to trot out. "People don't understand that Bob doesn't really care about public opinion," says a former NHLPA employee. "He's not like Al [Eagleson]. His responsibility is to his membership, and if the media or public don't like that, too bad."

As the owners had hoped, players came under intense pressure. "I was brought up in Canada," says Kirk Muller, whose NHL career began in 1984. "My dad's a postman. All of sudden you're a pro hockey player, and you're on strike. I felt the average guy couldn't relate to that. I was saying, 'I know exactly where I come from,' and it was tough knowing there wasn't a lot of sympathy for a pro hockey player. I'm no different from the blue-collar guys back home, but when this stuff hit it was that we were crazy, just spoiled pro athletes. That was a tough thing to swallow."

As the strike dragged on, players had to deal with cracks in solidarity. Despite an appeal that teams not practise on their own, lest they be seen as anxious to play again, the Edmonton Oilers conducted group workouts. "Other teams that practised really made everyone mad," recalls one player, who requested anonymity. "We were unbelievably pissed off by that. We had an emergency meeting over that. I still get mad when I think of that, even today—they fucked us."

Gartner thinks the debate among players was healthy. "We had more discussion during the ten days we were out than we did before we walked out," he recalls. "When you have that many players, there's always going to be guys who think you're not approaching the negotiations in the right manner—'Why didn't you accept the last offer?'—that sort of thing. Usually when you get problems like that it's because players don't have enough information. The best way to speak to players like that is give them all the information and let them make their own conclusions."

In truth, both Goodenow and Ziegler needed a quick resolution if they were to hold their constituencies. Goodenow's war chest was limited; many of Ziegler's owners had financing of new arenas hanging over their heads. So Ziegler could yield on the trading-card issue as a bargaining chip while Goodenow had wiggle room on demands for more free agency. When the NHL president sent the NHLPA director a "final offer" on April 7, both sides got down to serious bargaining. Goodenow, Gartner, and Bryan Trottier met in New York with Ziegler and lawyer Tony Herman (NHL chief counsel Gil Stein was noticeably absent). After an all-day session, the sides reached an agreement that saw the players realize some modest gains on playoff pay, trading-card rights, and side issues, while the owners were able to resume the playoffs and plan ahead for the real showdown in 1994—when owners would not be caught underestimating their opposition. By April 11, the first league-wide strike in NHL history had officially ended when players voted to accept the new CBA. Play resumed the next day.

"Never underestimate how tough it was for Goodenow to sell the players on a strike," says former Calgary GM Craig Button. "He did a great job of getting the players that the owners couldn't afford to stay out. But had management simply shut down the game for the rest of the year, we'd have destroyed his credibility. Once players saw what happened when Ziegler settled, the league guaranteed his credibility and made the 1994–95 lockout possible."

Many believe that, despite having misjudged the threat from Goodenow, John Ziegler did his best work in salvaging the playoffs from the mess of the strike. "This was his finest hour," said Stein. But he had lost the support of his patron on the Board of Governors, Bill Wirtz. At a crucial point in the final negotiations, Wirtz had ordered Ziegler to get a fax from Goodenow confirming the conditions for back-to-work before meeting with the NHLPA director. When Ziegler went ahead, meeting with Goodenow sans fax, he was upbraided on the phone by Wirtz, who also had Quebec's Marcel Aubut and Winnipeg's Barry Shenkarow on the line. Wirtz demanded to know where Ziegler had gotten the authority to negotiate without their go-ahead.

"Who do you think you're talking to?" Ziegler stormed back. "I'm the president of the National Hockey League, not some secretary."

Ziegler's impertinent outburst turned Wirtz against him for good. Owners who nursed grievances against Ziegler were now supported by the bellicose owner of the Blackhawks. When the playoffs ended, Ziegler handed the Stanley Cup to the Pittsburgh Penguins and was then handed his walking papers by the NHL. For his trouble, he received a $2-million handshake, plus a $250,000 annual pension for life starting in 1996. Predictably, Eagleson rallied to the defence of his friend. "He settled the strike, and they were playing hockey. If they'd taken a vote then, he would have gotten the Order of Lenin. Six weeks later, the owners are saying we have to sign players, and it's John's fault. They needed a scapegoat, and he was it." Within weeks, Wirtz himself had resigned as chairman of the Board of Governors, replaced by Bruce McNall, the free-spending owner of the Kings.

With the disappearance of the three amigos—Wirtz, Eagleson, and Ziegler—and the rise of Goodenow, an NHL era had come to an end. If anyone needed proof that a new day had dawned in business relations between players and owners, they needed only to look at the strategy adopted weeks later by Eric Lindros to control his own hockey destiny.

7

The Lindros Factor

It would be easy to confuse the Lindros family with a crew of piano movers. Eric stands six-foot-four and weighs 240 pounds; brother Brett (who played briefly with the New York Islanders) is six-foot-four and weighs 220 pounds; father Carl (who makes his living in the financial industry) measures up at six-foot-four and 230 pounds. Now, imagine all three—plus mother Bonnie—shoehorned around a battered old phone in the tiny bedroom of a 750-square-foot cottage on Georgian Bay in Ontario. There are closets with more elbow room.

"Yeah, it was crowded," recalls Eric of Saturday, June 20, 1992, a couple of months after the player strike and a full year after he had been selected first overall in the NHL amateur draft by the Quebec Nordiques. "There was an old rotary dial phone, and all of us were sort of waiting around beside it to see which team was going to call." Following a year spent in hockey purgatory—playing junior hockey in Oshawa and for the Canadian Olympic squad—unsigned Eric and his family were anxious for news of where he'd been traded by Quebec. He knew he was going to a team that would sign him to a lucrative contract and would be, he hoped, a Stanley Cup contender. But which team?

There had never been a hockey prospect quite like Lindros. His skills as both a scorer and an intimidator appear once in a generation; his self-awareness and business determination almost never. In a sport where players specialize either in racking up points or chalking up fights, Lindros could do both with breathtaking efficiency. He was special—and he knew it. As the family stood around the phone, the clan had used this skill set to bring a league that had previously refused to bend to the whims of any player—not Howe, not Hull, not Orr—to its knees. The lowly Nordiques had ignored the protestations of the Lindroses and selected Eric first overall in the amateur draft of 1991. Aubut had sworn Lindros would play in the fleur-de-lys of Quebec or nowhere. He had dreamed of using the big centre as the prime attraction in a new arena. But first he had to get him under contract. Only then could he raise financing for the building that would save his money-losing club.

After months of stubborn resistance, however, the Nords were finally giving up the pipe dream of luring the Toronto-born centre to *la vieille capitale*. Faced with an ultimatum—trade him or lose him in the draft the next day—Nords owner Marcel Aubut had finally opted for a trade. The gypsy year that began with the eighteen-year-old Lindros starring for Canada at the 1991 Canada Cup, returning to Oshawa of the OHL, then joining the national team at the 1992 Olympics in Albertville, was at an end. The Lindros family had won. But Aubut might still be able to replenish his roster—and boost the value of his team in a sale—if he pulled off a blockbuster trade. As the Lindroses gathered round the phone, there were stories of five-for-one, six-for-one... whole rosters seemingly in exchange for a single, singular player.

Having finally decided to move Lindros's rights, the Quebec owner then did Lindros's negotiating position a great service. To appraise the market value of his reluctant chattel, Aubut had taken the novel step of employing International Sports and Entertainment Strategies, a New York firm, to assess what returns the prodigious young centre could harvest for a franchise. Based on Wayne Gretzky's impact in California and Mario Lemieux's effect in Pittsburgh, ISES argued that a team acquiring the NHL's next superstar could expect to generate a multi-million dollar spike in advertising revenues, a healthy increase in season tickets (Lemieux had boosted Pens' crowds by 133 per cent), and jersey sales of at least half a million dollars. To say nothing of getting a new arena built.

ISES thought New Jersey was the team that could most benefit from Lindros's services, but the Devils' budget-conscious GM Lou Lamoriello wasn't buying. Toronto—where Lindros wanted to play—was undergoing an ownership transition and could not ante up for the player who'd grown up a few miles from Maple Leaf Gardens. As they jockeyed for position around the phone, the Lindros family had heard it had come down to two major markets: Philadelphia and the New York Rangers. The Flyers were financing a new rink and owner Ed Snider was angling to sell part of his franchise; Lindros was heaven-sent for the club. The Rangers, meanwhile, were always in the market for a star who might help them end their Stanley Cup drought. The Lindros family understood the implications of the ISES appraisal in a way few other hockey families had. After seeing Eric play like a young Mark Messier in the Canada Cup, they were prepared to ask for Messier's contract as a starter in bargaining.

Whoever wanted Lindros was clearly going to need deep pockets and a thick hide to deal with a family that was categorical about its desires. In a prequel to his NHL holdout, Lindros had earlier balked at going to Sault Ste. Marie of the Ontario Hockey League when he was drafted as a sixteen-year-old. The family and their agent, Rick Curran, sensed that Greyhounds owner Phil Esposito was more interested in using Lindros to sell the club to new buyers than in improving Eric's hockey or schooling prospects. So Eric refused to go to the Sault, playing in the U.S. instead. It was a primer on the exercise of star power, and much resented by the legions of players and fans who felt everyone ought to play by the same rules. Lindros's stand forced the OHL to change its rules about trading first-round picks so that the Greyhounds could eventually swap Lindros to Oshawa.

After two years of toying with OHL opponents in a Generals uniform, the OHL's player of the year was touted as the consensus number-one pick for 1991. NHL clubs scrambled to dumb down their teams so that they could pluck Lindros. Much to the chagrin of the Lindroses, the Nordiques finished last overall. According to the family, Aubut's attempts at losing on purpose—not the commercial restrictions of the small French market—were the reason Eric felt his future lay elsewhere. "If Aubut had owned the Maple Leafs, we'd have thought the same thing," says a family insider. "We didn't think he'd ever field a competitive team." But it was obvious that playing in the powder blue of the Nords was not going to be anyone's entree to financial superstardom in pro-sports marketing, either.

The people of Quebec took the snub as an affront. Books were written on the topic of the reluctant Lindros, psychiatrists were consulted; even Prime Minister Brian Mulroney—born a few hours east of Quebec City on the north shore of the St. Lawrence—weighed in to say that Lindros ought to wear the Quebec sweater. In the post-Meech Lake climate of Canada, Lindros the headstrong hockey star was transformed by the nationalist press into an Anglo boor, dissing the province and its people. Despite a reported $50-million contract offer from Quebec, Lindros refused to change his stance. Now, the months of threats, insults, and bare-knuckled negotiations would come down to a voice at the other end of the phone.

When the phone rang, it was Russ Farwell, general manager of the Flyers and Jay Snider, son of Flyers owner Ed Snider. Philadelphia had told Aubut they were willing to give up six players (Mike Ricci, Peter Forsberg, Steve Duchesne, Ron Hextall, Kerry Huffman, and Chris Simon), two draft picks (Jocelyn Thibault and Nolan Baumgartner) and $15 million for Lindros. He would wear the black and orange of the Flyers as soon as a contract could be worked out. Carl Lindros let Philadelphia know that the contract would be for more than $3 million a year. When he hung up on the Flyers brass, he thought he had a deal in principle.

But the palpable sigh of relief that circulated in the Lindroses' summer home after Farwell's call lasted only a few hours. Within minutes of accepting the Flyers' proposal, the mercurial Aubut received what he considered a superior offer of players and money from the Rangers. So Aubut traded his prime asset a second time in the wee hours of June 20, this time to New York. John Ziegler—who would formally give up the NHL presidency to Gil Stein in three days—was forced to call in an arbitrator, Larry Bertuzzi, to settle the dispute. Stein charitably ascribed the stalemate to Aubut's flawed English: "Marcel occasionally misses the meaning of a word or two in English...." After waiting so long, the Lindros family wanted a quick resolution to Aubut's action. After a weekend of reflection, Bertuzzi decided the Flyers had won the rights to the reluctant superstar.

(This also caused a flap at the NHL, because new president Stein was a former Flyers employee. When the decision was announced, Rangers president Stanley Jaffe phoned Stein to accuse him of calling Bertuzzi to sway him during his deliberations. A miffed Stein explained that he had never intervened to deliver Lindros to his old boss and resented the implication. The Rangers hastily backed off their accusations of bias, but remained convinced there had been hanky-panky.)

At the time, the six-for-one-plus-$15-million trade was considered a blockbuster on the scale of Gretzky's move to Los Angeles; in retrospect, its magnitude has only grown. The deal vaulted a poor team, the Nordiques, into a Stanley Cup winner within four years (albeit in Colorado, as the Avalanche). Forsberg is now a star many GMs would choose over Lindros; Thibault was later traded by the Avalanche to Montreal for a true Quebec icon, goalie Patrick Roy; Ricci has become an emotional leader on the San Jose Sharks; Simon is an effective NHL forward; and Duchesne won a Stanley Cup with Detroit in 2002. But the Flyers weren't complaining either. With Lindros, they ended a five-year absence from the post-season in

1993, making it to the Cup final within five years of the trade (where they lost to Detroit). As for Lindros, though he has battled injuries and (some would say) never completely fulfilled his awesome potential, he remains a rare blend of power and skill, with 367 career goals at the end of the 2005–06 season. And his economic power has shaped the game.

At a time when superstar veterans such as Gretzky, Messier, and Lemieux were worth $3 million or $4 million a year, Lindros planned to jolt the NHL by winning a rookie contract on a par with all three. Curran had discussed the strategy with him during the Albertville Olympics. "The numbers that he signed for, I walked around with for at least three months in an envelope," recalls Curran. "I had taken it with me to the Olympics to show Eric and talk about where I thought we should be." If he'd been an ordinary prospect, Lindros's position might have seemed weak; he'd sat out much of the season after the Olympics, and if he'd gone back into the draft he'd likely have been selected by the awful Ottawa Senators (the Anglo version of the Nordiques). One member of the Flyers management team said as much to Curran in the first negotiations in Syracuse, New York. "How do you justify what you're asking for a nineteen-year-old who hasn't played an NHL game?"

But other factors tipped the leverage in favour of Lindros. The Flyers had given up half a good hockey team in the trade and had not made the deal conditional on signing him. Ed Snider, the Flyers founder and owner, was actively financing a new arena for a club that had missed the playoffs three straight years; he was also attempting to sell all or part of the club. Losing Lindros would have ended those dreams. As well, Snider had staked his reputation on acquiring the hyped prospect who could turn the team around. Asked by the Flyer official to justify a contract as rich as Messier's, Curran said, "Me justify it? You're the ones who just gave up six players and $15 million. You're the ones who say how valuable he is."

Still, the Flyers were reluctant to give in. The deal Carl Lindros thought he had on the phone on draft day was stalled as Philadelphia pondered its offer. Some in their management were concerned. So was the NHL, wary of the salary spiral since the Gretzky deal. The spending by the St. Louis Blues and the Rangers on young free agents was upsetting the salary grid. So was the money awarded to rookies under the unrestricted rules of the day. Finances aside, many in the game also couldn't abide rewarding a player who wouldn't follow their standards. If the draft process was good enough for everyone else, it should have been good enough for Lindros. This attitude perhaps reflected the conservative roots of the sport in Canada where, unlike in the U.S., the interests of the group tend to be more highly prized than those of the individual. "Canada is notorious for chopping down its tallest wheat," said former Oilers-owner Peter Pocklington as he headed south in search of new opportunities away from his country's quasi-welfare state. Giving in to Lindros's demands was viewed by many hockey people as an incursion of American values into a quintessentially Canadian enterprise. It was impertinence that could not go unchecked.

But the Lindros deal was also a benchmark for Bob Goodenow. He was staking his leadership on driving agents and players to get the maximum from each negotiation. He believed in finding vulnerability and pressing the advantage. When he looked at the Flyers, he saw vulnerability and—in the fifth-largest U.S. media market—the ability to pay for a star. "He was unique," recalls Goodenow. "An amazing athlete. The clubs were making strong statements about him, the values put on him by Aubut and Philadelphia, about what he meant to their franchises. In the end, they were all correct." Goodenow kept in touch with Curran on the progress of the talks. Curran reported headway, but said it was going to be slow. Goodenow suggested, "You won't get it done till you meet with Mr. Snider."

Seeking to break the impasse, the Flyers owner flew to Toronto, hoping to whittle away at Lindros's demands. When the two sides met, Snider asked Curran why they were unwilling to move from their initial demand of the Messier model. Curran reminded the Flyers founder of the price he'd paid for Lindros, and pointed out that he had the club over a barrel since it had made the Quebec deal unconditional: "I could have walked in here and asked for $5 million a year and you'd have been stuck with that. But I haven't done that. I've given you the figure I've carried with me in my pocket for five months, before the trade. I'm not asking for any more than what I have on the paper."

Curran, Carl Lindros, and lawyer Gord Kirke then left the room. While some members of the Flyers management team were still upset by the temerity of Lindros and Curran, Snider got the message. Yes, it was a lot of money, but the upside was enormous for the club too. Snider needed only to consider what Gretzky had done for the Kings, and Lemieux for the Penguins. "That's how the deal was done," says Curran. "Mr. Snider just held up his hand and said, 'They're right.' He had the wherewithal to recognize what it was. Bob [Goodenow] was absolutely correct in his assessment. Mr. Snider was the closer."

"He has bent the game of hockey to his will," wrote the *New York Times Magazine*. "For the first time, a player demanded the right to choose his employer, and, by dint of what was essentially a one-man job action, forced the NHL to honor that choice." Lindros's $2.5-million signing bonus and $18 million over six years made him one of the five best-paid players in the league, and he'd not played an NHL game.

"I don't think you can underestimate how important the Lindros signing was," says agent J.P. Barry. "He fought the system, pushed it to the limit. It was just, 'I want it, give it to me.' I think it turned the eyes of a lot of players who had been performing in the league for four or five years." Adds Bob Goodenow, "There's no question the Lindros contract showed what the value, the impact could be for a fresh person coming into the NHL. And it was respected and understood by Lemieux and Gretzky. Eric was unique, an instant impact player."

Predictably, NHL management figures were shocked. "That deal bothered me most," said Neil Smith, GM of the Rangers at the time. "We thought we had him, but we wanted forty-eight hours to negotiate before we agreed to the trade. Then we heard what Curran and the Lindroses wanted: they wanted Messier's contract. Messier's an

MVP, he's won five Cups, he's led us to the President's Trophy his first year in New York...and here's this guy coming out of junior who wants a five-year deal. It was so exorbitant. And he gets it. That really bothered me."

Flames co-owner Harley Hotchkiss, current chairman of the NHL Board of Governors, concurs: "I was really disappointed to see it. My main concern about these contracts is that we have a team game. Good as Gretzky or Lindros are, it's still a team game, and we're overemphasizing the value of one player. That leads to great disparities in incomes on a team, and it's not healthy. It diminishes the sense of loyalty players have to the team. On our '89 team that won the Cup, we had great players, but it was a team effort without one superstar getting so much of the money and glory."

Larry Pleau points to the irony in the Lindros trade to Philadelphia. "He was the greatest thing since sliced bread. But maybe the greatest thing since sliced bread was actually one of the six players going the other way—Peter Forsberg."

Sather, then in Edmonton, saw the Lindros signing as part of a disturbing trend. "It was one of those million-dollar deals for an unproven player who had big time written all over him. The other part you've got to remember is that Philadelphia had a brand-new building, they had all these [luxury] boxes to sell. The theory I've had through all this is that it wasn't the negotiations of the contracts, but the rapid changing of the NHL buildings. Everybody was building new buildings for a couple hundred million bucks and putting in 100 to 150 skyboxes. You had to have star players to attract the big buyers to those boxes. The theory was that you could bring in so much more revenue that you could afford to pay the players. That started to drive the price of players, even unproven ones."

In his first season with the Flyers, the nineteen-year-old Lindros proved excellent value, scoring 41 goals and 34 assists on a team that finished out of the playoffs—and that despite missing twenty-one games with a knee problem. Opponents were awestruck. "I used to think Mark Messier was strong," veteran centre Mark Lamb told Roy MacGregor for his book *Road Games*. "There's no comparison. He's as strong as a bull. You just can't stay with him." Within three years, Lindros, though still battling injuries, had led the Flyers to the conference finals; the new $210-million First Union Center was ready to open with its luxury suites filled; and Snider had sold two-thirds of the team, the Spectrum Arena, and the First Union Center to the cable-TV company Comcast at an enormous profit. None of this, it can be argued, would have been accomplished without the ferocity and scoring exploits of number 88. "Ed Snider always got value from signing Eric," says a family insider. "It was a great deal no matter what he paid."

(Rick Curran wasn't around to share in the Lindros exploits; he was let go by the Lindros clan shortly after the negotiations on the Flyers contract. The sides split over a number of concerns the Lindros family had—including Curran's involving a trading-card company when he secured a mortgage on his new home near Philadelphia.)

The signing and marketing of Lindros became an instant blueprint for introducing a young star into the league. More than goals and assists had to be considered: rookie players were suddenly measured on their ability to get arenas built, market skyboxes and luxury suites, boost cable-TV contracts, and sell replica jerseys. The Lindros signing became the template for the selection and signing of the top draft pick in 1993, Alexandre Daigle, who went to the Senators.

As well as things went in turning Lindros's number 88 into gold, so they went badly for Daigle, the Victoriaville, Quebec, product. The whopping new deal Daigle got in Ottawa—and his failure to deliver—ended up precipitating a second NHL labour stoppage within two years. "In a sense, Lindros begat Daigle, who begat rookie salary cap when they needed a compromise on entry-level players to get the CBA done in 1995," says J.P. Barry. "Lindros, it was sort of okay with the owners, because he performed. But Daigle was the last straw—he got the big dollars but in their eyes never really stepped up and proved himself."

"In 1993, we had to sign our first-round pick, Todd Harvey, to a one-way contract at a million dollars a season because of Daigle," recalls Craig Button, then–director of scouting for the Minnesota North Stars. "That was a lot of money on hold to rookies who hadn't proved a thing yet. It's a gamble. That's one of the reasons we later convinced [owner] Tom Hicks to use that [rookie] money to go after proven free agents such as Pat Verbeek and Mike Keane instead, players who helped us win the Cup [after the Stars moved to Dallas]."

Certainly, the Lindros elements—a desperate ownership trying to finance a new arena via a charismatic young star—were in play for Ottawa in the summer of 1993. The Senators had won a frantic contest to finish last overall and claim first pick in the amateur draft (they'd lost a stunning 70 games in their first NHL season, playing with the meagre scraps offered by the rest of the NHL clubs in the expansion draft). Such was the haste of the godawful Senators to obtain the first pick that owner Bruce Firestone encouraged his club to tank the remaining games of the season. In a barroom chat with reporters, Firestone said, perhaps not entirely in jest, that his team would play without a goalie in its final game. He also stated that the competitive nature of coach Rick Bowness in trying to win games was hampering the team's long-term goals, namely, grabbing last place and Daigle. (As a result of the Firestone fiasco, the NHL went to a lottery system to determine who would get the top pick in the annual draft instead of automatically awarding it to the club with the worst record.)

Firestone and co-owner Rod Bryden intended to grab Daigle with that first selection. The handsome, bilingual centre had tallied 45 goals and 92 assists in his final year with the Victoriaville Tigres, making him the CHL's player of the year. He was also said to have a mean streak. Of equal importance, perhaps, he was coveted by the two other teams in cities with large French-speaking populations, the

Canadiens and the Nordiques. The Nords—still smarting from the Lindros rejection—were said to be willing to give up the rights to unsigned Swedish sensation Forsberg in exchange for Daigle. But this fervour only deepened Ottawa's desire to land the six-foot-one centre with movie-star looks.

Not everyone on the Sens' scouting staff was gaga about Daigle; some wanted to draft hulking defenceman Chris Pronger from Peterborough, or a shifty forward from the University of Maine, Paul Kariya. (If only, moan Sens fans today.) The Quebec Junior League had a reputation as a place to chalk up easy points, they argued; it was a perfect league in which to ignore defence and develop bad habits. The dissenters might have been listened to if not for something that happened in the final weeks of the season. The financing for the Senators' new arena, the Palladium, fell apart over financing of an overpass to connect the project on the west side of Ottawa with the nearby provincial highway. Considering that the Senators' pitch to the NHL in 1991 had been contingent on developing a new arena and the surrounding real estate in Kanata, this news was a death knell.

Without a glossy new money-maker to call home, the Sens would be stuck forever in tiny Civic Arena, wedged under the football stands of Frank Clair Stadium like a pizza carton beneath a door. With fewer than ten thousand seats to sell, the Sens would be doomed to the basement of the NHL in perpetuity (or until the league moved it to some American city in the Sunbelt). Having waited fifty-eight years for the return of NHL hockey to Canada's capital, neither Bryden nor Firestone wanted to see the franchise die a second time.

Faced with imminent financial collapse, Bryden and Firestone needed more than a hockey player; they needed a sales pitch to get the financing back for their arena. Bryden had heard about the marketing study conducted by Marcel Aubut during the Lindros negotiations, and understood the connection between acquiring the right player and having investors and advertisers sign on the dotted line. One look at the possibilities available on draft day convinced the pair that, of the top choices, only Daigle could be marketed to the people who would help build the Palladium. They liked his hockey skills and his media savvy. Typical was his reply to reporters on how he differed from Eric Lindros. "I drink my beer," Daigle replied, an obvious reference to Lindros's arrest for having spat beer on a girl in a nightclub near Toronto.

Daigle's agent, Pierre Lacroix, was also conversant with Aubut's ISES marketing study. As the NHL clubs converged on Quebec City for the 1993 draft, Lacroix was preparing a contract for Ottawa that would encompass every facet of Daigle's value, from points to media appearances. If the hockey world was rocked by the Lindros deal, it would be taken aback by the contract structured by the cagey Lacroix and Ottawa management. (A year after signing Daigle to the Sens, the clever Lacroix was hired by none other than Marcel Aubut to become general manager of the Nordiques.)

The deal consisted of not one but two separate agreements stretching over five years. For playing hockey, Daigle received a $2-million bonus payable over four years, plus a salary rising from $1.05 million in the first year to $2.65 million in the fifth. The second contract was a marketing deal that paid Daigle an additional $4 million over five years—against anticipated earnings from a joint marketing campaign with the Senators. In short, the Sens were so confident in Daigle's ability to follow in the commercial footsteps of Gretzky, Lemieux, and Lindros, they guaranteed him $4 million from advertising and promotion in hopes of earning much more themselves. This buyout of his marketing rights—a source of money usually controlled by the athlete or the NHLPA—was a calculated risk. According to *Road Games*, Ottawa figured that once it had earned $19.25 million from flogging Daigle's image, they would have recouped their entire investment of $12.25 million. Surely he'd get to that plateau and beyond. And they would have found enough investors to revive the Palladium project.

The Palladium plan worked fine. Using the promise of Daigle leading Ottawa to their first Stanley Cup since 1927, the club oversubscribed a new offering on the building and got the federal government to donate $6 million in start-up funds. The 18,500-seat Palladium—soon to be called the Corel Centre—opened in 1996, three years late and considerably over budget. But it arrived, and Daigle was key. As for the marketing plan, there was a hitch: Daigle would have to play like Gretzky, Lemieux, and Lindros to get the endorsements.

Instead, Daigle became arguably the biggest bust ever as a first-overall draft pick. Only twice did he hit the 20-goal mark or manage more than 50 points—this at a time of profligate scoring in the NHL. Worse, he was either hurt or indifferent for most of his four and a half seasons in Ottawa, where he developed a reputation as a soft player who dreamed more of being a famous actor than a great hockey player. The Senators' ambitious marketing scheme was best summed up in an unfortunate photo shoot where Daigle dressed in drag as a nurse. The gold turned to dust for the Sens, who moved him to Lindros's Flyers in 1997–98. Things went no better in Philadelphia. Daigle was eventually traded four times before finally retiring in 2000. (An attempted comeback with Pittsburgh in 2002 also went nowhere.) Ottawa never came close to recouping its $4-million advance.

The marketing shortfall and arena cost overruns were among the problems that eventually led the team to seek bankruptcy protection in 2003 to escape an estimated $300-million debt; but the precedent of the entry-level contract signed by Daigle was now the problem of everyone in NHL management. The new standard for a top pick had increased twelvefold in four years. Agents were now insisting on the "Daigle Deal" if a losing club wanted to sign a glittering young client. Paul Weiler of Harvard explains the dilemma facing owners after such precedent-setting contracts: "The NHL owner gets 100 per-cent of the additional benefit of having the best team or the cheapest payroll. But he bears only 1/30th of the harm that his decision inflicts on the collective league product, harm that often outweighs the sum of the individual team gains."

When Boston's Harry Sinden heard about Daigle's $12.25-million package on draft day in 1993, he said, "He's fortunate that we didn't have the first pick, because he's about $11.25 million richer than he would be [with us]." Glen Sather, squeezing pennies in Edmonton, growled, "It's sick. The guy who offered this deal should be thrown out of hockey."

The Devils' frugal GM, Lou Lamoriello, still bristles at the Daigle deal ten years after it was done. And Neil Smith says, "The Lindros deal showed that you can't get a franchise going without this kind of guy. With no stars or a winning team, we had no leverage. So Ottawa said, 'What choice do we have?' Pierre Lacroix ate them up on that deal. And the Daigle deal caused the rookie salary cap in the '94 CBA."

Bob Goodenow could afford to be philosophical about Daigle. "The careers of some players don't match their forecasts," he said in 2002. "With Daigle, the question of guaranteed contracts was one of the situations, clearly, that flowed into the events of 1994–95."

Yet even as the NHL squealed about the Lindros and Daigle deals, the decisions made by the Flyers and Senators reflected an optimism in management about new revenue streams. While general managers were bemoaning the inflation in salaries, owners were pushing the envelope in franchise values, arena financing, naming rights, and marketing possibilities. At the start of the 1990s, a wildly prosperous decade in the stock markets, the NHL was finally bullish on hockey's future. The modest, Presbyterian NHL was about to go Hollywood.

John Ziegler was history when Daigle signed his deal, replaced as NHL president by Gil Stein. Television and arena deals were bumped up to the top of Stein's agenda. But the NHL's true mover was the new chairman of the Board of Governors, L.A. Kings owner Bruce McNall, who had supplanted Bill Wirtz at about the time Lindros signed with Philadelphia in the summer of 1992. If anyone typified the high-rolling, entrepreneurial style of the decade, it was the man who had parlayed a coin collection into ownership of the Kings.

McNall had a reputation as a boy wonder: as a twenty-four-year-old he had outbid Aristotle Onassis and former French president Valéry Giscard D'Estaing for the world's most famous coin, the $420,000 Athenian Decadrachma. He'd counselled the mega-rich Gettys and Hunts to buy coins as a hedge against inflation. He had homes everywhere that mattered, a Jetstar 731, and the sort of cachet in the world's film capital that money can't buy. The high-school loner, fat and unloved, had become the coolest sports mogul in Tinseltown.

McNall's credo was that you had to spend a million to make five million. Hence the Gretzky trade. "I always thought that if I bought the best possible coins in the world, I'd be in good shape," he told *The Sporting News*. "In a funny way, that's the same as the hockey business. If you want the best team, you have to go out and get the best player....Luc Robitaille is a great kid and a good player but ask anybody on the street and they'd probably think Luc Robitaille is a type of salad-dressing." His fellow owners proved a ready audience, many of them eager to abandon Ziegler's plodding ways for the company of their NFL and NBA counterparts. In their zeal to get on board with McNall, however, no one thought to ask how one superstar could be divided into twenty-four pieces.

McNall was gung-ho for more expansion after Ottawa and Tampa limped into existence. He pointed out that Ziegler's idea of putting out a casting call for new expansion owners and hoping for the best had been a disaster in the Ottawa and Tampa expansion of 1992–93. Only two of the bidders in Ziegler's Follies had said they'd pay the price, and both nearly expired from financial mismanagement the moment they received their new teams. According to McNall and Stein, the NHL needed to identify key owners and markets it wanted and go after them. With the right people and corporations in the NHL's Board of Governors, U.S. network TV would come running, as the cable carriers had done when McNall brought Gretzky to Southern California.

The kind of gilt-edged owner McNall envisioned was not likely to wait in an anteroom with a dozen other sweating candidates while the governors sipped coffee and planned their parties. This was a buyer who needed to be cultivated and pampered. Such an owner was, in fact, located about thirty miles from McNall's front door. The Disney Corporation had just scored a big hit with its hockey film *The Mighty Ducks*. Its marketing department was considered omniscient, and its communications companies would open doors previously closed to the ragtag NHL. In addition, the city of Anaheim (where Disney is headquartered) had a new state-of-the-art arena set to open with no tenant. Michael Eisner, the head of Disney, could score points with the local politicians and ease approval of new Disney projects by dropping an NHL club in their laps. Using the success of *The Mighty Ducks* film as an opener, McNall began selling Eisner (who had sons who played hockey) on the benefits of joining the NHL. There was side action involved as well. Perhaps as important to McNall, Disney would have to pay him a large fee if it invaded his territory. Minnesota owner Norm Green had already agreed to indemnify McNall for $25 million if he moved the North Stars to Anaheim. For a cash-starved McNall, the deal was made in heaven.

For a second market in the American Sunbelt, McNall aimed at the chairman of Blockbuster Video, Wayne Huizenga, to add an NHL club to his Miami Dolphins, Florida Marlins, and Joe Robbie Stadium. The idea of Huizenga's vast network of Blockbuster stores hawking NHL videos linked nicely with the Disney involvement on the West Coast. And South Florida was overflowing with transplanted hockey fans, retirees from Canada and the northeastern U.S. Huizenga's vision was that the ultimate sports coup lay in controlling all the major sports teams in a market under one roof. "Huizenga had a great idea," says Mike Gillis. "He might have pulled it off, too, except the politicians in southern Florida wouldn't let him build in the area he chose for his buildings."

Eisner and Huizenga were intrigued by McNall's nerve and panache. The problem was going to be asking Disney and

Blockbuster to pay $50 million each to join the NHL. "We should pay them!" exclaimed Rangers governor Stanley Jaffe of Paramount Pictures (who had first-hand experience with Disney) when he first heard about the deal. Jaffe was quickly muffled by his fellow owners. Then there was the trick of convincing Eisner also to indemnify McNall for invading his proscribed territory—after all, the Devils had paid the Rangers and Islanders $12 million to move into the New York/New Jersey market. Unless it wanted a lawsuit from Tampa Bay, Ottawa, and San Jose, the NHL had to charge the same $50-million fee levied on the Lightning, Senators, and Sharks. But Disney was aware of its leverage, and Eisner was reluctant to kick in like some plebian Phil Esposito or Bruce Firestone.

Arguing that Eisner and Huizenga might bolt if the NHL tried to stall, McNall was able to get immediate acceptance of the two new franchises at his first league meeting as chairman in late 1992. The Kings owner was able to placate Eisner by having his $50-million expansion fee split between the league ($25 million) and McNall himself ($25 million as indemnification). Huizenga, too, shelled out the $50 million; the complaints of Tampa-board-member Phil Esposito that Miami was his territory were filed in the wastebasket. Finally, Ottawa and Tampa—eyes firmly on the prize of Alexander Daigle—were guaranteed that the worst team in the league would indeed still draft ahead of the expansion clubs in 1993.

The deal, done in secrecy over several months, was presented in December of 1992 to a shocked and impressed public at the Breakers, the same hotel that had witnessed John Ziegler's rummage sale of franchises two years before. "This is huge," a relieved McNall told the *Los Angeles Times*. "The magnitude—I don't think most people in sports realize how big this is. Even me, I'm not sure I understand." McNall and his fellow owners were now in bed with the big boys of corporate America. The long-sought-after network-TV contract was so close they could almost taste it. The expansion fees and the promised lucre of marketing would easily cover any increase in salaries to Lindros or the other stars of the NHL. A league

that had been labelled Mickey Mouse was now going to be promoted by Mickey Mouse.

It didn't take long for the players to remind the league of the
salary implications of bringing such blue-chip partners into the fold.
Within days of the announcement, Bob Goodenow wondered how a
business that was seemingly on death's door during the strike in
1992 was now such a great investment that Disney and Blockbuster
couldn't wait to pay $50 million apiece to join. What happened to
all that red ink caused by players' salaries? Had it dried up with John
Ziegler's tears?

This contradiction would haunt the league as new owners signed
on, pushing the value of an NHL franchise through the roof. When the
Kings were sold for $113 million in 1996 to Philip Anschutz, it
marked a fabulous appreciation on the $16 million McNall had paid
to acquire controlling interest eight years earlier. Norm Green's sale
of the Dallas Stars that year for $84 million was a tidy step up from
the $30 million he paid when the Gunds sold the club in 1991. The
moribund Quebec Nordiques, who paid $6 million to join the NHL in
1979, were sold to Colorado interests for $75 million. Every sale
spoke of the underlying profitability in owning an NHL franchise. In
2002, *Forbes* magazine estimated that thirteen teams were worth
$150 million or more, topped by the Rangers at $277 million, the
Flyers at $250 million, and the Avalanche at $243 million. Even lowly
Canadian teams held value, said *Forbes*, with the Senators worth $96
million, the Flames $92 million, and the Oilers $81 million.

By the mid 1990s, the NHL was in the curious position of trying
to look destitute to players, politicians, and the public while convincing potential investors to pay $80 million for the lucrative benefits of
owning a team. "The NHL wants to suck and blow at the same time,"
said one prominent agent.

The league would doggedly keep to McNall's aggressive business
plan for expansion and salaries that he proposed in 1992—even after
the coin dealer was found to be counterfeit himself. In 1997, McNall
was sentenced in U.S. District Court to seventy months in federal

prison after pleading guilty to two counts of bank fraud, one count of wire fraud, and one count of conspiracy. He had defrauded a number of financial institutions to the tune of $236 million. (His purchase—with Gretzky and actor John Candy—of the Toronto Argonauts of the Canadian Football League also cost his former star player millions of dollars.)

Through this suck-and-blow process, there was one constant in the owners' handbook, a holdover from the old days: when in trouble, blame the players. But this tactic wouldn't work coming from a president like Gil Stein, a remnant from the old NHL order. To update their methods, the Board of Governors needed to look outside the hockey tent for a front man. They needed someone who could crush the upstart Players' Association, protect franchise values, and restore what the owners viewed as the natural NHL order.

8

The Commish

Gary Bettman is perched in a front-row seat in the spacious owners' suite at Calgary's Pengrowth Saddledome. To his left sits Flames co-owner Harley Hotchkiss, Bruce McNall's successor as chairman of the NHL Board of Governors and a man who helped bring NHL hockey to Calgary from Atlanta in 1980. To Bettman's right is the Flames' new president, Ken King, a former publisher of both Calgary's major daily newspapers. Hovering on the periphery is Bettman's PR man, former reporter Frank Brown, his head glistening beneath the lights of the suite. It's late November, 2001. On the ice, the surprising Flames—with 13 wins and 32 points in their first 23 games—are playing the powerful Dallas Stars. In a city known for its power meetings, this hockey night out is a tough ticket.

Bettman is in town to assess the health of a franchise that hasn't won a playoff series since its Stanley Cup win of 1989. Crushed by the discrepancy between the Canadian and U.S. dollar, hindered by their low-budget ineptitude on the ice, the Flames are considered by many insiders to be a prime candidate for relocation as Bettman makes his flying visit to southern Alberta. Hotchkiss and the six other Calgary owners said earlier in the year that they will sell the team if they can't resolve the handicaps of their small market and the punitive exchange rate. After a summer of veiled threats and frantic marketing, the Flames reached their season-ticket goal of 14,000, giving them access to the NHL's Canadian currency-equalization scheme, piloted by Hotchkiss. Bettman has reassured reporters earlier in the day that he's still bullish on Calgary and the Canadian cities, but there is only so much they can do without government assistance. Something has to give.

Heads in the owners' suite follow the puck into the corner behind the Flames goalie Roman Turek. The only head not craning in Turek's direction belongs to Bettman. Dressed in a tailored dark-blue suit and crimson tie, the commissioner is instead consulting the Palm Pilot in his lap. While the hometown crowd moans at Benoit Brunet's goal for Dallas—the eventual game winner in a 3–0 Stars triumph—Bettman is preoccupied with other business flashing across his data organizer. There is the looming confrontation in 2004 with Bob Goodenow and the NHLPA, the huge debt loads of Ottawa, Buffalo, and other franchises, the ever-widening gap in payrolls between the NHL's haves and have-nots. The booing of the usually docile Calgary crowd rouses Bettman; instinctively, he turns from his Palm Pilot to make small talk with Hotchkiss.

A man caught between product and process is the accepted view of Gary Bruce Bettman, the NHL's first commissioner. Hockey people say he has no true passion for the sport, that he's a technocrat borrowed from the NBA. They see him as an American interloper in Canada's national game, a servant of the U.S. power-brokers in the NHL, a functionary who has bloated the league with unnecessary expansion teams. They joke that his caustic style has driven good people away from the league, and that he sleeps in his suit.

There's some truth in all these characterizations, but they shortchange the man; a true portrait of Bettman is more subtly shaded. Yes, the fifty-year-old Bettman is consumed with his NHL duties, a self-confessed workaholic who commits "190 per cent" to the job. "He gives good phone," laughs former Stars owner Norm Green.

"When I was selling the team [in 1996], he was available every day. He'd call back within ten minutes. He came to Dallas to help me meet with Don Carter, who owned the arena. He was sensational." Boston's Harry Sinden concurs: "I don't remember a time when he wasn't involved in putting something together to save a franchise. He's probably spent 75 per cent of his time since he became commissioner trying to help Ottawa or Buffalo or Pittsburgh, whoever needs help. He's done a hell of a job."

And yes, his relentless desire to succeed occasionally gives him the air of a man too eager to impress. But beneath a public facade described by writer Roy MacGregor as "hyper-relaxed," Bettman has a keen mind and an ironic wit. Not as naturally gifted or charismatic as his mentor, David Stern, commissioner of the NBA—under whom he served for twelve years—Bettman has developed a more comfortable speaking style in his ten years at the helm of the league. In mid-snit he's still like a man who has forgotten to remove all the pins from the collar of a new shirt. But media conferences that were once glacial and edgy are now more give-and-take, as a bemused Bettman accepts zingers from reporters with a wry smile—and gives as good as he gets.

Many traditionalists see Bettman as the symbol of all that's wrong with pro hockey, but they are longing for a time that will never reappear. Hockey today is all about business, and Bettman has taken the NHL to new heights. If Bob Goodenow at the NHLPA had a two-year head start on his adversary, Bettman has largely closed the gap. Since accepting the NHL job in 1993, he's transformed a lodge run on the whims and vendettas of powerful owners into a more modern business model. When he took over, the NHL faced an ugly lawsuit over allocation of a surplus in the players' pension plan, a class-action suit over Alan Eagleson's cozy relationship with the NHL, an FBI probe of that relationship, a failed attempt by Stein to have himself inducted into the Hockey Hall of Fame, impending charges of fraud against McNall, the chairman of the Board of Governors, and many other brush fires. Bettman and his staff dealt with it all, losing the pension suit but saving the league untold embarrassment and millions on other fronts. The key, says Ed Horne, president of NHL Enterprises, was Bettman "taking a sport that was operational and turning it into a marketing organization."

Having assumed control of a business that still relied on paper and telephones, Bettman overhauled the league's technology and communications. He bolstered the staff at the head office in New York, doubling the budget for personnel and technology from the $9 million the NHL spent in 1992–93 to $18 million. He negotiated a TV contract with Fox for $80 million in 1994, returning the league to mainstream U.S. TV; that deal was surpassed by the deal with ABC and ESPN Bettman won in 1999, which reaped an unprecedented $600 million for a league that once congratulated itself on scraps from obscure cable outfits. He largely discouraged the time-honoured NHL tradition of owners and GMs addressing collective bargaining policy on an ad hoc basis. As Toronto's Pat Quinn discovered in 2002 when he ventured the opinion that labour talks would end in Armageddon, loose lips can cost you: Quinn was docked $100,000 for his public musing. "One of [Bettman's] qualities has been keeping discipline about talking to the media," notes Flames owner Hotchkiss. "He's tough-minded and he acts as if he has his own equity invested. That's the greatest thing about his leadership."

Until Buffalo and Ottawa fell into bankruptcy in 2002–03, it could also be said that Bettman had been a successful stock promoter—the stock being franchise values. He has overseen a steady climb in the equity of NHL teams. Preaching the liquidity and desirability of an NHL franchise to expansion applicants and new buyers alike, he helped franchise values soar from the mid-$50-millions to as much as $266 million (the value *Forbes* recently placed on the Detroit Red Wings). These numbers kept otherwise restless owners from complaining about losses on day-to-day operations. "Franchise values have risen at a healthy rate," Chuck Greenberg, a sports lawyer in Pittsburgh, told journalist John Saunders in 1992. "As a result, even though franchises don't cash-flow in an attractive way, owners have been able to make back their money and a nice profit when they sell their franchise." While the 2003 bankruptcy sales of Buffalo and Ottawa have clearly shaken confidence in NHL Inc. and in Bettman himself, there has been no public move to unseat him from his office on Avenue of the Americas in downtown Manhattan.

As the first period ends in Calgary, Bettman mixes with local luminaries and oil-patch executives, then heads off for an interview. Perching casually on a stool—as casually as Bettman can perch—he thrusts his hand into a box of popcorn, which he eats with frightening intensity. "I'm yours," he says to the Calgary reporter, as public-relations man Brown lingers on the periphery. While Bettman's answers this night are variations on themes he has articulated before, there's a measured enthusiasm in the byplay with the reporter. Pinning him down on specifics is like trying to check Gretzky: just when he appears trapped in the corner—on revenue-sharing, for example, or a salary cap—he escapes with a "but really, I don't like to look at snapshots of a situation. I like to consider a series of things that might have caused a situation."

There is one pointed message this night, however, one he's delivering across the league. He wants to flush Bob Goodenow from hiding to start talks towards a new collective agreement. "I asked the Players' Association months ago to begin negotiations sooner rather than later, but that's something they haven't been inclined to do. It's my belief that the longer you let things go, the harder they are to fix. I know we still have two seasons to go before 2004, and I really don't want our fans to fixate on it."

Bettman knows that while owners judge him on their equity, history will judge his commissionership on how he handles the showdown when the current CBA expires in September 2004. He knows the owners are not paying him to find a safe middle ground in the next deal with the players. Hotchkiss—a moderate by league-ownership standards—says nothing less than a completely new way of doing business with the players will satisfy him. Bettman surely understands that his employers will not get everything they want.

How he translates their scorched-earth philosophy into a new deal with the players will determine his legacy. But then, he's probably known that from his first day on the job.

Bettman was hired at the Florida meeting of the NHL owners in December 1992, becoming the league's first commissioner after a series of presidents (he insisted on the commissioner's title to underscore the new powers he hoped to wield). As they welcomed him, the sour taste from the first league-wide players' strike was still fresh in the mouths of the owners, a taste only partly sweetened by the pleasant addition of Disney (which owned the new Anaheim franchise) and Blockbuster (which owned the Florida team) to their number. Bettman was not brought from the NBA to pal with Bob Goodenow or his Players' Association.

Since cashiering John Ziegler in June 1992 for sins both real and imagined, the owners had allowed sixty-four-year-old Gil Stein to handle their affairs as president, which included McNall's Anaheim and Miami expansion and the negotiation of the ABC/ESPN television contract. But Stein was not a young man, and the NHL was looking for someone to front their business for at least the next decade. Stein, a Philadelphia lawyer, had too many enemies as a result of years riding shotgun for Flyers owner Ed Snider. To many in the NHL's inner sanctum, the Snider faction was considered soft on salaries, dating back to the WHA days (compared to reactionaries such as Bill Wirtz and Dr. John McMullen, he was practically a socialist). Then there was the unpleasantness of Stein trying to engineer his own election to the Hall of Fame, a PR disaster that sealed his fate.

A new face was needed to break with the sorry recent past. The job description was spelled out by John McMullen, the Devils owner (who also owned baseball's Houston Astros). McMullen and Stein had lunch just after Stein had replaced Ziegler. Fresh from the turmoil of the players' strike, they talked about what the NHL should do in the next negotiations with the players. McMullen groused that the hockey players hadn't lost a cent in their job action in 1992, and was adamant that they should be locked out the next time. "When they miss two paycheques, they'll agree to anything we want," Stein quotes McMullen. Stein reminded the Devils owner that the lockout tactic had not worked in baseball in 1981. In fact, it produced a fifty-one-day labour stoppage that ended only when the owners' lockout insurance ran out. "That's true," replied McMullen, "but if we'd waited two more weeks we would have had them." The man who replaced Stein was obviously going to need to fight to produce cost certainty in hockey.

McMullen's linking hockey and baseball players went beyond his ownership in the two sports. The NHL and MLB had many similarities, including the growing discrepancy between large and small markets created by local TV money. To a staunch Republican like McMullen, the players' associations in both sports were formidable foes. The solidarity of players meant that no meaningful constraints on salaries—or on owners' spending—existed in either sport. Baseball's union had long been among the most potent in North America, thanks to its brilliant executive directors, former Steelworkers economist Marvin Miller, and then lawyer Donald Fehr. Over nine separate labour stoppages, the solidarity of the baseball union had never been breached, driving frustrated owners to more and more frenzied schemes for control.

Miller and Fehr had managed, since the mid-1970s, to extract free agency and millions in salaries for baseball players. (In the late 1980s, the union accused owners of colluding to restrain salaries and won $270 million in damages.) Along the way, the owners, like their hockey brethren, had been unable to negotiate any brake on salaries. That allowed owners such as the Yankees' George Steinbrenner to indulge himself with a $160-million payroll while teams such as the Montreal Expos made do with $25 million. Competitive parity became a sad joke in baseball, and the Yankees used a lineup of purchased and developed stars to capture four straight World Series starting in the mid-1990s. The popularity of baseball, high in the 1980s, plunged as a result.

Bob Goodenow had made no secret of his admiration for Fehr's mighty union when he led the hockey players to the picket line in 1992. Goodenow made every effort to emulate the solidarity and success of the MLBPA. A Don Fehr in hockey was McMullen's worst nightmare. Making it more galling to the Devils owner, the NFL and NBA owners had gained relative control of spending their sports. The NFL had effectively broken its union in a 1987 strike, negotiating a "hard" salary cap for both veterans and rookies, meaning that a team's payroll is capped at a fixed percentage of the league's annual revenues. A court decision in 1993 gave players the right to move from club to club as free agents, but the salary ceiling still gives NFL teams cost certainty, if not roster stability. There are no guaranteed contracts in the NFL, and there's no salary arbitration either, two pillars of the NHLPA. Rookie salaries are capped. And the NFL runs only one small farm league (NFL Europe); development costs of most players are absorbed by the American college programs, who can hold on to a player for up to four years.

These labour agreements have boosted the value of NFL franchises to dizzying heights: the expansion Houston Texans paid $750 million for the right to enter the league in 2002 as the NFL's thirty-second franchise. There's a waiting list of a dozen cities— including Los Angeles—ready to pay that and more to attract either an expansion club or an established team looking for a new home. Labour peace has made the NFL a licence to print money.

The NBA under David Stern also enjoyed a salary cap, although not the hard cap of the NFL. Payrolls were capped for NBA teams, but there were exceptions. Thanks to Bettman's earlier work, NBA teams re-signing established veterans could use the "Larry Bird clause." Named for the great Celtics forward, this rule let teams exceed the salary cap to re-sign designated stars on their roster. Nor was there any restraint on rookie salaries, which made possible such enormous deals as Glen Robinson's seven-year, $115-million rookie pact. But the NBA—unlike the NHL—pays next to nothing in player-development costs: again, colleges and high schools produce their players. While NBA owners griped about cost certainty, they still had much greater control of the bottom line than hockey owners—and basketball owners had a six-year, $4.6-billion-a-year TV contract.

For all its problems, baseball also received a large chunk of TV cash. It had its status as the American pastime, and it had a crucial congressional exemption from antitrust rules, a fanciful labour decision from the early part of the twentieth century (baseball was determined to be a sport, not a business) which MLB commissioners have lobbied strenuously to protect. Hockey was on its own in Congress and in the TV marketplace. Such was the universe Gary Bettman entered when he first sat behind his desk as NHL commissioner in 1993.

Bettman grew up in Queens, one of New York City's five boroughs. "When you are my age and you grew up in New York City you had a choice—there were two teams in all the sports," he says. "So you would pick your favourite hockey team, football team, baseball team, basketball team. I went with all the expansion teams, the Mets, Jets, Nets, and Islanders." In school in the 1960s, Bettman was virtually the only kid in his class from a single-parent household. "It's very common today, but it wasn't then. I didn't have a way to get all the history and tradition from someone else. So being a fairly practical person, I started at the beginning with those expansion teams, so I had it all going forward. I was a big Islanders fan, although the first hockey game I went to was a Ranger game at the old Garden. I used to go with my go card, this little student government card. For three bucks you could go sit all the way upstairs. You'd go early, bring a bag lunch, and do your homework waiting for the game to start."

After high school Bettman headed to the hockey hotbed of Cornell University in Ithaca, New York. "I was a season-ticket holder there for the four years. Watching a game in James Lynah Rink is spectacular. You had to sleep out in line for a day or two to get your tickets, which I did religiously. I was there just after Ken Dryden. Many people think he was the goalie for the undefeated team, but in fact it was Brian Cropper." Bettman met his wife, Shelli, while both were Cornell undergrads (their son Jordan is now a student at the same school). After leaving Big Red, he obtained his law degree from New York University School of Law. His law career began at the prominent New York firm of Proskauer Rose Goetz and Mendelssohn (coincidentally the NHL's legal firm); in 1970 he gravitated to the NBA, where he rose to the rank of third-in-command. Working for the innovative Stern, Bettman concentrated on the collective agreement with players. His work in the NBA—and Stern's recommendation—drew the attention of NHL headhunters as they sought a replacement for Ziegler in 1992.

There was much in hockey to attract the old Islanders fan to the job when the NHL's search committee came calling that year. Yes, the average salary had crept up to $570,000, but NHL attendance was flourishing. Yes, rookies such as Eric Lindros and Alexandre Daigle were winning huge contracts, but revenues from the new arenas around the league were kicking in. Yes, the Players' Association was gaining strength, but expansion moneys were bountiful. Yes, cost controls were problematic, but by 1994 *Sports Illustrated* was trumpeting "Hockey Is Hot, Basketball Is Not" on its cover. The opportunity was there to create a partnership between owners and television to grow revenues and fan support. The baseball example was ample proof that adversarial attacks on an entrenched labour force are disastrous. It seemed a propitious time to become the NHL's first commissioner.

Unfortunately, the NHL players' strike of 1992 had done little to quell the owners' desire for absolute power and revenge. Before Bettman arrived, the battle for the hearts and minds of the owners had largely been won by hard-liners such as McMullen, who saw the NHL's glass as half empty, not half full. Viewing a workforce of

Canadian farm boys and Euros on green cards as business partners was anathema to the Reagan-era capitalists of the NHL. Despite the opportunities for a partnership with players, there would be no sharing of wealth or power with Bob Goodenow's NHLPA for Bettman in 1993.

Some players still shake their head at the NHL's folly. "The one thing that stands out for me is that the owners don't know their enemy," points out Kelly Hrudey, who endured both the 1992 strike and the 1994–95 lockout. "When they picked a fight with us, it changed everything. If you pick a fight with a hockey guy—that's all we know, fighting and following. I'm not a PA member any more, I could care less, but I still get a little angry when I hear ownership picking a fight again. I think you could settle this as a business negotiation. But when it's all about greed...I mean, why is it that only one side is greedy?"

But once the greedy-player concept took hold with owners, it took on a life of its own. Though strong-minded business people in their own domains, owners in the major team sports tend to exhibit a pack mentality in times of stress. "The owners operate like sheep," observed former baseball commissioner Peter Ueberroth as he left office in 1991. "Sheep go in one direction or the other. Right now, they're going in a spending direction. There'll come a time when they run out of money and, choking with losses, they'll try to go in the other direction."

Though he ran baseball, not hockey, Ueberroth had accurately described the owners who hired Bettman as commissioner. They were stampeding towards a lockout of players that would save them from their own poor spending habits. Faced with the breakdown in a labour system they'd dominated for seventy-five years, the hard-line faction directed Bettman to force a showdown. They wanted a deal that guaranteed cost certainty and competitive balance. Not only did they want it for themselves, it was going to be the prime selling point in attracting four new expansion teams at $85 million apiece. Unless they could convince well-heeled

American businessmen that labour costs were under control, the final, lucrative phase of expansion proposed by John Ziegler in 1990 would be a bust.

To give the new commissioner a chance to get established, the owners and the union agreed to extend the existing CBA through the 1993–94 season, marking fall 1994 as the likely time for owners to close the doors. The owners' principal objective in the lockout would be to secure a tax on payrolls, a levy that would range from 100 to 200 per cent of the amount by which a payroll maximum was exceeded (as is now done in MLB). As well, they wanted to do away with salary arbitration and put meaningful restraints on rookie salaries.

To gain public approval for their strategy, the owners emulated Jack Adams from 1956–57 by pointing out the players' new levels of pay. In the wake of Gretzky's new three-year contract at $8 million a year in L.A. and Mario Lemieux's $33-million contract in Pittsburgh, the NHL claimed player demands were forcing them to jack up ticket prices. The average fan, said NHL spokesmen, was being squeezed out of the rink. If you can't afford tickets, they suggested, blame Eric Lindros's contract or Scott Stevens's jumping teams as a free agent.

The connection is flawed, says sports law expert Paul Weiler of Harvard. "Professional athletes are the beneficiaries, but not the cause, of the increase in ticket prices," he writes in *Leveling the Playing Field*. "The true economic interaction between players and fans is that when ticket and other team revenues go up, this causes salaries to rise, rather than vice versa.... The price of tickets is ultimately determined by the interplay of supply and demand in that consumer market."

Weiler cites the example of baseball, where average salaries rose from $50,000 to $400,000 a year between 1976 and 1986, yet the price of the average ticket dropped in real dollars. Conversely, when TV and gate receipts sank in the post-1995 strike era, the average player salary dropped by more than $100,000. If one accepts that salaries, which are determined by league-wide forces, cause ticket prices to rise, then the price of a hockey ticket should be the same (adjusted for currency) in every city. In fact, ticket prices vary widely according to demand in local markets. Some cities use variable pricing for more or less desirable opponents. Toronto and New York charge the highest prices while Calgary and Nashville are at the low end.

Weiler points to the movie business as an example of elasticity in ticket prices. *Titanic* cost $210 million to make, yet its ticket price was the same in cinemas as that of *The Blair Witch Project*, which cost $600,000 to make. Why? Because they had to compete side by side in Cineplexes across the continent, and *Titanic* could not allow *The Blair Witch Project* a competitive advantage when filmgoers were making their choice at the ticket counter. The pricing of hockey tickets, says Weiler, has everything to do with local competition from baseball, football, basketball, the symphony, theatres, and cinemas, and less to do with player salaries. As long as there is no resistance to price hikes, clubs will introduce them—and blame the players.

One thing was indisputable, however. Higher ticket prices were putting a night at the rink out of reach for a lot of blue-collar people, the bedrock of fan support. According to Team Marketing Report, a business publishing and research firm based in Chicago, a family of four paid about $240 to attend an NHL game by 2002. And large salaries were separating players from the common people. In 1967, a hockey player making $19,000 was earning about three and a half times the average worker's salary in America. By the mid-1990s, a hockey player making $1.5 million was earning almost fifty times the average worker's salary. And while the average worker's salary was going down in real terms, the earnings of hockey players had increased tenfold. Suddenly kids from small towns were in the same bracket as CEOs, not blue-collar workers. This was a source of resentment that the NHL would look to mine—one for which players had no ready answer.

"It's the hardest part of a labour disruption," says Hall of Fame player Mike Gartner, a key figure in the NHLPA during the work stoppages in 1992 and 1994–95. "I realized early that there is no sympathy whatsoever for an athlete. And I don't know if there should be any sympathy if players make $1.6 million a year. You can argue that it's a short career, but it doesn't wash with the public. Don't even go there. Don't expect any sympathy."

In the summer of 1994, the players were setting aside a war chest from the licensing moneys Goodenow had stockpiled for the Players' Association. "That's why it was so important that we kept the money from the trading cards in 1992," recalls veteran defenceman Brad McCrimmon, then with Hartford. "The money we made from that fight gave us the money for the big fight we knew was coming in 1994."

Despite the media boost it had received in the spring of 1994 from the Rangers' first Stanley Cup win in fifty-four years, the NHL and its players were on a collision course for a lockout on October 1. The rules of engagement were delivered in a memo to players and agents:

Please be advised that the NHL, effective on or about September 1, 1994, plans to unilaterally impose the following measures on NHL players:
1) Mandatory two-way contracts
2) The elimination of salary arbitration
3) The elimination of guaranteed contracts and buy-out provisions.
4) The reduction of the players' playoffs and awards fund from $9 million to $2 million.
5) The elimination of all per-diem allowances
6) Roster size reduced to 17 skaters and 2 goaltenders, major league roster reduced to 22 players
7) Force players to pay the first $750 of the medical cost per insured person and co-insurance of 70% (NHL) to 30% (insured person) to $10,000

8) The elimination of the senior player benefit. Force players earning in excess of $350,000 to pay 50% of the annual pension contribution

9) Compulsory currency conversion. Players traded between a Canadian club and a U.S. club shall have the amounts of their salaries and bonuses converted to the currency of the country to which the player was traded.

10) Clubs will no longer pay for players to travel from summer residence to the club's home city prior to training camp and at the conclusion of the season

11) NHL's discipline increased to $50,000

12) Players required to wear only approved NHL apparel off the ice. League will dictate "skates, sticks, helmets etc." for all players

13) Mandatory community service, public appearances and commercial appearances.

It was a declaration of war.

As training camp loomed, talks between the league and the NHLPA about a salary cap or payroll tax went nowhere; the players wanted proof of the owners' financial distress. The NHL declined to open the books. Liberal free agency, meanwhile, was a non-starter with the owners, who still believed the union's solidarity would eventually collapse if the players were forced to stay out for an extended period. Players professed themselves happy with the current CBA, but believed that owners would be pressured to talk only when the NHL's package with Fox TV began in early 1995—and when the owners' strike insurance ran out. Goodenow also assured his members that the owners would eventually be forced to negotiate because of the massive debt many were carrying from new arenas.

There was a bizarre atmosphere as players reported for training camp in the fall of 1994 fully expecting to be locked out in weeks. "It was a bit of a twilight zone," recalls Gartner. "There was nothing to vote on, really. They had taken away our insurance, our pension benefits, but we showed up anyway. It was a surreal experience, because we knew we were training for nothing."

In truth, both sides were vulnerable as the deadline arrived. The league's lawyers were concerned that the standard NHL player's contract had no exceptions for labour disruptions. Teams could still be liable to pay the players' salaries, even if the clubs legally locked them out. If the players' salaries were missed for three weeks, the players could give the owners a notice of default and declare themselves free agents. The prospect of all their players being tossed into the open market petrified the owners, who didn't trust themselves not to poach one another's stars. So as training camp ended, a cautious Bettman announced he was merely suspending the start of the season, not calling for a lockout. If the players gave notice of default, Bettman was prepared to start the season and continue negotiating behind the scenes. When Goodenow failed to force action on this default clause, the owners chortled in delight: they could now lock out their players and not have to pay them. They had already bested the NHLPA director. Or so it seemed. The lockout was on, with both sides ready for a lengthy disruption.

Typically, the NHL couldn't see things from the NHLPA's point of view. Yes, the marquee players would have prospered in a free-agent free-for-all, but the move would have been costly to the rank-and-file players, the ones prospering under the current conditions. With no scarcity of talent, players on the third and fourth line or extra defencemen would have been cheap for owners to pick up or discard. And Goodenow, who counted on these blue-collar players for his support, would have been portrayed as a director for the rich players, not for the journeymen. In the interest of union solidarity, Goodenow never pursued the default strategy, even though it might have caused the NHL to buckle sooner on the union's demands.

For the association, there was also grave concern about how long it could maintain solidarity in the face of pressure from the owners and—more pointedly—the public. "In any sports-union battle," notes Mike Barnett, then Gretzky's agent, "the union is only as strong as its support from star players." The concern over the major stars was largely addressed when Barnett had Gretzky's contract structured so that he received most of his 1994–95 salary as a bonus before the start of the regular season. This eliminated the possibility of Gretzky mounting a mercy mission with Goodenow for "the good of the game" to end the lockout prematurely; instead, Gretzky and a number of other high-profile players went to Europe on a barn-storming mission, far from the firing line and the stares of disapproving fans. Meanwhile, worries that other superstars such as Mario Lemieux, Jaromir Jagr, Raymond Bourque, and Eric Lindros might try to circumvent the PA to cut their own deals proved unfounded. Goodenow had sold his message.

Adding to the public antipathy for the players' position was the concurrent strike by baseball players, who were resisting payroll caps and an end to salary arbitration in their sport. When ballplay-ers would not end their strike, the owners of MLB cancelled the end of the 1994 season and the World Series. Hockey players were thus linked with their striking baseball brothers in the public mind, even though they were locked out, ready to go back to work the moment the owners opened the gates again. It was a subtlety lost on most fans. Gary Roberts, then with the Flames, was heckled by irate fans at the grocery store and while dining with friends at a restaurant. "You lose if you get in a shouting match with the guy," Roberts sighed. "You lose if you walk away. And if you get in a fight, you end up in court. I've been staying out of the public."

"I was on a radio show in Vancouver that winter," recalls Mike Liut, by then working for the NHLPA. "And the host raised the issue that no matter what happened, the players would never get back the money they were losing in the lockout. I said, 'The one thing you must respect is the players' decision to take a chance. He's put his money where his mouth is. It's a very principled person who does that, and you have to respect him.'"

As 1994 ended without a settlement, time was rapidly running out on the chance to play a meaningful schedule and playoffs.

Players had by now lost about 40 per cent of their salaries, and were hunkering down at home, scrimping and saving while trying to stay in game shape. "Way back when, they told us to prepare for a lockout," said a chastened Rangers goalie Mike Richter. "They told us it would be a long one, and I was like so many other guys: I never thought it would happen." One of Richter's teammates summed up the frustration: "Why don't we just admit what we all know? We got our butts kicked!"

Other players got an eye-opening taste of life beyond the rink. Kings goalie Robb Stauber tried selling cars. "The cars I sold, I would give away a hockey stick or sign things for them. That was the only way I could get them to buy. The first few days out there, I didn't know what I was doing. A couple of guys helped me out."

With new arenas either opening or expected to open in a dozen cities, the ownership group faced severe pressure as well. The crucial American network-TV package on Fox was scheduled to start its coverage in January. Any delays there could be very costly, added to the millions already lost by CBC TV on *Hockey Night in Canada*. The schism between hawks and doves on the NHL Board of Governors was threatening to make acceptance of any proposal moot. The hawks felt that, having endured this long, they might as well go all the way to the bitter end; the doves felt the season and the business were salvageable by a settlement. At one meeting of the negotiating committee in 1994, owners renewed their vow to crush the players, only to have former players Bobby Clarke and Phil Esposito—now in management—make passionate pleas not to underestimate the resolve of the players. Asked about a deal that would help the league's smaller markets, McMullen growled, "To hell with the small markets." Boston's Harry Sinden expressed his frustration at preparing yet another proposal for the players: "This is the final, final, final, final, final offer," he groused.

It wasn't. By January 1995, with the public saying "a plague on both your houses," talks between the NHL and the PA finally resumed in New York City. In an effort to end the stalemate, Bettman and his assistant Brian Burke backed off the concept of a payroll tax and the end to salary arbitration, but held firm on limited player movement in the prime years of a player's career.

Goodenow and the executive of the NHLPA had to walk a fine line: concede on some issues, but make it seem to his weary membership that their sacrifices had been worth four months of waiting. The easiest tack was to give way on rookie salaries. After all, none of the players to be affected by this move were as yet NHLPA members. Giving ground on a rookie salary cap would allow for greater benefits to veteran players in the union. "The players were not that opposed to [a rookie cap]," says Barnett, "because it gave teams insurance that if a player couldn't play, he'd end up on a two-way contract (between the NHL and the minors). But if he proves himself on the ice, the teams get value."

The final negotiations came down to a late-night session between the bulldog Goodenow and the terrier Bettman. While a media throng, six hundred NHL players, and the twenty-six owners awaited the result, an outline of the hockey business for the next decade was hammered out in closed-door sessions. NHLPA people at the head office in Toronto felt that if the talks came down to stamina, Goodenow would outgrind Bettman. But Bettman was equal to the task. By dawn, word circulated that the men had a tentative deal to take back to the Board of Governors.

But even at this late moment, owners such as Abe Pollin of Washington and Bill Wirtz of Chicago still tried to hit a home run, proposing that players must accept an earlier offer from owners or else. "That's the dumbest motion I've ever heard," hissed an exasperated Flyers owner Ed Snider when Capitals owner Pollin proposed his changes to the deal Bettman and Goodenow had hammered out. Bill Wirtz led a charge against the proposal that players become unrestricted free agents at thirty-one, not thirty-two. The Chicago owner led a group of fourteen owners—either hawks or small-market teams such as Quebec, Hartford, and Winnipeg—against the deal ratified the night before. (The fourteen owners were nicknamed the "needy and the greedy" by ESPN's Al Morganti.)

Again, Bettman had to go back to Goodenow to ask for more concessions. "Gary Bettman did an unbelievable job Monday," said one NHL governor. "Then we had enough people dumb enough to make him go do another unbelievable job on Tuesday night." Goodenow might have used the obvious rift in the Board of Governors to prolong the talks. But player rep James Patrick of Calgary summed up the frustration of the players: "If there are all those changes, and it is a take-it-or-leave-it offer, I don't know if it would go through." Goodenow realized it was make or break for the season when Bettman returned from his spanking by the owners. He compromised one last time on the age of unrestricted free agency, bumping it from thirty-one to thirty-two. On January 11, Bettman was able to take back another proposal to the fractious owners, one that was indeed the "final offer."

Since the last governors meeting, the media had reported on the last-ditch moves by Pollin and the other hawks to squeeze more from the players. Pollin whined that a board member had sold him out in the media. "I can't believe my partners would do this to me," he protested. Stung that the public was thinking that they had held up resumption of the season, the owners quickly ratified the second tentative agreement by a 17–9 margin. Players followed suit by week's end, concluding the 103-day stoppage. Joe Nieuwendyk summed up the feelings on both sides. "We lost money. They lost money. And the fans lost the game they love."

Nearly everyone conceded that, in his first crack at collective bargaining, Bettman had won a good compromise. "Bettman is so much more commissioner than hockey deserves it is a laugh," wrote an admiring Mike Lupica of the *New York Daily News*. "Some people have suggested that Bettman might get a pink slip when this is all over. He should get a medal." Bettman had Goodenow concede a cap on rookies' salaries for the first three years of their careers, the maximum going from $875,000 in 1996 to $1.075 million over the years of the deal, with no free agency or arbitration. He had allowed no significant free agency before age thirty-two for players until

1999, thereafter not until age thirty-one. Group Two free agents—those on their second contracts or later, but younger than thirty-two—could become restricted free agents, but teams signing them would have to provide compensation in the form of five first-round draft picks. And any team matching the competing offer could retain its player, rendering competitive bids virtually pointless except in escalating salary levels.

While he hadn't done away with salary arbitration, Bettman won the right for teams to walk away from up to three arbitrators' decisions in two years should they not like the settlement. The NHL continued to restrict free agency by keeping the entry draft at nine rounds, with the rights of American high-school and college players, as well as European draftees, held in perpetuity.

Goodenow was pilloried in some quarters. "He can proclaim a bloody victory," snorted Al Strachan of the *Toronto Sun*. "Then the players will look at what he gave away. Hockey players always know who lost the fight." Lupica derided Goodenow as "a stubborn light-weight...out of his weight class...he was in over his head with Bettman from the start." Jack Todd of the Montreal *Gazette* was blunt. "The players lost, but there is no reason to bleed for them.... It's not like he's going to have to run down a recipe book on 101 Things You Can Do With Kraft Dinner."

For his part, Goodenow saw a clear outcome from the prolonged struggle. "The lesson is that the players would not be intimidated. They were going to be professional from start to finish. Any attempts not to negotiate with them will be unsuccessful. There's a lot of commentary about what we gave up. But the CBA is still a work in progress."

Indeed, clear eyes saw that, while he may have surrendered on some fronts, Goodenow had preserved the essentials for generating higher salaries: free agency, salary arbitration, guaranteed contracts, no salary tax or cap, the right to license players' images for profit—in short, nothing to save owners from themselves when need met greed. "By getting a deal without a salary cap/luxury tax, the players

effectively put the onus on owners to run their businesses effi-
ciently," noted Eric Duhatschek in the *Calgary Herald*. "Some will
try, but others...will not be able to change the spending habits of a
lifetime. All it takes is a handful of free-spending teams and all the
contracts you couldn't comprehend before...will appear almost log-
ical in two years."

Goodenow had also preserved the concept of scarcity for those
free agents who became available and for entry-level players. A keen
student of Marvin Miller, Goodenow had noted a telling passage in
Miller's autobiography. "To me," wrote Miller in *A Whole Different
Ball Game*, "a large supply of free agents each year would defeat one
of the purposes of free agency, namely the bidding up of salaries.
Luckily, Oakland's owner Charlie Finley—who generally was
ignored—seemed to be the only one smart enough to recognize that
opening the flood gates by making all players free agents would
work to the owners' advantage."

Hockey owners, too, fell into Miller's trap of scarcity. By putting such stringent conditions on unfettered free agency, they
guaranteed a bidding contest for those few who hit the market. As
well, by preserving a nine- or ten-round entry draft, they reduced
each team's access to the best young talent to one-twenty-sixth of
the available talent pool in the world. Again, scarcity made desirable entry-level players more expensive. Should a club be unable to
draw on its farm system to replace a player when injuries hit, the
cost of acquiring one from another club became prohibitive.
Outside Europe, there would be virtually no unattached, worth-
while prospects. Looked at in these ways, Goodenow's deal in
1995 was not a defeat. Far from it.

Some owners sensed as much when players reported for work
again in late January. Arthur Griffiths of Vancouver lamented the
failure to win a salary cap: "[We] were headed in that direction, but
at the last minute—and I don't want to get into specifics—it got off
track. And we ended up with a situation that wasn't in the best interest of managing these businesses." "The cap on rookie salaries helps

a bit," said Quebec owner Marcel Aubut. "But clearly, it's insuffi-
cient for the long-term stability we need." "The lockout didn't last
long enough to solve the problems of the industry," observed Norm
Green, owner of the Dallas Stars. "We should have been tougher,"
said Calgary's Harley Hotchkiss. "We needed to get a solution for
everyone, a system that works if you run the thing well. There's still
significant room for inflation."

Hotchkiss's comments were prescient. It took another eight
months of lawyering for the final proposal to be signed, and less than
two years to have the worst suspicions of the chairman of the Board
of Governors borne out. By the time the NHL headed off to its
Nagano Olympics experiment in 1998, Hartford, Quebec City, and
Winnipeg would be former members of the NHL, transferred to
North Carolina, Colorado, and Phoenix, respectively. Minnesota,
Nashville, Atlanta, and Columbus would be granted expansion franchises to play by the year 2000, taking the NHL to thirty teams.

As time passed, other wrinkles in the CBA showed that Goodenow
had done better than reported by critics such as Al Strachan. For
instance, the NHLPA kept the expiry date for the next deal in mid-
September 2004. That date comes a full two and a half months after
teams need to qualify their players' contracts for the next season,
and six weeks after salary-arbitration season. In effect, the teams
would have to guess or gamble on a labour disruption when decid-
ing which players to retain and at what price. It's likely that
two-thirds of the NHL players will greet September 15, 2004, the
drop-dead date for a new CBA, with a guaranteed contract in hand.
That prospect makes any labour disruption seem a lot less threatening to those players. In addition, the players won the right to stage a
World Cup of Hockey just prior to the September 15 deadline. The
revenues garnered from this event would assist players through any
lockout imposed by owners.

One of the stars in that World Cup was likely to be Joe Thornton.
The tall, gifted centre from St. Thomas, Ontario—who was not even
born when Wayne Gretzky was traded to Edmonton—could write

his name in hockey history with a big performance. It wouldn't be the first time Thornton had made history. As a rookie, he proved that the 1995 CBA, won at such cost in dollars and tears, was no impediment to the sorts of contracts that have tilted the economic balance between labour and management in the NHL.

9

No Ordinary Joe

The Boston Bruins' brain trust sat in the stands of the Ristuccia Memorial Arena in Wilmington, Massachusetts, during training camp in September 1997. The hockey men were watching a slender rookie with curly blond hair flowing from beneath his helmet. The Bruins had been the worst team in the NHL the season before, missing the playoffs for the first time in thirty years. Their hopes for revitalization rested on the shoulders of Joe Thornton, a lanky centre who'd just turned eighteen. As a film crew watched, assistant GM Mike O'Connell turned to his boss Harry Sinden. O'Connell's brow was creased with worry at the performance of the Bruins'—and the NHL's—top selection in the 1997 draft.

"He gets his chances all the time, and he misses all the time," said O'Connell, as cameras rolled for the documentary *The New Ice Age*. "He misses the net."

Sinden nodded in silence.

O'Connell continued, "I was saying to Cheesy [former Bruins goalie Gerry Cheevers, now a broadcaster] we should take a film of Allison and show it to Thornton and say, 'This is what you're going to be if you don't get your act together.'"

Jason Allison, like Thornton, was a big offensive centre out of the OHL who'd been a bust as a first-round pick in Washington. While he was about to have a breakthrough season in 1997, Allison's name was still synonymous with failure as O'Connell, Sinden, and their staff looked on. Thornton, a consensus number-one pick a few months before, now seemed destined for a similar fate. To the men who'd staked their reputations on him, Thornton appeared out of shape and unfocused.

Making Thornton's lacklustre play more painful was the production of the Bruins' other first-round selection, Sergei Samsonov, selected seven spots later. The stocky, speedy Samsonov had come to camp without a contract, eager to prove he deserved the same money Thornton had received in his rookie contract. After playing in the International Hockey League the year before, the young Russian speedster was looking like the prospect worth millions; Thornton, counted on to fill seats in Boston's Fleet Center, was looking like an embarrassment. "He's a quick little bastard, isn't he?" O'Connell said to Sinden as they watched Samsonov. "Nice play—Jesus Christ, what a play. Did you see that play?"

The NHL amateur draft is guesswork at best; number-one prospects (Joe Murphy, Greg Joly, Doug Wickenheiser) sometimes flop while unheralded kids from later rounds find themselves in the NHL. That's the gamble you take assessing talent that won't fully mature for another five years. For the Bruins, however, Thornton's mediocrity seemed more than just a poor choice from the June draft. Yes, they needed to regain their customary spot in the playoffs. But they also had an expensive new arena, the Fleet Center, built in the shadow of the Boston Garden, with seats in need of filling. That required star power, the kind Thornton promised. Now, on the steaming ice of the Ristuccia Arena, he was looking very ordinary as the older players treated him like a schoolboy. Could Samsonov, a European, get skeptical New Englanders to part with the money for personal seat licences and souvenirs? Not likely. But Thornton...

Of greater concern to Sinden (the Bruins president and GM since Bobby Orr's early years) was the contract he had given Thornton to keep him from returning to junior hockey. In three decades in the NHL, Sinden had earned a reputation as a negotiator who parted with his owner's money only under duress. Name the tightwad joke and players have applied it to Sinden. Even the great defenceman Raymond Bourque was unable to pry his true market value out of Sinden. The lowered benchmark set by Bourque, the NHL's top rear-guard, retarded the salaries of all NHL defencemen for years. Sinden had always been the first to condemn inflationary contracts.

For Thornton, though, Sinden was a changed man. "Everybody in the league thought, this is great, our first big deal under the new entry-level cap, he has to go to Boston, so he's going to have himself one hell of a time," Sinden recalled years later. "Everybody's waiting for us to tell Joe Thornton to go take a hike. But I said to Mike O'Connell, 'We're going to sign this kid, I don't care.' We'd had a miserable year, ended last, and we got a chance to get a player who, consensus, was the next great one. This is what had happened to all the other teams, or many of them: 'We're going to do what we want. To hell with Boston.' But in the case of Thornton, I said, 'Come on, we're signing him, whatever it takes.'"

Sign Thornton he did, to an entry-level salary of $925,000 a year for three years, the maximum allowed under the 1995 CBA. No problem there. The devil was in the bonuses. The CBA describes eleven categories of bonus for entry-level players (goalies have five). The A list, as agents call it, has the usual goals, assists, points, and Calder Trophy voting. The swing categories include ice time, plus/minus, and power-play production. The model for top prospects before Thornton had been the contract signed by Jarome Iginla in Calgary. It set marks of $50,000 for hitting 20 goals or 35 assists or 60 points as a first-year player. Mike Barnett, Thornton's agent, bumped the payoff to $250,000; should Thornton hit just two of the six agreed-upon categories in his first year, he would make $1.8 million in "balloon" bonuses. If not, he would have to hit three of the six marks to reap the $1.8 million in year two; four of the six in year three. Sinden and Barnett also agreed that the bonuses would be rolled over, allowing the developing Thornton three years to collect on them. Once a bonus was attained, Thornton could not get the same category the following year. The total deal could average the same $2.25 million a year won from the Senators by Daigle, a contract Sinden had excoriated in 1993.

Sinden was—and remains—unapologetic. "I told them, 'From now on, I don't care what happens to you because of this contract. I let all kinds of players go over the years because I wouldn't pay them. I tried to do the party line, hold salaries. But you signed your players at whatever.' Now they can tar and feather me. I got a chance at the best player since Lindros, and he's come along really well. He has sold seats. Everyone is excited. We weren't going to sign him for nothing. We could not risk him going back into the draft."

Not only did Sinden give Thornton this newfangled contract, he eventually awarded a similar one to Samsonov as well. "I didn't hide the fact from the commissioner. I was going to do this great thing." Sinden allows himself an ironic laugh. "He was disappointed when I told him. But he doesn't run a team."

Agent Rick Curran felt there was more to Sinden's about-face than met the eye. "He and [former Bruins defenceman] Al Iafrate had a pretty unique relationship," recalls Curran. "And he was asked to stand up in an arbitration case and tell Iafrate that, because of an injury, he wasn't going to get paid. I don't think Harry really wanted to do that. I was told later that he was pissed because he had to carry the ball for the NHL, and he didn't feel good about it."

It took a while for Sinden to succumb to self-interest on the Thornton case. "Ominous" was how he first described Barnett's new bonus model. "I brought it home to read, and I wasn't sure if I was going to digest it or throw up." Barnett kept preaching that it would pay out only if Thornton produced at levels reached by very few eighteen-year-olds. For a vulnerable GM such as Sinden, the outcome was inevitable. The entry-level cap on rookies was a paper tiger; the bonus structure Barnett proposed would guarantee that rookies—at least those who produce—would be paid as well as Lindros and Daigle.

"There's a bonus in the contract model for the player being a top-nine forward on the club," points out agent Ritch Winter. "But you're not going to sign an eighteen-year-old player unless he's already one of your top nine. So that clause is almost like an automatic bonus for eighteen-year-old kids on weak clubs. Then he only has to hit one more in the first year to collect the balloon payment."

Sinden was content to pay Thornton top dollar—if he produced. Still, it was hard for him to smile when he was over a barrel. "I think one of the problems with the people making these decisions is their own security," concedes Sinden. "They take the position it would be a hell of a lot better to have those players on the ice for their own sake than to hold the line and end up out of the playoffs. That's human nature. I didn't have that problem. My relationship with our owner was that I didn't expect he'd fire me if I signed Thornton or not. But a lot of other managers, you can imagine."

"Boston wanted Joe," recalls Barnett, now running the Phoenix Coyotes on behalf of Wayne Gretzky, the Coyotes' part-owner. "Harry was very open about it. They wanted Joe to satisfy the fan interest as well as to help on the ice. It was pretty likely, though, with [new coach] Pat Burns and his feelings about bringing rookies along slowly, Joe was going to be more of a marketing piece in the first year." Restricted ice time meant there was little or no chance for the Sault Ste. Marie Greyhounds star to earn bonuses or awards that would put him above the rookie maximum. Even the greatest prospects are hard-pressed to thrive as eighteen-year-old kids against the men of the NHL.

"If you looked at Bryan Berard," says Barnett of the number-one pick by Ottawa in 1995, "he went back unsigned to junior, then came back as a nineteen-year-old, stronger, more experienced, more confident. He won the Calder Trophy as the NHL's top rookie after being traded to the Islanders. There was little likelihood of Joe winning the Calder at eighteen, and even less likelihood of him hitting

any of the minimums [20 goals, 35 assists, 60 points]. Only five players have done that in the year they were drafted, guys like Yzerman,
Turgeon, Lindros."

Barnett told the Bruins that Thornton was better off going back
to junior, then coming back at nineteen, when he had a more legitimate shot at the bonuses. But the Bruins wanted—needed—
Thornton in the big time, even if he wasn't ready. "So I told them, if
he plays as an eighteen-year-old, let's give him a second shot at the
bonuses as a nineteen-year-old when he legitimately has a chance to
do it. Through negotiations, we were able to get to where what he
didn't get in the first year, he could get in the second or third. This
was the way to give the Bruins the security they needed on non-
guaranteed salary."

As Barnett had predicted, Thornton struggled in his first year,
achieving no bonuses. In his second year, he reached only the ice-
time bonus ($250,000); in the third year, though, with more than $3
million available in rolled-over bonuses, he hit the bonanza by scoring twice in the final game of the season. "Harry says, 'You guys had
me, and you nailed me,'" smiles Barnett. "It's easy to say they got
beaten up in the deal, but I think when you look back on it, they paid
only an ice-time bonus in two years. If they had had to pay out $3.5
million per year in the first two years, it would have been different.
But the levels were high enough that it didn't happen."

The Thornton contract may have seemed reasonable to Barnett,
but Sinden's acceptance of it riled many of his fellow managers (even
if Thornton's debut filled the chairs at the Fleet Center, and the pockets of owner Jeremy Jacobs).

For all the wrangling in the acrimonious lockout of 1994–95, all
the carefully lawyered phrases, all the hard-won concessions, Sinden
was admitting that teams were no better off than they had been
before the lockout. Faced with a player he desperately needs—to fill
a building, get a new TV contract, or win a title—an owner or general manager will find the money. And an agent with a hot property
can and will drag the last dollar from a deal.

"It's almost like as soon as the CBA was done, they found a loop-hole and drove a truck right through it," said former San Jose GM Dean Lombardi. "We were supposed to have a cap on rookies, but it didn't really work out that way. Nobody anticipated, when you signed a top-ten pick, being exposed to $7 million or $10 million. Thornton started it with $3 million or $4 million, and then Vincent Lecavalier was up to $10 million or $11 million."

In short, the NHL's desire to control all the hockey talent on the planet backfired. Heeding former Major League Baseball union director Marvin Miller's contention that having fewer, not more, free agents creates scarcity, and therefore higher salaries, agents such as Don Baizley, Barnett, and Don Meehan argued successfully that it was better business for a club to retain its stars than to replace them. Little had changed since Bob Goodenow took the gloves off the NHLPA in 1991. And all the pundits who'd said the players were losers in the lockout needed to look again. The Thornton contract was a watershed in the post-lockout era; the her-alded entry-level cap had lasted less than two years before Barnett blew it apart.

"Look who was the most vocal about Randy Sexton making the Daigle deal in Ottawa," says Neil Smith. "Harry Sinden and Mike Milbury, both in Boston at the time. Three years later, faced with the same dilemma, Harry does the Thornton deal. When I went to nego-tiate Manny Malhotra's rookie deal with the Rangers the next year, I blamed the Bruins for why we were all in trouble on this rookie thing. Harry got mad at me, as he always does. You can't say any-thing critical about him, but he can criticize you."

"Harry's tremendous," says Larry Pleau of St. Louis. "We all admire him, but he had a new arena, Thornton was their number-one pick, and they had missed the playoffs. It's not just one freaking person doing this; it's all of us to blame, every one of us. I don't blame the players, the agents, or the Players' Association. That's what they're there for. We're the ones who've driven it. We have to get it together in our own local markets."

Barnett, of course, was hailed by his fellow agents, who now use the Thornton model when negotiating a rookie contract. "They'd say, 'I don't know how you did it,' or 'Jesse James wore a mask'— those sorts of things," smiles Barnett. Most rookies have not used the Thornton model to get rich quickly, but those who flourish in their rookie years can put a team in serious trouble if it doesn't get insurance protection. Edmonton's Mike Comrie was able to garner $3.5 million in bonuses for the 2001–02 season, based on his entry-level contract, a sum the Oilers had not covered with insurance. The amount was reduced by a million when the Oilers missed the play-offs. In 2002–03, Comrie hit on three bonuses and reaped $3.5 million. Even then, the Oilers were hard-pressed to find the money to pay his bonuses. (Ironically, Comrie's father, Bill, a furniture-store magnate, is a part-owner of the Edmonton club.)

Similarly, the Atlanta Thrashers were hit with a bill of more than $8 million when their flashy rookies Ilya Kovalchuk ($4.375 million) and Dany Heatley ($4 million) both cashed in their first-year bonuses in 2001–02. Kovalchuk, who scored 29 goals, and Heatley, who notched 26, also pocketed the $1.3-million maximum salary.

Barnett's creative approach to the Thornton contract was one of many indications that, while the CBA hammered out two years earlier may have mounted roadblocks to the players' wealth, a skillful agent working with the NHLPA can find a way around them. "The NHL insisted on three-year contracts for entry-level players in the CBA," says Don Baizley. "For the life of me, I don't understand why. Why couldn't they sign a marginal prospect for just one year and an option? For a contract supposedly idiot-proof, why did they insist that entry-level players must get three-year deals?"

While Thornton and Barnett shattered the rookie cap, the NHL's latest round of free-agent salary escalation began in earnest in 1997, and Baizley played a major part in it. Before the 1994 lockout, Wayne Gretzky had received $8 million a year and Lemieux about the same, but most hockey people viewed them as exceptions and worth the money. The ceiling for other top stars hovered in the range of $3 million to $5 million. Baizley and a few other agents changed that in the summer of 1997. Using the game's best young players, they pushed the top end of the salary structure past the Gretzky/Lemieux benchmark into the $10-million range.

Buoyed by expansion money, new arenas, and Gary Bettman's rosy prognosis for TV and the Internet, owners were persuaded to go on a spending spree. Linking the presence of a superstar to potential earnings in a cable-TV deal or an Internet tie-in, owners forgot the hard lessons of the lockout. The prospect of a Stanley Cup winner married to a Fox TV contract or an AOL website was exactly the future Bruce McNall had spoken of so glowingly. Here it was, the chance to harvest easy dollars and catch up with the NFL, NBA, and MLB.

Soon there were big contracts for old reliables such as five-time Cup winner Mark Messier, who got $6 million per year in July 1997 from a desperate Pat Quinn in Vancouver; Quinn hoped Messier would help $5.5-million man Pavel Bure reverse the Canucks' slide. Philadelphia took a $10-million flyer on hulking twenty-two-year-old centre Chris Gratton, who'd scored 67 goals in four years with Tampa (and who would be shipped back to the Lightning eighteen months later). The Rangers acquired injury-prone Pat LaFontaine at $4.8 million to recapture his previous glory on Broadway. (LaFontaine was injured again that season and retired.)

But the locus of activity in the summer of 1997 was Don Baizley in Winnipeg, a city that had just lost its team, the Jets, to Phoenix. As a collegiate player in Manitoba, Baizley had started representing players when the Jets began play in the WHA. Using European contacts, the bespectacled lawyer soon was handling contracts for Anders Hedberg, Ulf Nilsson, Lars-Erik Sjoberg, and other Jets. His signature deal was signing Hedberg and Nilsson—Bobby Hull's linemates in Winnipeg—as free agents in 1979 with the New York Rangers. At a time when the highest NHL salary was thought to be $350,000, Baizley got the Swedes their $750,000 signing bonuses and $225,000 salaries with the Rangers. "That was a big number at the time," he recalls.

A former litigator and arbitrator in insurance cases, Baizley began assembling a roster of hockey stars with his low-profile style and bona fide contacts, all the while retaining his other legal work. By the mid-1990s, he was perhaps the most respected player representative—he prefers the term "sports lawyer"—representing Peter Forsberg, Joe Sakic, Paul Kariya, Teemu Selanne, Theo Fleury, and many others under the banner of the firm Thompson, Dorfman and Sweatman. By 2002, he was responsible for $64,332,727 in contracts. "He may be the consummate agent," says Neil Smith. "He's like Anthony Hopkins—he's a class act."

In 1997, Baizley had Forsberg, Sakic, and Kariya all entering restricted free agency—that is, Group Two free agency for players under thirty-one years of age. This meant another club could lure them away with an offer sheet (for five first-round picks) or their former team could match the offer to retain their services. Rumours swirled that Colorado could not afford both Forsberg and Sakic as well as their $4-million-a-year goalie, Patrick Roy. Forsberg, a coveted twenty-four-year-old centre, had led the Avs to a Stanley Cup with his sweet playmaking and fierce determination. Better yet, the tenacious Swede wouldn't be an unrestricted free agent—able to exploit a free market—for six more years. Sakic, meanwhile, was among the top forwards in hockey, a slick scorer and offensive genius with one of the deadliest shots in the game. Sakic would be unrestricted in just three seasons, making him a slightly less valuable commodity than Forsberg to Colorado. Either Sakic or Forsberg would have been the centrepiece of his new club for years to come.

Avalanche GM Pierre Lacroix targeted Forsberg as the team's priority in the signing season of 1997, hoping to tie him up in a long-term deal as a showpiece in the club's new Pepsi Center. Forsberg and Baizley preferred a shorter deal, one that would allow them to react to a swiftly changing marketplace. After weeks of
, Colorado signed the man they'd received in the 1993 Eric

Lindros trade to a two-year deal. Forsberg's salary was bumped up in the first year; in the second, he'd be paid a handsome $5.5 million, meaning he would have to receive a qualifying offer from Colorado of at least that much—plus 10 per cent—when he renegotiated.

With the Avs choosing to sign Forsberg first, Sakic was left available to all comers on July 1. "Joe being Joe, he was not overly excited," recalls Baizley. "But he wasn't going to take less money than Peter got." By the terms of the 1995 CBA, any club could make Sakic an offer; if Colorado declined to match, the other team was obliged to surrender five first-round draft picks.

To that point, the system had been seriously challenged just once, when Winnipeg had to match Chicago's offer for Keith Tkachuk in 1995, a deal that cost the Jets $6 million a year. Sakic's realistic options were limited to re-signing at Colorado's price or sitting out for a long time. "Everything was quiet for three weeks," recalls Baizley. "Then, out of the blue, Vancouver comes along and signs Messier at $6 million. The Rangers are really in a spot. They have to replace Messier, and they've got Joe sitting out there. There's a timing issue, because Paul Kariya's also looking for a contract in Anaheim, and [Rangers president] Dave Checketts and [GM] Neil Smith have to move fast. And there's a perception that Colorado's ownership might not have the ability to match the offer."

Neil Smith remembers the management conferences at MSG that summer. "I had one guy above me, way above, who wanted us to sign Kariya. And I said, 'I'm not going to do it. Disney is not going to let him go. We're just escalating salaries and wasting money.' Disney scared him off. But I couldn't talk him out of trying to sign Sakic when he was restricted. He'd heard that the owners of the Avalanche, their stock was way down, they'd never be able to match. Sakic would have been great with us, the centre of our team. So we made an offer. But they still matched."

The Rangers offered a stunning $15-million signing bonus and $2 million a year for three years—huge by NHL standards, but a pittance to the giant Cablevision firm that owned the Rangers. Clearly,

Rangers owner James Dolan thought the signing bonus enough of a poison pill to discourage Colorado. A winning Rangers club in the playoffs would make the money back on cable TV. But the Avs didn't flinch, and Sakic was re-signed to the record-shattering deal. "The Sakic signing told other teams that a club like the Rangers just might do it, they might take a run at your guy," says agent Ritch Winter. "It left people thinking if a player's worth $9 million to other clubs, I'd better offer my player $8 million. But not $6 million, because the Rangers might try something on me."

Though Sakic and Forsberg re-signed in Colorado, Paul Kariya remained on the sidelines in Anaheim as the 1997–98 season began. The captain of the Mighty Ducks had potted 44 goals and 99 points the season before and was a franchise player, as well as being the key to Canada's entry at the 1998 Olympics in Japan. But while Sakic had benefited handsomely from the Rangers' bold move, there were no suitors to help Kariya escape the clutches of the Disney Corporation. As Neil Smith said, Disney was almost certain to match any offer, and making an enemy of Mickey Mouse was not considered good business. Kariya retreated to his Vancouver family home as the season began; the stalemate dragged on for weeks, then months. Kariya was tight-lipped, except to say he was going to play with the Olympic team in Nagano the next February. The Ducks, off to a slow start, shrugged. Kariya then said he was not going to play for anyone until after the Games—if he played at all that season.

That was the clincher for the Ducks. While Gary Bettman might be upset that the team wasn't using its leverage with Group Two free agents, Anaheim needed to act out of self-interest. In a serious slump and seeing more and more empty seats at the expensive Arrowhead Pond, Ducks president Tony Tavares swallowed hard and came up with a contract. Despite missing ten weeks of play, Kariya agreed to a two-year deal, for $5.5 million and then $8.5 million. (Unfortunately, he was cross-checked by Gary Suter of Chicago days before the Olympics and missed the rest of the season with post-concussion syndrome.)

"I didn't expect Kariya to get an offer sheet," recalls Baizley. "The exercise of going through the offer sheet, then seeing it matched, you have a situation where a team has exposed its own locker room to the fact that they're willing to pay a premium for a player who's never played there before. To not get that player and have all the rest of that happening makes no sense."

For the reasons Baizley outlines, offer sheets have failed to attract franchise players in all but three prominent cases. The first was Tkachuk; then came Sakic; the third offer sheet grew out of a personal rivalry between Detroit owner Mike Ilitch and Carolina owner Peter Karmanos. Ilitch's centre Sergei Fedorov, the Hart Trophy winner in 1994, was another restricted free agent in the summer of 1997. Fedorov, then twenty-eight years old, initially wanted Forsberg's contract terms from the Wings. But the signing of Sakic upped his expectations. At that level, the Red Wings balked. As the season started, Fedorov, like Kariya, was unsigned and waiting for a helping hand to lift him into the $10-million range. He, too, volunteered to play for his nation in the 1998 Winter Olympics to enhance his bargaining position. It was while playing for Russia in February 1998 that the Hurricanes, the team relocated from Hartford to North Carolina, made their move.

The Canes, playing in a temporary home in Greensboro, North Carolina, needed to make a splash. The dashing Fedorov—who was spending time with Russian tennis star Anna Kournikova—seemed a perfect fit. But there was a personal animus at work as well. Karmanos, who is of Greek origin, and Ilitch, who is of Macedonian, had clashed as they ran rival operations back in Detroit minor hockey. Karmanos's Compuware teams and Ilitch's Little Caesar's clubs were bitter rivals. Karmanos also felt that Ilitch had prevented him from winning an expansion franchise before his successful purchase of the Hartford Whalers. The Canes owner could attain two goals in making a bid for Fedorov: acquire a star player and put a burr under Ilitch's saddle.

Karmanos and Fedorov's agent, Mike Barnett, created a poison pill for Ilitch: $14 million in signing bonuses, to go with $2 million a year for five years. The catch was that if Fedorov's team made it past the conference semifinals—a likelihood for Detroit, unlikely for Carolina—Fedorov would receive an additional $12-million bonus. Such a stunning contract would not only upset the balance in Detroit's payroll, but across the NHL salary structure itself. Yet Fedorov was a unique player Detroit felt it could not do without. Reluctantly, the Wings matched the Carolina offer. Sure enough, the Wings won the conference semifinals and the $28-million one-year payment kicked in. The pain of resisting Karmanos's hostile bid was salved somewhat when Detroit went on to win the Stanley Cup over Washington that spring and Fedorov received "only" $2 million a year till 2003.

The Kariya and Fedorov contracts signed in early 1998 brought Pittsburgh's phenom, Jaromir Jagr, into the millionaires' leapfrog. The 1995 Art Ross Trophy winner and two-time Stanley Cup champion was receiving $5.1 million a year from the Pens, but his agent—again, Barnett—insisted that he not be surpassed by his peers, such as Forsberg, Kariya, and Fedorov. With Mario Lemieux's health a concern after bouts of cancer and back surgery, the Penguins and Barnett went to work on a new deal that brought Jagr's pay up to Kariya's $8.5 million and pushed it in future years to $10 million a season. "The first Jagr contract that took him to $10 million really led the market to the double digits," says agent J.P. Barry, at the NHLPA at the time. "All these emerging young stars were able to say, 'I'm his age.' Kariya could argue himself into that pay range. Forsberg. Lindros."

Jagr's market-moving deal jump-started the Flyers into talks to extend Eric Lindros's deal. It was no secret that the $10-million signing bonus and first-year salary for Chris Gratton had caught the attention of the Lindros clan, and there was concern in the Flyers' head office that the big centre might jump ship when his entry-level contract expired that summer. Having led the Flyers to the 1997

Cup final (where they lost to Fedorov and the Wings), Lindros knew his market value was at its apogee. Not wanting to lose him, the Flyers extended his deal for an average $9 million a year for the next four seasons.

And so went the salary spiral. By the time the ink was dry on Lindros's contract, Forsberg's deal with the Avalanche was up again. Baizley had been as adept at reading the market as Forsberg was at reading goalies; by going for a short-term contract, Forsberg was able to cash in at $30 million for three years in Colorado. Kariya followed him to the $10-million level shortly thereafter. The rising tide soon raised the NHL's salary ceiling for the best players beyond $10 million; when Jagr nailed $11 million from Pittsburgh, all the great scorers rose: Pavel Bure, Teemu Selanne, John LeClair. The "cost certainty" preached by Bettman at the conclusion of the 1994–95 lockout was in tatters.

Had goal scorers been the only ones reaping the riches, NHL managers might have rationalized the signing spree. Traditionally, defensive forwards, goalies, and defencemen—crucial to any Stanley Cup team—were overlooked while scorers carried off the big contracts. But players at other positions were now raising the bar as well.

"I remember saying to a number of GMs that the only $10-million player on my team would be the guy who can play goal," says Ritch Winter, who represented Buffalo's Dominik Hasek, perennial winner of the Vezina Trophy. "Those days he played sixty-five to seventy games a season plus playoffs. He was on the ice for 95 per cent of your prime moments. They'd always point to Roy making $4 million as the most a goalie could make. But I wouldn't listen to that, especially after Dom won back-to-back MVPs. Whatever you thought of goalies, that put him in the elite class of players—who were making $10 million a year by then."

Winter had had to convince his client to climb the golden stairs before his contract expired in 1998, when he would become an unrestricted (or Group Three) free agent. "Dom had a desire to stay in Buffalo. I tried to get him to test the free-agent market—who knows what he would have got on the open market?—but he thought the owner [John Rigas] was a nice guy, and he had come to him early." (It turned out Rigas was spending other people's money, but that's another story.) "So we did the deal with Rigas, [GM] Darcy Regier, and the Sabres people."

The Sabres were a small-market team, but they had opened a new arena and knew their acrobatic goalie could keep it filled. As well, Hasek would be unrestricted when his next contract expired. In the end, the Sabres gave him a $4-million signing bonus and $31 million over four years—all guaranteed. It was the contract that paved the way for goalies to be paid like the men who try to beat them with slapshots and dekes. Hasek rewarded the Sabres' loyalty by leading his small-market team to an unexpected Cup final in 1999.

That was also the year St. Louis's Chris Pronger brought defencemen into the holy land. While Raymond Bourque remained trapped in Sinden's pay scale like a fly in amber, the tall St. Louis defenceman shot past him with not so much as a competing offer sheet as leverage. The Blues—like so many other clubs—had a large new arena and wanted to make sure the future Hart and Norris trophies winner remained the core of their club. Their owner, Bill Laurie (an heir to the Wal-Mart fortune), was worth $2.5 billion, rich enough to keep up appearances with his brother-in-law, another Wal-Mart heir named Stan Kroenke, who was using his fortune to run the Colorado Avalanche. "Pronger was able to successfully argue that with the Hart Trophy as MVP he was as valuable as any forward in the league," recalls J.P. Barry. "He used the Jagr deal to launch himself into that salary area."

"We decided to go out on a limb," says Blues GM Larry Pleau. "This is what our ownership felt comfortable with. I can give you ten different reasons why we did it. But what are you going to do? I'm not saying it's right or wrong, but every organization's doing the same thing. It sure didn't help the Kings when they went to sign Rob

Blake, and they blamed us for having to trade him rather than pay him Pronger's number [$9.5 million a year]."

Soon after Pronger's deal, Colorado awarded Blake, another Norris winner (whom they'd acquired from the Kings), a contract worth $9.3 million a year. He was joined in the upper echelons by two-time Norris winner Brian Leetch, who won $8.7 million a year from the Rangers.

Even though the NHL's promised revenues proved less substantial than imagined, and a number of big signings, such as Valeri Kamensky, who moved from Colorado to the Rangers, flopped in new surroundings, teams still invested heavily in free agents. Journeyman players felt the effects of thirty clubs bidding on a finite number of competent veteran defencemen. Colorado plugger Jon Klemm left the Avs as a Group Three free agent for a three-year deal at $2.5 million a season with Chicago, while Sean O'Donnell followed the same path to Boston for three years at $2.5 million per in 2001.

Bob Boughner, a fourth or fifth defenceman in Pittsburgh, was lured to Calgary that summer by a $2-million-a-year free-agent salary. "It was funny," he says, "I got a bunch of calls from people in Ottawa saying that they announced on national TV that I was signing with the Senators. They had to have a retraction on TV. I would have been surprised by the money I got if I was the first to sign. But once Klemm and O'Donnell signed, it set the market for a guy like me. It was quite a day. I had to sit down and have a stiff drink when it ended."

Perhaps the most controversial signing in the post-1995 period was that of Detroit's rugged right winger Martin Lapointe, who became an unrestricted free agent in the summer of 2001 through a unique provision. Under the CBA, ten-year veterans making less than the average salary at their position were eligible for unrestricted free agency when their contracts expired. When his four-year deal with the Wings ended, the twenty-eight-year-old Lapointe was in the enviable position of being free to sell himself at the prime of his career—something almost no one had been able to do. The contract he received also illustrated why owners were deathly afraid of even journeymen such as Lapointe—who had scored more than 20 goals only once in his ten years—hitting the open market.

"At the time we signed the deal with Detroit, we didn't know how much the average salary would be," says Lapointe's agent, Gilles Lupien. "We crossed our fingers and hoped it would end up where we wanted it to be. Detroit kept phoning, they were going pretty high, trying to get him to sign before he became a free agent. But Martin wanted to see how much money was involved as a free agent." Based on what others in Lapointe's category of physical forward with limited scoring were receiving, he might have expected something in the mid to high two millions. But Lupien was able to sell other teams on Lapointe's intangibles.

"Everybody but the people who run teams base performance on how many points you get, how many goals," says Harry Sinden. "Well, we don't. If he gets goals, that helps. But you have to look at the overall contribution to the team. Martin's a character person. He comes to play every night. He came from a winning program. And we needed at his position." Lupien and Lapointe also benefited from the fact that Boston was afraid of losing the Ville St. Pierre native to Montreal, a club they play many times a year.

On July 1, 2001, Lapointe met Lupien at the agent's office in the Montreal suburb of Rosemère. The bidding quickly came down to three teams. Detroit had asked Lupien for the right to match any deal that was proposed. Lapointe happily agreed. The Canadiens' management drove to Lupien's office to woo him in person. Meanwhile, their division rival Boston made an offer of $5 million a year for four years, about the same as Montreal's offer.

"Boston made that offer at nine o'clock in the morning," recalls Lupien. "By doing that, we were sitting pretty comfortably. But I had told every team we were going to be open till six o'clock at night to hear their offers. And I told them if Detroit matches, then we're going to Detroit. But at the end of the day, Detroit looked at Boston's offer and said, 'Holy shit, we won't match that.' So we decided on Boston, because it was a good future with the team."

There were shock waves in the NHL when Lapointe's four-year, $20-million deal was announced. While a gritty player, he was not among Detroit's top six forwards and had never been considered for All-Star teams or individual awards. The inflationary pressure of such a contract was bound to have repercussions for teams signing or going to salary arbitration with role players.

As in the Thornton case, Sinden was making no apologies. "We got into a bit of a bidding war with Montreal. We matched Montreal's offer, and he wanted to come to Boston. So, yes, it was too much to pay for him, but he's a good player, the team thinks the world of him. And we had the money. In this business, if you can keep your player cost to 60 per cent or less of revenues, you've got a chance to make it. The problem is that only two or three clubs do that. We had room to do that even with Lapointe's deal, even though it was out of character for us to overpay."

Lupien summed up the new dynamic in contract negotiations: "It's like the teams say, 'Sometimes we've got the power and sometimes you've got the power.' That day, we had the power."

Sinden had company overpaying that summer. The same week Lapointe struck gold, Jeremy Roenick inked a five-year, $37.5-million agreement with Philadelphia, Pierre Turgeon received $32.5 million for five years in Dallas, and Alex Mogilny was given a four-year, $22-million contract by Toronto.

"I think, in many cases, eyebrows were raised," said NHL commissioner Bettman of this rash of high-priced signings. "And if at the end of the day this is not something workable in this league, we'll have to take another look at this system." Bettman's right-hand man went further. "I think some of the contracts are dollar amounts that are too high for the sport," said Bill Daly, the NHL's chief legal officer and executive vice-president. "And dollar amounts that the revenues can't support in the long term."

While Sinden and former Rangers GM Neil Smith don't see eye to eye on many things, both know the perils of needing free agents to keep their market happy. After gambling on Adam Graves back in 1991, Smith had added veterans such as Mark Messier, Mike Gartner, Glenn Anderson, Kevin Lowe, and Steve Larmer to his Rangers roster. The moves paid off in a Stanley Cup in 1994. But after the rules changed in the 1995 CBA settlement, his thirty-one-year-olds were all staring at unrestricted free agency. "I got caught in the changes between the 1992 CBA and the 1995 CBA," he admits. "Suddenly, I had all these players who could leave or I had to pay them free-agent money. Between those two contracts, we were a good team. After that '95 CBA, I thought I had a little rope, but Cablevision wanted to win this year, every year." Smith was fired in 2000, six years after bringing the Rangers their first Stanley Cup in fifty-four years.

Perhaps nothing captured the fuzzy math of negotiating better than a filmed session of contract talk between Toronto's assistant GM, Bill Watters, and Tie Domi's agent, Don Meehan, in the summer of 1997. The veteran Domi was the Maple Leafs enforcer, a five-foot-nine dervish with a fanatical following in Toronto for his willingness to fight the NHL's toughest men. The twenty-eight-year-old had had a grand total of 28 points in the 1996–97 season. Watters, meanwhile, was operating in a vacuum as interim GM, waiting for new Toronto president Ken Dryden to name a full-time replacement. (He wound up appointing himself to the job.) Watters wanted to renew his scrappy winger for $1 million a year. On the surface, Domi had little leverage beyond his popularity.

But Meehan had found a flaw in Watters's armour. Toronto had just signed second-year winger Sergei Berezin—who'd scored 25 goals with 41 points—at $1.5 million a year. While Berezin's production appeared to dwarf that of Domi, Meehan figured out that Berezin had just four more points than the Toronto slugger at even strength. "It brings the distinction down to four points when they're on the ice on a five-on-five basis," Meehan told Watters.

"Twenty-eight is to forty-two as four is to six and two is to three.... Unless you're going to stick to the Berezin story, let's stick to the numbers," Watters admonished Meehan.

"What you're doing, Bill, is to ignore the 275 [penalty] minutes."

"We'll find somebody who can get 275 minutes."

"I don't want to have to be [telling] the Toronto community that you'll get somebody else to do it as well as he does," said Meehan.

While Watters could have pointed to Domi's minus-17 plus/minus or his undisciplined penalties, he instead sought middle ground. "The function here is to make a deal. You want $1.5 million, you're not going to get it. I want a million, I'm not going to get it."

But Meehan wouldn't be dissuaded from comparing his pugnacious grinder with 28 points to the slick scorer at 42 points. "As much as you can say to me you know we're not going to pay it, you've got a problem on your hands because you've set a precedent on Berezin. Like it or not, he's there."

Indeed he was. So was the prospect of explaining to Leafs fans that the club preferred a sporadic Russian scorer over their darling enforcer. In the end, Watters offered Domi a contract for $1.43 million a year for five years. The Domi-equals-Berezin strategy worked like a charm.

When the contract numbers were presented to Domi, he paused for effect and then said, "This is all U.S.? ... Let's get it done!"

Deals such as Domi's left veteran managers equally incredulous. "Teams accept the agent's comparables too freely," said Harry Sinden. "'So-and-so is as good as the other player in St. Louis. We want the same money.' Even though your club has half the income, half the revenue of St. Louis, they pay him." Sinden, who wears a hangdog look at the best of times, shakes his head sadly. "The only people dumber than us are the people in baseball."

10

Perils of Arbitration

S o, let's see who else is in Denis Gauthier's class," said Calgary Flames GM Craig Button. It was early in 2002, and Button was at the computer in his office at the Saddledome, punching data into the NHL's computer program: "Defencemen... more than four years' experience, less than six...more than 100 games played in that span...average ice time seventeen minutes a game... defensive-type defenceman...okay, let's see who we have here." Button hit the send key and his computer instantly ranked two dozen NHL defencemen in the 2002–03 season by their plus/minus ratings.

"There we go. You have Colin White of New Jersey, he's the top ranked at plus-38 over five years. He makes an average of $675,000. Dan McGillis of Philadelphia, he's second at plus-30. Jay McKee of Buffalo, plus-27, he gets $1.433 million. And so on down to Deron Quint of Columbus—he's minus-53 over six years and makes $625,000. Let's see, the lowest average salary there is Radoslav Suchy of Phoenix at $475,000. The top man? Wow, Dan McGillis got that big $3-million deal from Clarkey a couple of years ago. But it looks like the median salary is about $900,000.

"Here's our guy, Gauthier, just after Chris Phillips in Ottawa. He's ninth-rated, plus-12. Takes a lot of penalty minutes, but that's his style. Did you know his mother is one of the Rougeau family? The wrestlers? Yeah, she manages them. Where was I? Right, he's not going to score a lot for you. His current deal, he's getting $675,000. So who will he be looking to compare himself to?"

Button is playing comparables, the NHL's favourite game, before an upcoming salary-arbitration hearing with Gauthier. If you wish to survive financially in the modern NHL, you must master its intricacies. In the era of salary disclosure, arbitration rights, restricted free agency, and qualifying offers, a player's worth is ultimately determined by his standing amongst his peers. In the Gauthier arbitration, slated for August 2002, Button and Gilles Lupien (agent for the rock-hard defenceman) will make their cases for where the Flames' first-round pick in the 1995 draft should be ranked. Lupien will seek to show that the twenty-four-year-old Montreal product is comparable to McGillis, McKee, Phillips, Rhett Warrener ($1.5 million), Brendan Witt ($1.66 million), Zdeno Chara ($1.550 million), and Hal Gill ($1.25 million). Of that group, Gauthier is ranked below all but Chara and Witt on the NHL's exclusive computer model. Button, meanwhile, will try to group his third-best blueliner with players such as the fourth-rated Suchy, sixth-ranked Brent Sopel ($475,000), and Nashville's Andy Delmore ($550,000).

"Of course," says Button, "if you add a couple of different statistics, you may get a different result. Let's put hits and shot-blocks in there." He keys in the new categories and *voilà*, a different ranking appears onscreen. This time, Gauthier—a noted shot-blocker and bodychecker—zooms up to fourth in the class of comparables. "There you go. What you're trying to do in this exercise is get the truest picture of your player for the arbitrator to judge his worth. That removes the subjective stuff we used to have in arbitration...you know, he drinks too much, he missed the team bus, he needs help putting on his helmet. You try to tip it as much to your side as you can. But you have to be careful to get the right picture or you can lose big time."

"If you bring up the proper comparables," points out Rangers boss Glen Sather, "they prove to the arbitrator that the player is not worth that kind of money. You can forget it if the player is successful and scores 40, 50 goals in his peak season. But if you've got the good comparables you should win or be able to make a deal beforehand."

Button grabs a ring binder filled with past decisions and pulls out the case of Washington's Brendan Witt. The Caps defenceman was twenty-five at the time of his hearing in August 2000 and coming off a solid season playing with Calle Johansson. In the final year of his contract, Witt—like Gauthier a stay-at-home, physical player—made $1 million. When he decided to go the arbitration route, the Capitals made a two-year offer. Witt was looking to make $2 million and then $2.2 million. The club was offering $850,000 and then $900,000. Witt's agent, Mark Hall, selected seven comparable defencemen to bolster his claim, including Keith Carney of Phoenix, Richard Matvichuk of Dallas, Gill of the Bruins, and McKee of the Sabres.

The Caps GM, George McPhee, had his own list of comparables, but only one player—Jason Marshall of Anaheim—was on both lists. Clearly it would come down to who could paint a better picture for arbitrator Claude Foisy. Foisy had adjudicated a similar case between David Karpa and Anaheim in 1997, a case that defined the value of an aggressive defensive defenceman. Both Washington and Calgary relied on Foisy's reasoning in that award, in which he used the criteria of penalty minutes per game, ice time per game, and games played. Much would depend on whether Hall could make the case that Witt was a bona fide top-four defenceman of this type in the NHL.

After hearing the sides plead their case, Foisy agreed with Washington's list of comparable players, not Hall's. The gamble to elevate Witt's comparables had failed. "The player has argued," wrote Foisy, "that by reaching the top four defenceman plateau, he has finally arrived. I am not prepared on the basis of one solid season to conclude that Witt is now a regular top four defenceman. Evidence of more consistency is required to reach that conclusion. I determine Witt's salary for 2000–01 to be $1,000,000 and $1,075,000 for the 2001–02 season." By aiming too high, Witt was stuck with the same salary he'd earned the season before.

When Gauthier's case was heard in Toronto before Michel Picher, on August 1, 2002, Lupien argued for $1.6 million for one year; the club offered two years at $900,000 and then $1 million. For the arbitrator, the key issue was Gauthier's durability. "The fact that he has played only two seasons at a level in excess of 60 games played, and has just completed his first season as a fourth defenceman...does not place him in the salary range of those more established players," decided Picher. Gauthier was awarded $1.1 million for 2002–03 and $1.3 million for 2003–04. Should he play more than 70 games in the first season, noted Picher, he'll get an additional $100,000 (Gauthier earned the bonus by playing 72 games in 2002–03). If he plays more than 70 the next year, he'll get $1.4 million: "The incentive is to relate solely to issues of injuries and the player's related durability," wrote Picher. Gauthier probably could have negotiated these figures instead of enduring the nerve-wracking arbitration process. While not exactly a loss for him, it's not a win, either.

"Of course, it goes the other way, too," smiles Button. Consider several highly publicized arbitration awards from the summer of 2001. Playing the comparables game, Group Two free agent Petr Sykora won a 389 per cent increase from the Devils in his salary arbitration, jumping from $675,000 to $3.3 million. Bobby Holik, also a Devil, was boosted to $3.5 million from $2.7 million. Pavol Demitra more than doubled his salary, from $1.8 million to $3.7 million, besting St. Louis in arbitration. Miro Satan of Buffalo, another offensive force, chalked up a two-year, $6.8-million contract in his hearing with the Sabres. Pittsburgh's Martin Straka translated 27 goals and 95 points into a two-year award worth $7.2 million. The players and their agents seemed unstoppable. What worried NHL officials about this trend was that, like the Kariya/Fedorov/Lindros class, these players all were restricted Group Two free agents. These were the players supposedly with little leverage, who were now jumping the salary bar via arbitration. This was the group that NHL owners thought they had stifled in the 1995 lockout settlement.

"So many parts of the agreement made sense," moaned Sharks GM Dean Lombardi, shortly before he lost his job after the 2002–03 season. "The idea was to channel money towards players as they gained more experience." Clearly that had been undermined by the free-agent and arbitration decisions.

"All you need is one or two comparable statistics in each category—power forward, defensive defenceman, scoring centre—and then you've got the bomb to obtain a good Group Two contract," says J.P. Barry, who has worked both as an agent and as a lawyer at the NHLPA. "An example would be Smyth and Sullivan." (Power forward Ryan Smyth of Edmonton signed for $2.525 million a year while Steve Sullivan used a breakout year to negotiate a $3-million deal with the Blackhawks.) "They get good deals in 2001, and then Sykora goes to arb that year. Now you've got the example of the previous two deals for twenty-five-year-olds who have offence—five or six years as a pro. Sykora goes in and he's got the example of these negotiated contracts, he has better comparables than they have, he's automatic to raise the bar. Sykora was never going to get that deal by negotiating with Lou Lamoriello in New Jersey." (Lamoriello subsequently shipped Sykora to Anaheim in the summer of 2002.)

Perhaps no aspect of the player-management tangle has been better manipulated by the NHLPA than players' arbitration. Says Sather: "The PA has picked the players who they think are going to win in arbitration and put them up first. Once a guy wins, it sets up a precedent. The ones they think they will have the most trouble with, they bring last." Lamoriello adds, "I've always said I'd be for salary arbitration if we could take players to arbitration they way they take us. It could work if it were two-sided."

It's no wonder that salary arbitration was a hot-button issue for owners in the last CBA and will be again in the next talks. "Arbitration's terrible," says a disgusted Harry Sinden. "To put your business in the hands of a third party—you usually get killed even when you do it right. We had a case in 2002 where the guy who represented the Bruins, he did a Johnnie Cochran–type job, he was absolutely fantastic. And the union guy, his presentation was like nothing. But the arbitrator was dozing in the chair and we got clobbered. We might as well have sent in the damn numbers to the arbitrator and said, 'Here, call us when you decide.' We had a woman arbitrator once. She said, 'Ice time, what do you mean by ice time?' I think the NHL should look at getting rid of arbitration. Baseball's the only other sport that has it."

Nor is NHL commissioner Gary Bettman a big fan. "My problem with salary arbitration is I think the process can sometimes impact a relationship between a player and a team in ways that aren't constructive for either of them. If the player gets the money he wants, the team loses and the player is happy; but if the team wins and the player loses, it's not fair because they said all these terrible things [about the player]. It should be fair for both sides. Lots of players also choose not to go to arbitration because they don't think the arbitrator will give them what they want. They prefer to hold out. There are things that need to re-examined."

In 2002–03, the league tried to address an arbitration problem of its own making. In its zeal to improve game reporting, the league had been inadvertently aiding players who didn't put up gaudy numbers of the traditional sort. Since 1995 the NHL had been counting a range of new statistics: shots blocked, hits, turnovers, even-strength goals, and so on. There was considerable debate about the merits of these stats, but they quickly became a part of the business. Goodenow and the PA took the new stats and crunched them in their software programs to create whole new categories of bonuses and payment thresholds. Ironically, the NHL's goal of more accurate stats helped to buttress the arguments players and agents use in precedent-setting contracts. "The PA used those statistics to turn $600,000 defencemen into $6-million defencemen," says a member of NHL management.

(Such was the impact of the new statistics for arbitrators that the NHL unilaterally removed a number of them from game reports in 2002—a move the PA grieved. The association argued that the categories were an accepted part of the collective bargaining process and could not be eliminated without the agreement of the players. An arbitrator found in favour of the players and restored the categories in 2003.)

Arbitration particularly helps players who are not yet unrestricted free agents. "The first five years of your NHL career, you don't have any salary-arbitration rights," explains agent Tom Laidlaw. "You've got very little negotiating power when you come in under the entry-level system. You can certainly make a lot of money with the bonuses, but there's no guarantee—you have to perform. Then you get salary-arbitration rights, but as a restricted free agent you can't move freely from team to team with compensation and right to match. You really don't get freedom until age thirty-one, unless it's a special case like Martin Lapointe. And only then can you go to the highest bidder. As I say, it's a very restrictive system. That's why the leverage you get in arbitration has helped a lot."

It isn't only big names who have prospered in salary arbitration. Players such as Craig Darby of the Canadiens have used the system to get a one-way contract (no provision for minor-league pay), and Blake Sloan and Cale Hulse were able to negotiate rewards for contributions other than simple goals or points.

"My arbitration was a great experience," says Bobby Holik of the Rangers. "Partway through, [agent] Mike [Gillis] and I went for lunch in Toronto and he said it doesn't matter what we get, every player should go through with it. The earlier in your career you go through it, the better. It educates you. I got traded after two years in the league and I realized it's just business. There's nothing else to it. You get treated like a first-round draft choice and it's special. Then you get traded and, hey, I'm just like everyone else."

Under the NHL's system, Group Two free agents must request arbitration by July 15 if they can't agree on a new contract. The two sides file their salary proposals with the arbitrator; a hearing is held between August 1 and 15. In baseball, the arbitrator must choose between the player's request and the team's request; in the NHL, the arbitrator can choose a figure between the two extremes. "With all the other restraints that management has on the players, it's a player's relief valve," says Bob Goodenow. "It's an opportunity for the two sides to exchange information in front of a neutral third party. Most of the contracts get settled before a hearing. If they don't, you have to ask why the GMs couldn't find the market. I think there's a lot of bravado involved from the NHL. I don't see salary arbitration as being that troublesome."

It certainly wasn't a problem for NHL management when Alan Eagleson's NHLPA won salary arbitration as a concession from the owners in 1986. Without salary disclosure to drive the process, arbitration was a toothless tiger. With few concrete statistics to work with, arbitrators were left to sort through tales of heroic accomplishment (players) and character assassinations (management). Don Baizley smiles as he recalls the early days when he used his lawyerly skills in salary arbitration. "I went to arbitration twice with Jari Kurri in the 1980s," he explains. "You have to remember that Jari played on Wayne's line. Scored 71 goals one season, 68 another. Just a great player. I was there with my lawyer's brief, Glen [Sather] was there with his case written out on a napkin—and we lost twice. On one of them, the arbitrator, Gary Schreider, gave Sather everything he asked for. Even Glen didn't expect that. That tells you about my advocacy skills.

"We were saying that Jari should be compared to Mike Bossy of the Islanders without knowing what Bossy was making. I called Pierre Lacroix, Bossy's agent, and he said, 'I can't tell you, we signed a confidentiality agreement with the Islanders.' The arbitrator could go to the NHL offices and look at the contracts filed there; we couldn't. Even then, we weren't sure that the contract on file had the real numbers. The only contract we knew was the one Dave Taylor signed with L.A. [$6 million for seven years] in 1981. We tried to make the argument that that's what the best right winger in the NHL should make. But the arbitrators said that was then, this is now. How much is the top right winger getting now? We didn't know those things till salary disclosure." (In 1984, Wayne Gretzky approached Taylor's agent, Ron Salcer. "I heard about that deal you got for Dave," Salcer recalls Gretzky saying. Salcer replied, "But that was three years ago, Wayne. You make that much!" Gretzky shook his head: "I don't make half what Dave Taylor makes," he reportedly said. Of course, Gretzky later made up for being short-changed when Bruce McNall appeared.)

"I remember arbitrations where the GM would come in with his notes on a bar mat," recalls Mike Barnett, now the GM in Phoenix. "That would be it. We'd have a big binder, the whole deal." The early years of salary arbitration were better known for the acrimony they generated than for the salary levels they established. "I remember one time I went to arbitration," says a retired defence-man, "I had 43 points the year before, a great season, and all they could say was that I was an alcoholic. It was brutal." Others heard their skills ripped apart, their leadership questioned, their personal lives critiqued.

Until Goodenow streamlined arbitration, the process could be less than transparent. One reason Doug Gilmour left Calgary had to do with his salary arbitration in 1991. Miffed at not getting a deal, Gilmour played for the Flames the night before the hearing. During a break in the action, he looked up to the Flames owners' box. There, to his amazement, was arbitrator Gary Schreider, scheduled to hear the case the next day, being entertained by the club. Gilmour blew a fuse; at a post-game impromptu press conference, he said he was through in Calgary. Sure enough, he lost his arbitration and never skated for the Flames again; he was traded in a ten-player deal to Toronto.

Even when players won their hearings, they often felt they'd lost. Such was the impact of being dissected before a third party. "Gilmour went against Lou Lamoriello in New Jersey, and Lou just toasted him," recalls J.P. Barry. "He said Gilmour couldn't hold Dave Andreychuk's stick. And Gilmour still won $4.5 million—the largest award till then." Despite the salary boost, a bruised Gilmour left New Jersey for Chicago the next season as a free agent.

Lamoriello, who has run the Devils since 1988, is notorious for his confrontational style. The former Providence College administrator says it's all part of the game. "I don't believe you tear him apart, but some of us don't want to hear the truth, either. It shouldn't be something the player's never heard before. If he's soft, he's soft. If it's the first time he's heard it from you, shame on you."

Neil Smith doesn't like the adversarial nature of arbitration, but says there are few options left to management. "What are you supposed to do? I did arbitration and you'd swear that the guy sitting at the other end of the table was Gretzky, Orr, or Lemieux. He can't be little Timmy Taylor! The only way to counter that stuff is to be negative. But as soon as you do that, they say you ripped into him, took away his confidence. Well, don't get into the room if you don't want to hear it."

Faced with new restrictions on free agency for players under thirty-two after the 1995 settlement, the agents (and the NHLPA) had to find new levers for raising the salary bar. The first step was the game of Group Two salary leapfrog that commenced with Forsberg, Sakic, Kariya, Jagr, and the others in 1996–97. Once the bar for Group Two free agents had been pegged at over $10 million for scoring stars and $9 million for elite defencemen, the arbitration game commenced in earnest. Under the guidance of the PA, which chose its strongest cases and when to slot them in the arbitration schedule, benchmark examples were advanced to develop categories such as two-way forward, stay-at-home defenceman, emerging star, offensive defenceman. "All it took was one or two people to give Group Two players big contracts and then you were dead for arbitration," laments Lamoriello.

"The arbitration system has been perfected to a T," says agent Rick Curran. "And the guy who deserves a lot of the credit, and will not get it, is Ian Pulver [NHLPA's associate counsel lawyer]. We had such an advantage because Ian and his staff were so good, they'd perfected it. That's why so many teams want to get rid of it. The teams haven't educated themselves to the point that they could use it properly. It wasn't a tool they utilized; it was a tool they were getting their ass kicked with."

Pulver, who has been with Goodenow almost from day one, had his first arbitration in the case of Sergio Momesso of the Canucks. "Back then we did salary arbitrations in the middle of the year. I remember arriving at the Greenbelt Marriott in Landover, Maryland. George McPhee was there for the Canucks. We did that hearing on a game day. Sergio didn't skate. He did the hearing instead." (He lost.) As part of the 1995 CBA, the arbitration season is confined to August 1–15. Pulver and the NHLPA have made that timing work for them by putting their strongest cases first and using the results of the summer's hearings to give a boost to restricted Group Two free agents who need leverage as training camp rolls around.

The NHLPA also knew that while agents could share offers and proposals made to their clients, the league was restricted from colluding. "The union did an outstanding job of pushing things up," acknowledges Lamoriello. "It wasn't that ownership didn't adjust, it was that we couldn't adjust. Ownership can't get together to restrain salaries because of restraint-of-trade laws in the United States."

Major League Baseball owners learned that collusion was a losing tactic. In 1985 the teams agreed not to sign any free agents but their own. For trying to fix a salary grid in their sport, they were forced to pay $280 million (the estimated salary amount lost by Andre Dawson, Jack Morris, and many other free agents who were denied offers by clubs). Hockey owners were not about to risk similar penalties in their sport.

"The NHL was outmanoeuvred by the Players' Association on arbitration," says a high-ranking NHL management figure. "The process got away from us before we had a chance to adjust. We were working with a paradigm that was outdated, and they were a mile ahead of us." J.P. Barry, who secured over $200 million in new deals in 2001–02, agrees that the league never knew what hit it. "The NHL had this new CBA that they thought was going to control everything. Then, from 1995 to '98, the agents outnegotiated the GMs on Group

Two free agents. Then the arbitration system was fine-tuned. For years, the agents were coordinated and understood their leverage—they'd done their homework. It was definitely the agents who were leading the market. The league didn't pick up on any of that until about three years ago."

Barry says that the NHL has no one but itself to blame. "Why were teams giving huge contracts to players who were only coming out of their first contracts? These players had no technical leverage, but they got big deals anyway. Lou Lamoriello understood it: he hammered Patrik Elias and Petr Sykora on their second contracts. He said, 'I'm not giving it to you. You're going to take what I give you.' But the rest of them, they didn't use their hammer." Tom Laidlaw agrees. "Look at New Jersey. They've had a great deal of success, and they've controlled their budget. With this CBA, general managers have the ability to just say no. They don't have to give the players a certain amount of money."

Ritch Winter, an agent since the mid-1980s, concurs. "What I don't understand is how management has let the bar get raised so quickly. It's amazing how the minute one guy gets something, it's like all the GMs lose perspective. Lindros worth $3 million? Boom, Daigle gets $3 million. Curtis Joseph worth $8 million even though he has a save percentage of .908? All of a sudden the bar is raised everywhere. Ed Belfour's getting $6.5 million."

Walk-away rights were another part of the 1995 CBA that clubs have ignored to their detriment. Teams can walk away from a limited number of salary-arbitration decisions, making the player a free agent. "It was a gift from us, a freebie," says an NHLPA source. "They can let him walk or retain the player by matching 80 per cent of any other team's offer. But they never use it." In the eight years since that clause was negotiated, only Harry Sinden's Bruins have used it, to walk away from a 1999 decision when the arbitrator awarded Dmitri Khristich $2.8 million a year. Khristich became a free agent and signed with Toronto at $20 million for four years. (Sinden had the last laugh: Khristich lasted just eighteen months with the free-spending Leafs.)

Asked why more teams don't walk away, Sinden shakes his head: "There are a lot of tools in the CBA that people don't use. They're afraid of arbitration, so they pay the player more than they really should to avoid it. Most of them are afraid of the press. They're afraid of the fans. They run their business that way and most of them lose money."

As long as expansion money and arena-naming payments flowed in the late 1990s, teams could overlook the problems that arbitration had created. "We just took all that money and threw it back at the players," Cal Nichols, chairman of the Edmonton Oilers ownership group, told the *National Post*. "In fact, we probably doubled it up, and then threw it back at them. [The expansion money] was useful on one hand, but a curse on the other. Everyone got the same amount, but the bar went up on player salaries. We got poorer instead of richer."

And as many league sources will attest, the NHL was slow to react. The man on the firing line was often the team's general manager, a veteran administrator who had to balance the desire to ice a winner against the need to protect ownership's money. Established figures such as Sinden and Sather were largely immune from ownership pressure, but lesser lights were not so fortunate. "You have to remember how a team is structured," says former Rangers GM Neil Smith. "There's ownership, then there's the president of the club, and beneath him the general manager. The GM always has the president of the team between him and the owners. If things go well, the president takes the credit. But if things go poorly, the president blames the GM. The GM is always the one who gets dumped on. You can't win."

A Calgary team party in 2001 underscored Smith's point. About seventy-five people had gathered at an owner's home for a pool party with Flames president Ken King, new on the job. A big, jocular man, King likes to punch shoulders and squeeze hands. In a moment of exuberance, he dispatched his general manager, Craig Button, into the pool. Button's cellphone and data organizer also went into the pool. An audience of players, staff, and their families watched in stunned silence as Button emerged from the water, his clothes drenched and the tools of his trade ruined. Button's wife fled the scene in tears. It was a poor omen for the president-GM relationship: King later sacked Button, in the spring of 2003.

"It's taken a while for NHL management to understand that the old managerial model doesn't work," says an NHL source. "It's so much more a managerial position, not a talent-evaluator one. Look at the Boston Red Sox. They hired a twenty-seven-year-old lawyer to be their new GM because they realized that being organized and a good handler of people is as important as knowing who can go to the opposite field better than another guy."

Cashing the last of $320-million worth of expansion cheques (from Nashville, Columbus, Minnesota, and Atlanta) had finally made the NHL wake up to its managerial shortcomings. After years of awarding over-market Group Two contracts and treating salary arbitration haphazardly, owners increasingly found banks reluctant to extend more money and creditors unwilling to wait for payment. Moody's Investors Service announced in 2003 that it considered the NHL a weak credit risk, the poorest of the major team sports. Moody's estimated the NHL teams' total debt at $2 billion; the pending labour negotiation and a weak broadcast contract prompted the rating. Elsewhere, J.P. Morgan's $45-million loan to the Columbus Blue Jackets can be re-evaluated if the average price of the previous five NHL team sales falls below $80 million.

As a result of these warnings and the collapse of the tech sector—an industry with ties to ownership, sponsorship, and luxury boxes around the league—management was now trying to apply the same diligence to arbitration cases as do the agents. Gary Bettman stresses the teams' understanding of their right to restrict free agents and to walk away from unsatisfactory salary-arbitration awards. "I think the teams are getting better at understanding that those are their options, and I think they're using them more."

One management strategy is to use the hammer on players not likely to benefit from arbitration, players such as Bobby Holik or Mike Peca, whose inspirational qualities can't always be quantified. "These are arbitrators who don't understand the value of a player," says Barry. "And Holik, even though he has big leadership value— checks, hits—there's a lot of things on his stat sheet when you compare him to Sykora or somebody else, the arbitrators go, 'Where's the bacon?' These guys don't watch hockey. You've got to bring tangible things. As well, if a player such as Daniel Alfredsson opts to go to arb, the team can extend the arbitrated contract into a two-year deal. So with someone like Daniel, you've got to be worried about stepping into a trap. He's been injured a lot and it would be a long two years if they got him at $3 million, $3.1 million." (Barry eventually negotiated $4.55 million a year for Alfredsson without arbitration.)

The arbitration system can also be made to work against goaltenders, because there was no benchmark Group Two contract before José Théodore's two-year, $11-million deal in Montreal in 2002. For that reason, goalies such as Nikolai Khabibulin passed on arbitration and held out for a new deal. Khabibulin held out on Phoenix for almost two full NHL seasons before being sent to Tampa, where he finally signed his new contract. Peca missed the entire 2000–01 season in a contract stalemate with Buffalo, an impasse finally resolved by a trade to the Islanders. Petr Nedved and Alexei Yashin also declined salary arbitration and were forced to sit out before getting new contracts in other cities.

"The Peca situation, Khabibulin, Yashin—that's not good for the sport," says Mike Barnett. "I think we're going to find more and more arbitrations directed at keeping players on the ice. I'd like to see arbitration move even further to a system that doesn't lend itself to players' having to withhold services. Whether through a third party or whatever, everyone would be on the ice in October for the good of the sport. Albeit a one-year deal. We need to keep refining the process."

Another new tactic was the hired-gun approach, with clubs bringing in lawyers and accountants such as Kevin Gilmore and Daniel Dumais, who specialize in contract negotiations and salary arbitrations. In some cases, these experts have supplanted GMs. "What you see now," says Barnett, "is many of those traditional GM's responsibilities fall into the lap of the assistant general manager, who is really the knowledgeable one on salary comparisons, arbitration, preparation, and all that. The day-to-day responsibilities of running a team are so complex, and in many cases the general manager is also the president. That's where we on the player's side had an advantage in the past.

"The first step was the Bob Essensa arbitration in the early '90s when the Winnipeg Jets hired Larry Bertuzzi," recalls Barnett, who was aided on that case by Bob Riley, Goodenow's law-school friend doing his first case for the NHLPA. "That was one of the first times a club used one. Their GM, Mike Smith, was a bright guy to hire an outside party back then. Now much of it's done internally, although there's still some outside people like Larry."

"I remember one time," says agent Tom Laidlaw, "I had Dallas Drake as a client in Winnipeg. They'd hired a young guy named Laurence Gilman, who's now in Phoenix doing their contracts. He got on the phone and said, 'I'm the new lawyer of the team.' I just went, Oh God, this is going to be different. Before, I was dealing with hockey guys—no disrespect to anybody when I say this, but I felt I could deal a lot more easily with a hockey guy. Now the emotions are taken out of it in most cases. Basically, it's, 'Here's the numbers, here's the player's rights.' Both sides fight hard using the CBA. It's not an easier process, but it's a much more professional one."

Other agents who've dealt with Gilman echo Laidlaw's appraisal. "Laurence won't talk to you till he's ready to," says Mike Gillis. "Some guys just answer the phone and let the agent start the process before they're prepared. Laurence only talks when he's ready to talk. You don't end up with a hasty deal that both sides are uncomfortable with."

Says Gilles Lupien, "Six or seven years ago, for agents it was, 'We have the power to do what we want to do.' Now general managers and assistant GMs are managing the money and the team. Before they were only managing the team. The money? 'Oh, we don't care about that so much.' Now they're working a lot more on the money side. You can see that salaries are not going up that fast now."

Ownership had also begun catching up technologically. At Bettman's initiative, general managers began using software to share information without incurring charges of collusion. "We have something called a contract-tracking system," says Sinden. "If I'm negotiating a deal with you and you make a proposal and I make a counter-proposal, I can put that up on the computer for other teams to see where we're at. If they're dealing with a similar player, we can see where we're going. We can't say, 'Don't pay the guy any more. He's not as good as my guy.' We can just put it up there—you can use it any way you want. In the old days, we keep it to ourselves."

With a few exceptions—the Bobby Holik and Bill Guerin contracts come to mind—the league had managed to put a lid on the top end of the pay scale in recent years. But the NHL's attempts to catch up came too late to stem the money tide created in 1995 by Group Two free agency and salary arbitration.

11

Haves and Have-Nots

t's June 2002, and the NHL Board of Governors are locked in heated discussion at Toronto's Royal York Hotel. The entry draft is a few days away, and Rick Nash of the London Knights, the consensus first choice, will nail down the most lucrative rookie deal since the imposition of the new CBA in 1995. The Blue Jackets' young winger could earn $8.561 million in his first three NHL seasons, more if he hits certain scoring and ice-time thresholds. A week after the draft, the New York Rangers will award Bobby Holik his five-year, $45-million handshake.

The NHL's average salary has increased from $733,000 to $1.4 million since 1994, a 95 per cent jump. The governors are troubled by this salary spiral, and by the 48 per cent increase in ticket prices during the same period. NHL commissioner Gary Bettman is talking tough about drawing a line on salaries. "The economics of the league don't work," he tells the owners. "There are two seasons left, and we intend to have two really good seasons. After that, we have to be prepared to do whatever is necessary to repair the model."

Bettman is offering players the carrot of early negotiations for a new CBA. The stick is a lockout come the 2004–05 season. This macho message plays well with hawkish owners pinched by stagnant revenues and increasing payrolls. But Bettman's aggressive stance merely plays into Bob Goodenow's hands, solidifying the director's contention that the NHL wants to break the NHLPA, not partner with it.

In the midst of the arguments, Chicago's crusty owner, Bill Wirtz, takes the microphone. A diminished force in the NHL since the demise of his running mates John Ziegler and Alan Eagleson, the imposing Wirtz nonetheless commands an audience when he speaks. Disgusted with the rookie bonuses teams have been shelling out of late, Wirtz announces, "Gentlemen, we have never paid these rookie bonuses in Chicago. And I can tell you we never will pay them. We think you're crazy to pay this money to untried rookies. In fact, we think doing business with you is bad for our reputation in the business world." And, with that, Wirtz got up, summoned his lieutenants, and strode out of the boardroom, leaving the NHL governors in shocked silence.

With owners in as many as half the NHL cities looking to sell all or part of their businesses, and two teams in bankruptcy, the governors are a nervous lot. "I think the major bobble clubs and management made was thinking they can buy something," says Devils GM Lou Lamoriello. "Your ego, your experience in other businesses, tells you that one more player will do it for you. And it becomes a runaway train." Agent Tom Laidlaw agrees: "Owners get competitive, and they want to win. Maybe they've had that same view in the business in which they got wealthy. But it isn't necessarily the case in pro sports."

Chicago investment banker Paul Much, who deals with many sports investors, says a lot of prospective owners are armchair quarterbacks. "Rightly or wrongly, they believe they can do a better job than the existing owners." Harry Sinden puts it this way: "They're chasing the Stanley Cup and they think that fifteen teams can win it and share it. It's going to be a fifteen-team tie, and we're all going to share it. But only one team's going to get it. The rest are chasing a rainbow." (As if to underscore his disgust, Sinden dumped three of his top players—Bill Guerin, Byron Dafoe, and Kyle McLaren—heading into the 2002–03 season, and the Bruins still made the playoffs in the Eastern Conference.)

How had costs escalated so quickly after the NHL owners shut down their business for almost five months in 1994–95 to achieve "cost certainty"? The owners push the idea that large salaries directly caused ticket-price increases. "We don't have an attendance problem," said Bettman, "but I'm concerned about the increasing ticket prices. There needs to be a system that allows clubs to respond to the [player] market."

Despite the commissioner's contention, ticket prices are more a reflection of revenues and the elasticity of local markets than of payroll. Bettman persists in linking the two, arguing for a salary cap or luxury tax. Which leads to a question: Whose numbers to believe? The league says salaries account for about 65 per cent of total revenues of $2 billion in 2002–03. The GM of one American team said his payroll represents 67 per cent of the club's total revenues. A study done in Pittsburgh says the NHL's player payroll is 56 per cent of operating expenses. Whomever you believe, the gloomy stats reflect the mood of hockey people. "I think we're heading for a lot of changes," says Florida Panthers governor Bill Torrey, who built the Islanders into a powerhouse of the 1980s. "We're fighting to keep thirty competitive franchises. That will be a tough task."

The NHL had earlier said that revenues in 1992 were $400 million while salaries hit $280 million, or about 70 per cent of gross. It leaves many scratching their heads. "Gary's always talking about these numbers that don't exactly add up," says Ritch Winter. "We need him to quit telling us about increases and percentages and show a little leadership. He and the owners have to stop being so fixated on Goodenow—'Will Bob like this proposal? Will Bob like that proposal?' Bob doesn't run their business. Gary needs to talk over his head to players and give them any good ideas he has for the next contract. And he needs to do it soon."

Bob Goodenow sits in his midtown Toronto office, watching storm clouds gather above the city—and his industry. The man who once worked in a converted shed at the back of Alan Eagleson's office is now surrounded by rich wood furniture and handsome fixtures. Leaning back in his chair, fingers tented across his chest, he describes Bettman as "the owners' commissioner" but otherwise scrupulously avoids inflammatory judgements. As the moments tick down towards the 2004 CBA, he's leaving provocative statements to others. He prefers to talk proudly about the collective agreement he helped broker in 1995. "It has worked for both sides, I think. It takes years to see the full cycle of a CBA. The owners have extended it twice—that speaks to a lot of things. What came out of the deal, everyone has opinions on. But the business has grown dramatically in terms of revenue, new arenas. A more mature industry came out of it."

Certainly, the NHL's figures reflected an industry in growth mode as the 2002 entry draft dawned. The number of fans attending NHL games increased during Goodenow's tenure from 12,769,676 in 1991–92 to 17,264,678 in 1997–98 and 20,373,329 in 2000–01. According to NHL figures, the revenue number for 1991–92 of $400 million had multiplied fivefold over ten years to more than $2 billion (during a time of low inflation). National TV contracts in both the United States and Canada had mushroomed from $50 million at the beginning of the 1990s to $760 million. Licensing and marketing opportunities were also burgeoning as the league provided its top stars to the Olympics in 1998 and 2002.

Corporate America liked the demographics of the league, since many fans were in the lucrative eighteen-to-forty-nine age bracket. Hispanic and female interest was up slightly as well. Even though the league lost corporate partners Nortel, Wendy's, and IBM in 2002, it developed nearly twenty other ties with blue-chip firms such as Dodge, Nextel, Southwest Airlines, and Sun Microsystems. Meanwhile, twenty-six teams were valued by *Forbes* at $110 million or more, and nine checked in at over $200 million—this in the throes of the worst financial downturn in North America since the 1970s.

As the 2004 CBA renegotiation loomed, however, the NHL painted a different picture for public consumption. With the Rigas family's financial implosion and criminal charges in the summer of 2002, the league tried to engineer the sale of the Buffalo Sabres first to Mark Hamister; when that collapsed they turned then to New York businessman Tom Golisano (who made his fortune, appropriately, in the cheque-printing business). In Ottawa, meanwhile, the ambitious plan proposed by Senators owner Rod Bryden for a limited partnership to reduce a $250-million debt collapsed in bankruptcy. Out of cash, the first-place Senators sought bankruptcy protection and needed emergency cash infusions to finish the season. Finally, Toronto businessman Eugene Melnyk swept in to buy the club for $100 million, even as his financial consultants advised strongly against the investment. Their concern: no cost certainty.

Other franchises experienced financial woes in 2002–03. "In St. Louis, we're just trying to keep ourselves above water," said Blues GM Larry Pleau. "I think it's known that we don't make money." Edmonton's thirty-seven owners faced cash calls, while Vancouver's chairman John McCaw put the Canucks up for sale. Throw in Pittsburgh's ancient arena, Phoenix's shaky ownership group, the travails of the other Southern-based U.S. franchises, and the financial challenges of the Islanders owners, and it's easy to see why Bettman held grim-faced press conferences and owners publicly wrung their hands, a daisy chain of woe for public consumption. "I'm not looking for a fight," Bettman intoned, "but the economics of the league are broken. We owe it to the game, and we owe it to our fans, to fix it."

Expansion, the salary explosion, and the notion that no matter how poorly you run an NHL club you're entitled to stay in business have all contributed to the NHL's instability, but many problems could be attributed to factors the NHL could not control: currency exchange, the stock-market collapse, and the financial malfeasance of some owners.

Yet few of these factors go to the heart of financial viability in a well-run franchise. "It's a matter right now of the owners controlling themselves," Florida's Peter Worrell offered. "Nobody puts a gun to their head and tells them to pay a fourth-line guy $4 million or $5 million. That's their decision. They've shot themselves in the foot for a long time, and now they want to put the blame on us."

The main source of the NHL's dysfunctionality is its flawed policy of revenue-sharing. Revenue numbers expose the underlying cause of the league's troubles with parity and competitive balance. While the NFL distributes 74 per cent of its revenues, the NBA 35 per cent, and Major League Baseball 25 per cent, NHL owners share just 12 per cent of revenues as the 2003–04 season gets underway. This winner-take-all philosophy has led to a growing rift between the NHL's profit centres (New York, Detroit, Dallas, Colorado, Philadelphia, Toronto, New Jersey), and its break-even operations (Buffalo, Tampa, Nashville, Pittsburgh, Ottawa). "If the Rangers had to pay $15 million to a pool shared by Nashville," asks agent Ritch Winter, "would they have spent as much as they have on salaries?"

"I don't want to see us come to a league of haves and have-nots," says Lou Lamoriello of New Jersey. Yet the league has become just that. Teams in small markets are essentially training grounds for stars who gravitate to the richest teams once they achieve leverage in contract negotiations. The starting 2002–03 payrolls reflected that imbalance. At the top end were the New York Rangers ($69 million), Detroit ($68 million), Dallas ($61 million), Colorado ($60 million), Philadelphia ($56 million), Toronto ($54 million), and New Jersey ($52 million). At the bottom were Nashville ($25 million), Tampa ($28 million), Ottawa ($30 million), Edmonton ($30 million), Buffalo ($31 million), and Pittsburgh ($31 million). The effect? Every year since 1994–95, when the last CBA was signed, a member of that first group has won the Stanley Cup; only one in the latter group— Buffalo, in 1999—has even reached the finals. The rule held again in 2003, when New Jersey beat Anaheim in the Stanley Cup final.

Both management and players agree that better distribution of revenues would lead to a better distribution of players. Vancouver GM Brian Burke articulated the frustration of making do with half as much. "I can't wait to find out if some of these guys can operate in a system where you can't just go out and spend what you want to spend. I can't wait for that day when it comes down to who can do their job." Until the NHL redresses its large/small-market conflict, says agent Gilles Lupien, the top talent will naturally migrate to the bigger markets. "Everybody in my hometown of Brownsburg [Quebec] would like Céline Dion to come and sing. But it's too small for her. What can we do? If the big markets in the U.S. are saying we want to have all the teams, and the players want to have that money, what are we going to do? If the McDonald's in Calgary doesn't do well, do all the other McDonald's chip in? Why should all the players have to roll back their salaries because Calgary is struggling?"

It's an oft-repeated observation that increased free agency has distorted competitive balance in the NHL and made it impossible to keep champion teams together. Because of free agency, it is indeed harder to maintain winning dynasties, such as the Canadiens of the late 1970s, the Islanders of the early 1980s, or the Oilers of the later 1980s. But are dynasties desirable?

In sports where team revenues and payrolls are comparable, free agency has allowed a wider distribution of winners. From 1976, when baseball granted its first form of free agency, the Blue Jays were the only repeat winners of the World Series, in 1992 and 1993, until market discrepancies pushed by cable-TV dollars in the late 1990s allowed the Yankees to buy enough premier free agents to win three World Series in four years. Before the Yankees splurged, both large markets (New York, Los Angeles) and small (Kansas City, Pittsburgh) took home baseball's biggest prize. TV revenues escalated, as did merchandising and stadium revenues; and baseball thrived because of the equalizing effects of free agency.

In hockey, where free agency was a mirage, only six clubs won the Stanley Cup in the two decades between 1973 and 1992; economic growth was steady but small. After real free agency arrived in the early 1990s, seven different teams won Cups in a decade, and nine others made it to the final. As a result, the NHL showed healthy revenue streams across the board. "It doesn't seem like it's random in the NHL," says sports economist Andrew Zimbalist. "You have nineteen years or so of these dynastic periods, and then, starting in 1991, you don't have them any more. Something systematic happened. Once salaries reflect competitive market forces, it becomes harder to hold a winning team together. It also becomes easier to assemble a winning team. If you're in the cellar and a Wayne Gretzky becomes available, you can buy him. Ironically, the salary explosion from free agency is one of the factors that's promoted this rotation at the top of the league. And I think the fan relates to seeing teams rotate at the top, having a sense of opportunity for their teams to win the Stanley Cup."

Many fans find it offensive that pro athletes receive huge salaries when teachers, social workers, and nurses make relatively little. Yet those same fans have no problem with owners (who don't risk their physical well-being) or others in the entertainment field hauling in enormous salaries. "Everybody went bonkers when Alex Rodriguez got $25 million a season with Texas," says sports-law expert Paul Weiler. "Nobody, except for a few entertainment specialists, knew that Tom Cruise was getting that much for each of the three movies he made that year. Or that Oprah was making $80 million a year. For that matter, how about CEOs? Until the Enron and WorldCom stuff, nobody was bothered that one CEO took home $750 million in salary and stock options in one year.

"We'd never dream of banning an actor or CEO from his job because he happened to have marijuana, yet we do that with athletes. We see sports as national pastimes with a special presence in our moral lives. That why we—wrongly, I believe—object to athletes being paid so much. That's why we blame them—wrongly—for our ticket prices going up. Athletes really do have influence on people's behaviour. You rarely see an entertainer, let alone an executive, as a role model for personal behaviour. Yet if Tiger Woods is driving a particular car, or wearing a particular shoe, that's what we go out and buy."

Clearly, hockey players have benefited from this celebrity. Has it made them lazy or indifferent, as some fans like to grouse? On the contrary. The peak condition of even marginal NHL players these days speaks to a dedication and professionalism not widely seen when Gretzky made his move to Los Angeles. After a short post-season holiday, most players train rigorously, then play a punishing schedule amid constant travel. The day in 1998 that Dominik Hasek signed a new four-year contract for $8 million a year, he stopped 32 shots and was the first star of a Buffalo win over Florida. Instead of going out to celebrate, he spent an hour and a half in the training room, working out.

As for rich players not putting out, Harry Sinden is unconvinced. "I'd say they've always been among the best in terms of getting your money's worth. I often ask myself, if I was making $10 million a year could I really put my face in front of a puck? I don't know. But a lot of these guys do. I think money has affected some players, but on the whole they put out every bit as much as they ever have."

"It's a man's game and these are truly dedicated athletes," says Bob Goodenow. "The careers of some players may not match their forecasts, but that doesn't make them any less unique. These are not just people walking down the street. They are exceptional, skilled players."

If fans resent highly compensated athletes, they think player agents and lawyers are repugnant. Devils GM Lou Lamoriello articulates the case against agents: "I'm bothered because an agent has more fear of losing a client than doing the right thing. I hear it all the time from agents—'I know you're right, Lou, but if I don't get the money that his friend on the team got he'll fire me.' God almighty, it's like your child coming home and saying his neighbour got something, and if I don't get it I'm finding a new father. Or else they say to you, 'This is my final offer.' And then there are five more final offers."

While some agents merit Lamoriello's wrath, many do a compe-tent, highly professional job. Don Baizley says "agent" no longer even describes what he and his brethren do. "Typically an agent is someone who brings two sides together. But in hockey, there's not much seeking out. Your rights are drafted and controlled by one team until you become a free agent at age thirty-one. And then they phone you, if you've got the right client.

"A player needs four things in this day and age," adds Baizley. "First, legal advice, contracts, that sort of thing. Second, financial advice. Third, investment advice. And fourth—if they're a superstar—they need marketing help."

The NHLPA has forced the NHL to become more creative, more efficient, and more profitable in its dealings with players. And since Eagleson left, it has prodded agents to do better for their clients as well. As Gilles Lupien says, the zeal of agents has helped owners increase the equity in the teams exponentially.

Not that agents have ever got recognition for their contributions. "In the early days, we were despised as pariahs," says Don Baizley, who started representing players in 1972. "They didn't want to touch us." In a famous incident from the 1960s, Punch Imlach, on the phone with an agent, put him on hold during negotiations, traded the player he represented, then resumed the conversation by saying he no longer had the player in question on his roster. "Would the agent please call the other club?" asked Imlach with a smirk. In another celebrated episode, a GM reportedly urinated on the pant leg of an agent who was standing at the urinal next to him.

It used to be hard to tell which was a bigger threat for players—management or their own representatives. Eagleson's firm was the dominant agency in the 1970s; sometimes he represented almost everyone on a single team. Dennis Polonich, now a player rep himself, was a client of Eagleson's. In the late 1970s, the five-foot-six buzz saw was involved in a stick-swinging incident with hulking Wilf Paiement, one that required he attend a meeting with NHL disciplinarian Brian O'Neill. "I walked in with our GM, Ted Lindsay," recalls Polonich, "and I look over at Paiement. Who's sitting with him but Eagleson's assistant, Bill Watters. My own agents! I guess they had to make a choice between clients. About the only good thing that came from it is I owed them a little money, and they never got it." Faced with such ethical shortcuts, young prospects had the choice of being a pawn to Eagleson, or risking that he might bury you with his management contacts.

Other agents were no bargain either, remembers former centre Mike Rogers, who had 519 points in 484 NHL games with Hartford, the Rangers, and Edmonton. "In my last year of junior with Calgary Centennials, I wanted to hire Herb Pinder as my agent," says Rogers, now a radio analyst for the Flames. "But my coach, Scotty Munro, told me I had to go with Dick Sorkin, another player agent. Scotty was being paid by Sorkin to send all his players to him. I told him I wanted to go with Pinder. He told me if I wanted to play in the play-offs I'd go with the other guy. He promised me that when Sorkin paid him off, he'd give me some of the money. It was crazy. I'd scored 76 goals and 140 points in my last year, but if I didn't go with the other agent, he was going to bench me." Rogers, who had three 100-point campaigns in the NHL, eventually ended up with Pinder when he left the Centennials for the Edmonton Oilers of the fledgling WHA. Sorkin ended up in jail for misappropriating his clients' money. (Famed tough guy Dave "Tiger" Williams was given the same "sign with Sorkin or you don't play in the playoffs" line when he played in Swift Current.)

In the mid-1970s, with big money flowing from the WHA, agents began recruiting players at younger and younger ages. Toronto agent Gus Badali—who once represented Wayne Gretzky—was perhaps the most famous of the early recruiters. Two years after signing the Brantford flash, Badali steered a seventeen-year-old Gretzky to the pro WHA's Indianapolis Racers, raising the hackles of many who felt he was robbing the cradle. Meanwhile, renegade WHA owner Johnny Bassett signed a raft of players too young for the NHL draft to his Birmingham squad. The Baby Bulls—Mark Messier, Mark Napier,

Rob Ramage among them—were considered a hockey heresy, but the NHL soon dropped the age of the draft from twenty to eighteen so there would be no more teenage raids against them.

Conditions improved for players and agents in the 1980s, recalls Mike Barnett, but there was still hostility from management and indifference from the NHLPA towards agents and player reps. A Calgary native, Barnett began representing players he met at his Edmonton restaurant. He recalls his motivation for leaving the hospitality industry: "As players had more responsibilities—Canada Cup, long season, contracts that were becoming more complicated—they needed representation. I took it as a personal challenge, something I wanted to do." He vividly remembers an early duel with Glen Sather over his first client, Marty McSorley. "You have to remember that in a city the size of Edmonton, Glen knew everything that was going on," laughs Barnett, who bears a resemblance to the late movie actor Alan Ladd. "He felt he controlled his players in a way you can't in a big city. McSorley had had a good year. I go in to see Sather and he says, 'I've got five guys who can do his job just as well at the minor-league level.' And I said, 'You may have to bring them all up, then.' He didn't like that, but we got the deal done. That's how I started representing players."

Barnett parlayed representing McSorley into his role as agent for McSorley's pal Wayne Gretzky. He eventually became the most prominent agent in the business, with stars such as Brett Hull, Jaromir Jagr, Owen Nolan, and Joe Thornton, and an office in Hollywood. His success piqued the interest of the International Management Group, founded by the late sports-marketing pioneer Mark McCormack. IMG—which virtually runs the pro golf and tennis worlds—took Barnett under its wing as the hockey branch of the company. Barnett left IMG in 2001 to join Gretzky's new management team in Phoenix.

Like Barnett, most top agents got into the business indirectly. While still a student at Queen's law school in Kingston, Mike Gillis helped an old teammate, Geoff Courtnall. "I initially said no," Gillis recalls, "but his wife was a good friend of my wife, and when she called us I couldn't refuse. He had a brother, Russ, and I ended up helping him, too. I did this one and that one and it really took off. At that point I had no intention of getting back into hockey."

Rick Curran started in the business at age sixteen by working summer hockey camps for Bobby Orr. Ritch Winter was in law school in California when he helped a Kings defenceman, Dave Lewis, who came from the same Alberta town, Drumheller. In 1972, Don Baizley was a young lawyer trying to help his buddy Jerry Wilson (father of future NHL player Carey Wilson) acclimate some European friends named Lars-Erik Sjoberg, Anders Hedberg, and Ulf Nilsson into the WHA in Winnipeg. Bobby Orr fell into the agenting game because of his turbulent falling-out with his agent, Eagleson. "I had a bad experience," says Orr. "I think there's a better way of doing it. I want to make that happen."

Before the Gretzky trade in 1988, agents battled not just management but a Players' Association run by a union leader not eager to push for his members. "I remember calling Eagleson to ask some questions for Dave Lewis," recalls Winter. "This was Alan Eagleson, the man who organized the '72 series, supposedly a great man. There was absolutely no interest in helping us out. That's when I realized what a problem we had."

Few agents besides Eagleson got rich back then. For most it was a lonely vigil in arenas, living rooms, on the phone with vindictive hockey managers, suspicious parents, and complaining clients. If they represented European players before the fall of the Iron Curtain, there was also the prospect of cloak-and-dagger efforts to get Russian or Czechoslovakian players to the West. Ritch Winter loves to recount the tale of spiriting Frank Musil out of the claws of the Czech national team in Vienna, with the secret police on his heels. Ron Salcer expedited the defection of Pavel Bure from the Soviet Union under the noses of the KGB in Vancouver in 1991.

Before the salary explosion of the 1990s, representing players was not lucrative. Even though agents received as much as 6 to 10 per cent of a player's salary for negotiating and providing financial services (the current standard is anywhere from 1.5 to 3 per cent for contracts, and up to 6 per cent if a player opts for financial management), it did not add up to much when the NHL's average salary was stuck in five figures. It helped to have a law practice or business to supplement—or support—the player agency. That's why agents such as Eagleson, Curran, and Don Meehan emphasized numbers of clients over quality of service.

Says Curran, who worked for Eagleson in the 1970s and with Watters in the 1980s, "This is how I used to think of it when there was Alan, Bill Watters, and me. We would invoice ten dollars. But we'd have to spend nine. And we'd make one dollar after going through all the time and trouble to collect the nine. You'd spend every night lying awake, wondering about this client, that client. Every time Norm Kaplan used to go into Peterborough we'd worry about which client he was stealing.

"The better way of doing it was when I bought the company [Branada Sports] from Bill Watters and downsized it. I dropped down to maybe twenty-five guys. You invoice five dollars but you spend two and you make three with a lot less aggravation. And because you are so much closer to your guys, you're able to give them what they're looking for. They're happier, you're happier, life is much better. That's the way it's been for me for the last ten, fifteen years. Best thing I ever did."

Another change has been the move away from player representatives personally handling players' finances. In the wake of Sorkin's troubles and Eagleson's jail sentence for fraud in 1997, most agents feel the risks and temptations of being a one-stop source for all a player's needs are not worth the aggravation. For instance, the Law Society of Upper Canada announced in the summer of 2002 that as a result of failed investment schemes, Don Meehan—who handles Jarome Iginla, Nicklas Lidstrom, Curtis Joseph, and many others—had undertaken that neither he nor his firm would hold themselves out to clients as financial advisers. Meehan's former partner in a series of investments involving hockey stars was earlier disbarred for not reporting the failure of investments or his secret shares in the deals. It was a warning to unqualified individuals that operating outside your expertise can be a career killer.

Mike Gillis feels there's no upside in acting beyond your expertise. "In the old days there were guys charging a client 3 per cent of gross, just to pay his Visa bill. Look, I'm not trained in financial management, so why should I even try to do it? The best thing is for a player to seek out impartial investment experts, not hockey agents doing it on the side." Gillis now works for Assante Corporation, which specializes in wealth management; while Assante has access to Gillis's clients, it must compete with other firms for the business of handling the players' money. Most agents in all sports these days help players farm out their financial affairs to third parties. That's not to say that players' money is always well managed; there are still stories of financial mismanagement by non-agents, but the instances of agents being the guilty parties has been almost eliminated—at least in North America.

The same can't be said about spreading around money to attract clients. Though the top ten agents handle the bulk of the profitable business, there are more than two hundred player representatives listed with the NHLPA, all anxious to sign the next Gretzky, the next Thornton, even if it means following a boy of twelve, signing him at fourteen, and nursing his ambitions until the draft at eighteen when the first cheques might arrive.

"There are two areas that concern me now," says Mike Barnett. "First, people coming into the business do not have the patience to build a clientele base over years. They want to get it all now, and they're prepared to do it at just about any expense. So they offer inducements, mostly financial, to families that are in many cases in desperate need of the cash.

"The second is how easily they'll be available for a player contemplating making a change. Many, many times we have players come to us and say, 'I'm thinking of making a change.' Either they'd call or they'd come up to the rink or they'd have somebody on their behalf, an accountant. My response was always the same: I appreciate your interest, but I'm not going to tell you anything that we're prepared to do, because it might influence your decision. You need to make your decision independent of what we're prepared to do. When you can tell me that you no longer have representation, then please let us be one of the people you consider.

"I was primarily worried about contractual interference. You start telling a player you're going to do this or that for him—I know it's done frequently, but there need to be actual lawsuits filed for tampering, contractual interference. The Players' Association needs to get a mechanism by which people have to be responsible for that type of illegal activity."

The Eastern European market remains a cutthroat environment for player reps. "There are payoffs between agents and players' families—$10,000, $20,000, even $50,000—going on in parking lots over there," says Ritch Winter, who's long had ties in the region. "First, it's created a climate where the Mafia can get involved. And second, how are you ever going to get that money back? A player might not generate that much money in fees for a decade, if at all. It's crazy, but people are doing it all the same."

"That's where it's going," agrees Rick Curran, "particularly with the European market. Guys are going out and buying their guys. And my point to [partner] Bobby [Orr] was, there's no sense getting into that, because the day you have to buy somebody, you're one day closer to the day you're going to lose him to somebody who wanted to pay more for him. A good agent has to look a client and his parents in the face and tell them what they need to hear. Not what they think they want to hear. The day you tell them what they want to hear, you've sold your soul to them. And eventually you're going to have a problem."

For a while, veteran NHL players were helping younger Russian, Czech, and Slovak players find representation. Now, to help naive kids from the former communist bloc avoid the perils of rapacious agents, the NHLPA stages summer information meetings in Europe. Young men born under the communist system or in the chaotic post–Cold War breakup are given guidance about the illegal activities and fraudulent claims of some "businessmen" preying upon vulnerable players.

The NHLPA has also instituted a certification program to ensure minimum standards in the business: before someone represents an NHLPA member, he or she must be certified. While the NHLPA has seldom invoked its power, it can decertify agents deemed to have crossed legal or ethical boundaries. In 1998, Dave Cook was decertified when it was found he'd used players' money improperly; mostly, though, the threat of decertification is implied rather than enforced.

Despite attempts to produce a code of conduct, agents haven't greatly improved their public image over the years. The illegal activities of Eagleson, Sorkin, and agents such as the notorious "Tank" Black in other sports did not help, either. Tom Cruise's portrayal of a rapacious agent in *Jerry Maguire* is still the accepted public image of the modern player rep. Ironically, the public is probably more resentful of agents these days than are the general managers they victimize. "Management today—most of them are former players," says Baizley. "They all had agents when they played, and they encourage their players to go out and get agents who know the marketplace. They don't want the players to feel squeezed or resentful after a deal where they might have gotten more."

The image of agents has also been hurt by the agents' singular success. Their ability to extract big dollars—and management's lack of success in preventing the same—has given agents a plundering image. Especially in endangered Canadian NHL cities, an agent winning a lucrative contract for his client is seen as a threat to the club's survival. It's a label Ritch Winter resents. "If you want to know why individual operators aren't making money, look at the decisions they're making," he protests. "The majority of their problems would be solved by GMs not giving five-year deals to thirty-four-year-olds. It's a matter of managerial competence, not agent's greed." Not surprisingly, NHL clubs try to hire successful agents to manage their teams. Barnett, Pierre Lacroix, Brian Burke, and Bill Watters are four agents-turned-managers. Baizley, Gillis, and others are routinely canvassed about their willingness to switch sides.

Gillis is a good example of the edge agents now bring to their dealings with management. While teammates and opponents from his playing days gravitated into management upon retirement, Gillis headed to Queen's law school, articled with a large firm in Toronto, and practised in the corporate world. His former teammates, however, were stuck like flies in amber in the NHL's closed shop. Now when Gillis faces them he has an advantage. "I think that playing with or against just about every general manager in the game today has helped," he says. "Understanding the game and all the situations a player and his team get into is extremely helpful. The combination of having played and being a lawyer has taken the two to a different level."

Contrast Gillis's development path with that of his old Bruins teammate Mike Milbury. After retiring from the NHL in 1985, Milbury stayed within the hockey fold in Boston. He guided the Bruins farm team, coached the Bruins for two seasons, and served as assistant GM to Harry Sinden before getting the job as coach of the Islanders in 1995. He added the portfolio of Islanders GM in December 1995. Burdened with undercapitalized owners and an old arena, the Isles under Milbury were a long way from the team that won four straight Cups from 1980 to 1983. Six coaches worked the bench while the team missed the post-season for seven consecutive seasons before 2002.

Along the way, Milbury—now nicknamed "Mad Mike"—squandered an all-star team of young talent in trades. Todd Bertuzzi, Eric Brewer, Roberto Luongo, Zdeno Chara, Bryan McCabe, Olli Jokinen, Bryan Berard, Zigmund Palffy, J.P. Dumont, Brad Lukowich, Taylor Pyatt, Tommy Salo, Darius Kasparaitis—all were dealt. Most of the players obtained for these players—Trevor Linden, Bryan Smolinski, Roman Hamrlik, Dmitri Nabokov, Mats Lindgren, Felix Potvin—didn't last long on the Island. The Luongo deal stings Isles fans most. The budding star goalie was sent to Florida so Milbury could pass up future megastars Dany Heatley and Marion Gaborik in favour of American goalie Rick DiPietro, who has yet to become a starter for the Isles. The team got new owners (computer magnates Charles Wang and Sanjay Kumar) in 2001; that allowed Milbury to spend generously for Alexei Yashin, Chris Osgood (now in St. Louis), and Mike Peca. Those moves put the Isles in the playoffs, although they haven't yet made it past the first round. (The playoff failures cost head coach Pete Laviolette his job in the summer of 2003.)

While Milbury has changed strategies and players every year of his eight-year rule to little effect, he still seems to enjoy job security. Many player reps point to him when they argue that the NHL needs to address the competencies of its own executives before it attacks players. "Maybe what the NHL needs is to hire the top fifteen agents to be general managers," says Ritch Winter. "After all, if I was always losing with my team, wouldn't I look to see how the opposition was doing it?" (The NHLPA, concerned about the defection of Mike Barnett to the GM's job in Phoenix, has requested that agents who wish to switch sides wait nine months before doing so.)

Despite the increasing respect they get from management and the media, most agents downplay their success. "It wasn't because agents were smarter than management," says Baizley. "These people were paying the salaries because they were projecting that they'd have the money. They saw these new revenue streams from arenas, expansion, the Internet, and merchandising, and maybe the revenues weren't what they were projected. But that's what created the salaries."

Says Winter, "Am I brilliant? I was only brilliant the one day in Jihlava in the Czech Republic when Dominik Hasek failed to show up for a meeting. I was brilliant because I listened to my partner who said this guy is worth looking for. And so we went to find him—he was at a movie house, watching a film. He did the rest. Any agent that tells you he's the world's greatest advocate is lying. If you represent Miroslav Bednar, you're not going to get one penny more than he's worth. But if you represent the best goalie on the planet.... It's all in recognizing what you have."

"I think the teams had the money to give," concurs Gilles Lupien. "And they gave, and they gave. And then they said, 'Oops we have to stop now. We need new rules.' I don't think so. I think teams have to hold to budgets. Some teams are doing it. How come the CBA works for them and doesn't work for others?"

Sports economist Andrew Zimbalist has studied agents in all the major leagues and says the hockey variety generally understand their place in the universe. "A lot of them will toot their own horn, but I think the more honest ones, like Steve Bartlett, say, 'Look, this is a simple job. I fell into this and I got lucky. I go in there and I've got some background and I do a little bit of homework and I push. There's not much more to it than that.' If you are going to be a good agent, you've got to study the CBA, you've got to see if there are loopholes, and you can play some psychological games with the owners and so on. But I only see that as the difference between a signing of $1.5 million and $1.6 million."

Ritch Winter helped organize an association of some—but not all—of his fellow agents to influence the NHLPA's position going into the 2004 CBA talks. "The collective agreement negotiated by the NHLPA in 1995 reduced young players' rights considerably," he says. "There was a rookie cap, no movement before thirty-one, a lot of things that weren't friendly to players. But then agents went in there on an individual basis and came away with precedent-setting deals, contracts that moved the market. It was agents who did that, often in spite of the CBA. The Players' Association was helpful, but unless agents did the job with the information, we never would have grown."

Andrew Zimbalist disagrees: "I don't think the agents caused the change. I think the change happens because the players negotiated a 1995 agreement with veteran free agency, and decided to use salary disclosure. Plus, you have a union chief who's going to use salary arbitration. So you have a new structural circumstance that enables bargaining to take place, and you bring an agent into that environment. The agent is the handmaiden of the salary increase, but he's not really the cause of it."

Another contentious issue for player representatives is the pressure they receive from Goodenow and the NHLPA at contract time. Detroit defenceman Chris Chelios renegotiated his own contract with the Red Wings in the summer of 2002. Chelios admitted the PA urged him to get market value for his services, signing for more money rather than staying in Detroit, the city he preferred. After re-signing with the Red Wings, he appeared to question the wisdom of pushing the bar ever higher on salaries. "You always have the thought that something stupid's going to happen like Holik," he told the *Toronto Sun* in the wake of Holik's mega-contract. "To me, that's stupid... getting that much money. It's good for the PA. I guess we're happy with that, but it's just ridiculous."

Then there's Gilles Lupien's assessment: "The player's association never put any pressure on me to sign the player at a certain amount. It never happened. We've got our computers and we see where the player should be and the players are telling us now. It's a big difference. The players are talking. During our days we used to take the plane with two or three beers in our pocket. Now the players go to the plane with a computer. 'If I score 50 goals, I'll make this much.' It's more the players telling us how much they want now."

"Kids are coming in today more businesslike," agrees Kirk Muller, who entered the NHL in 1984. "We came into the league, we didn't know a whole lot. It took us a few years to get onto things. But kids today, they're much more onto the issues. You've got to be involved now. There's certainly way more people involved in the meetings than when I first came in."

As the 2004 showdown approaches, more and more teams are tightening up. After the extravagance of the Joe Thornton contract, Sinden's Bruins played hardball with three of their stars in the summer of 2002. They allowed Bill Guerin to depart for Dallas as an unrestricted free agent. They turned down the salary demand of Byron Dafoe, who was looking for $6 million per year, and the free-agent goaltender sat out half a season before signing at half that salary price with Atlanta. Likewise, disgruntled defenceman Kyle McLaren, a restricted free agent, sat out much of 2002–03 awaiting a trade (he eventually was dealt to San Jose). Around the league, a handful of other veterans—Pat Verbeek, Mike Vernon, Igor Kravchuk—were not signed at all, and drifted into retirement or headed off to Europe to play.

Was the recent tightening the first salvo in hockey's looming showdown, or just a blip? Will the entrenched positions lead to a disrupted or perhaps even cancelled 2004–05 NHL season? Will the two sides find common ground before the league grinds to a halt? Ritch Winter has his own take on the impending drama: "Gary Bettman keeps saying he wants to create an idiot-proof CBA this time out. Why doesn't he just get rid of the idiots instead?"

12

A Better Mousetrap

Ken Dryden, the Hall of Fame goalie turned president of the Maple Leafs, tucks his long legs beneath the Formica table at the Mars delicatessen on College Street in Toronto. Hip-replacement surgery and seven years at the helm of a hockey institution have slowed him somewhat, but he still displays the calm, reasoned approach he showed while winning six Stanley Cups in eight seasons with Montreal. The local Toronto media may despair over his lengthy answers and aversion to sound clips, but his careful smarts have helped him survive everything from the child-abuse scandal at Maple Leaf Gardens to Pat Quinn's throttling of photographers to the Leafs' repeated failure to capture the NHL's top prize in this city of great hockey expectations.

The NHL news this summer day of 2003 is not good. Ottawa and Buffalo are seeking bankruptcy protection, attendance is down in many venues, several teams are for sale, and talks on a new CBA are far off. At the suggestion that all this will inevitably lead to the disappearance of Canadian teams such as the Flames and the Senators, Dryden's calm exterior disappears. "You can easily say, 'That's the way the forces of the world are going, that's just the way it is,'" he says. "It's wonderful to hear the players or the agents say that it's inevitable—'Ten years from now there's not going to be a Calgary Flames or Ottawa Senators. No big deal.' What a load of crap that is. Find an answer, forget the inevitability.

"I think it's much more interesting to imagine a way in which the Flames or Senators could survive. It was unimaginable ten years ago to think the NHL could survive with an average salary of $1.5 million. Saving the Canadian teams is dead simple relative to what's been done in the last twenty years."

Dryden takes a sip of juice. "You can talk about having a nice little Green Bay–type franchise in a modern, futuristic NHL. What's the plan to find a way to see that that happens? Who's actually looking to find a way to save Canadian teams? Are governments? Outside of this new Alberta lottery, not really. The media? No. Are players? I haven't heard those voices. Are the agents? I haven't heard those voices. Who else is trying to save the Calgary Flames or Ottawa Senators for the next fifty years? Right now it's only coming from one place. The NHL."

Even as Dryden was making his point, Gary Bettman was bluntly warning players that talks on a new CBA must start soon—or else. "The system needs to be overhauled," he told *The Hockey News*. "We know exactly what's wrong with the system so we don't have to be dealing with band-aids. We know what has to be fixed."

Despite Bettman's tough talk, NHLPA director Bob Goodenow prefers to wait and allow market forces to determine player compensation. "We dealt with this issue in the lockout," says Goodenow. "We don't believe a salary cap is in the best interest of the sport. There should be a marketplace. The clubs and players should have the ability to decide values."

Responds Bettman, "Free markets don't have minimum salaries. Free markets don't have salary arbitration."

Meanwhile, Wayne Gretzky laments the salary spiral he inadvertently helped to launch: "The money is astronomical now. It's hard for the average person to fathom." Mario Lemieux, who owns the Penguins, agrees: "All I know is, as a business, we can't keep up.

Tickets are expensive now and every year we keep charging more. There has to be something that makes more sense. I want to see the NHL more like the NFL, where every team can succeed and every team can compete." NHL owners such as Harley Hotchkiss, chairman of the Board of Governors, talk bravely about rewriting the CBA to produce an NFL-like balance. But as agent Gilles Lupien points out, what's the use of a contract if the NHL then ignores it? Hall of Fame forward Mike Gartner agrees: "If you sit down with an honest GM, he'll tell you that this contract in its present form—if used properly by management—is a management-friendly contract. All the restrictions are in place that a team can control the contracts they sign with players. The only thing that takes it out of their hands is salary arbitration. But they have the ability to walk away from an arbitration award they don't want to sign."

It is not an easy time to own an NHL franchise. Buffalo and Ottawa are emerging from bankruptcy protection; Dallas, Anaheim, and Vancouver were openly for sale during the previous season; Nashville, Pittsburgh, Atlanta, and New Jersey are unofficially looking for new investors. As the league heads into collective bargaining with its players, the hot sports property of the late 1990s has turned cold. The uncertain North American economy and the pending spectre of a lost season in 2004 combine to make the NHL a poor buy.

"It's definitely a buyer's market right now for NHL teams," Marc Ganis, president of Chicago-based SportsCorp Ltd., told the *National Post*. "Financial institutions are not putting up a lot of money to help support the acquisition of NHL teams, in part because there have been quite a few NHL teams in very serious financial distress. The fundamental reason for all of this is that the economics of the industry are all screwed up. Players are getting paid substantially more than they should be as compared to the revenues the teams generate."

Ganis points at the NHL's modest revenue-sharing (12 per cent, versus the NBA's 35 per cent) as a reason for the deep freeze. "When you have that kind of situation and you have limited revenue-sharing, it's a recipe for a bad economic result. There's an expectation that the

2004 season may never take place. So there are quite a few people with substantial wealth that would like to be in the NHL, but they don't want to buy a team a year before a major labour dispute. They'd rather pay more money in '05 with certainty than take the risks now."

Not everyone feels that hockey is a bad long-term buy. Dean Bonham, who runs a sports consultation business in Denver, feels that a new CBA and the technology boom from interactive communications will make the league a winner. "I would suggest to you that the NHL offers the most upside potential of any league," Bonham told the *National Post*. "My belief is that the glass is half-full because you can buy those franchises today for less than what they'll be worth five to 10 years from now. The most thorny and important issue the NHL has to deal with is that the NHL has to find a way to solve the problem of out-of-control player costs. If they can ever get the player cost issues in line with the revenues of the teams, in the long run this could be quite an investment."

But first, the NHL must get past the next collective bargaining session. Would the eighty-six-year-old league survive the work stoppage projected for the fall of 2004 if it goes on and on? If play stops for a year or more, will fans in the Southern U.S. care whether the sport returns? What about teams whose equity shrinks to virtually nothing over a twelve- or eighteen-month standoff with players? And with as many as six hundred players being potential free agents going into the negotiating session, might a new, competing league incorporating major Canadian, American, and European cities rise from the NHL's ashes?

Despite Bettman's emphasis on a salary cap, the principal issue NHL owners must address is what the league should look like in future. As rescue worker (rather than builder) these past few years, Bettman has been short on vision beyond 2004. The real financial windfall for hockey lies in the hockey-crazy markets of Europe, not in the American Sunbelt, yet this option has been largely overlooked. The NHL remains essentially a collection of city states that will serve their own interests first.

"I don't believe it's possible [to remain at thirty clubs] without some kind of imposed salary structure," says former Canucks owner Arthur Griffiths. How will the league protect its Canadian franchises with the improving Canadian dollar still worth much less than the American? Does the NHL want a winner-take-the-spoils approach to player salaries, with big stars taking home the lion's share, as in the entertainment model? Does it want a rotation of clubs at the top of the standings, or a return to dynasties? Who are its core fans: the Don Cherry traditionalists who embrace fighting and physical play, or the NBA-styled fans who want offence and skill? Should the NHL control so many players via the draft, or would a greater free market in mid- to lower-ranked players be in its best interests? Will the league build in safeguards against its teams running up huge debt against the equity in their clubs? And can the NHL partner with its stars—as NASCAR and the NFL have done—to assure a profitable future?

The absence of vision in these many areas has made fans apprehensive about the future and distrustful of both sides in the endless wrangle over money. Typical of the conventional thinking of NHL people is the way they view the amateur draft—a lottery that rewards failure and punishes corporate creativity. To understand why the draft doesn't work, consider why it was introduced in 1967. Primarily, it was intended to address the weakness of the poorer teams by giving them first crack at eligible prospects. As any fan of the Flames or Oilers knows, however, if these teams draft a player with the talent of Joe Nieuwendyk, Jason Arnott, or Al MacInnis, that player will end up with a big-market team sooner or later.

If the draft is really a good way to spread talent, why do Detroit, New Jersey, and Colorado keep coming up with top talent despite drafting late in the first round? And why do the same weak teams keep fumbling their opportunities at the top of the draft? Granted, the old sponsorship system wasn't perfect because kids were being signed in their early teens. (Today, agents are the ones doing the under-age recruiting.) Yet, under the old system, the Boston Bruins, the worst team in the NHL in the 1960s, still managed to sign Bobby Orr in an open competition.

Some argue that if you had free competition for all, or almost all, players, the rich teams would lock up most of the talent. Yes, teams like the Rangers and Red Wings would be active in pursuing talent, but they have only so many jobs. Most players would rather start in the NHL with a smaller-market team than be buried way down the depth chart of a rich team.

The other rationale for the draft was that it would put a damper on the salaries given to untested talent. The fear was that general managers and owners wouldn't be able to control themselves, that some cuckoo would hand out a million dollars a year to an eighteen-year-old who had zero chance of being an NHL regular for five years. As we've seen, the draft has done little to restrain rookie salaries.

While NHL clubs wait to see whether their pick turns out to be Wayne Gretzky or Brent Gretzky, first-rounders can hit team budgets to the tune of a million dollars a year plus tens of millions in bonuses. Add the sums handed out to players drafted in rounds two through nine and you end up with financial commitments that, for small-market clubs with limited revenues, are burdensome.

If there were only one round of the draft each year and the rest of the players were free agents, that would also drive down the cost of talent. Clubs today can access just one-thirtieth of the available talent when they need a replacement player. Otherwise they must sign a free agent or make a trade. Agents would cut prices for players if they knew there were twenty kids competing with their client for a single job.

The drafting of eighteen-year-olds also hampers the development of young stars who have no hope of being competitive in the NHL for a few years. Instead of following a natural growth curve that would see them ready at twenty-one or twenty-two, prospects are rushed into an unrealistic development cycle or thrust straight into the NHL

)or team and little support. The result is evident when you

play "Where are they now?" with the draft picks of, say, Edmonton over the past decade: Jason Soules, Joe Hulbig, Scott Allison, Tyler Wright, Jason Bonsignore. The same is true of Vancouver's list. Or Montreal's. Or Chicago's.

Finally, the current system rewards incompetence, giving a team the top pick even when its scouts messed up, its GM traded poorly, and its coach misused his assets. If you want parity, better to distribute the management talent—not the hockey talent—more evenly across the league. Hiring five terrific scouts at $100,000 each, instead of twenty recycled players at $30,000, is a better way to get the jump on other teams than sinking money into Central Scouting.

To avoid antitrust legislation, the NHL could have a one-round draft. All other players would be free agents eligible to sign with any team when they could add real value to that team, not at some arbitrary point early in their career. A one-round draft would be a boon to the NHL, as well as to the junior leagues, which would be able to keep their top players longer.

None of the old arguments for the draft make much sense; teams acknowledge as much when they let players re-enter the draft. But that's the way it is in the inbred culture of the NHL, and the unproductive nature of the draft probably won't even be on the agenda when CBA proposals are discussed.

For now, the league remains fixated on the idea of putting a brake on the salaries it has handed out under the 1995 CBA. "There are no controls on player costs," says Bill Daly, the NHL's vice-president and chief legal officer. "We're committed to changing that system."

The league's public posture indicates that it still regards its players as a problem, not an opportunity for a profitable partnership. "Our biggest source of revenue is ticket sales," Bettman has said, "and since our biggest expense is player salaries, the tremendously inflationary rate at which salaries have increased had an impact on ticket prices. My hope would be that in the immediate future the union would sit down and engage in serious discussions over how to solve the problems that are plaguing our industry."

Challenged by Bettman's tough talk, players have responded with their own. "We want no payroll tax, and we want no salary cap," declared Dallas defenceman Darryl Sydor, the team's player representative. "If either of those is on the table, there's nothing to talk about. There's going to be a lockout." Hardly words to reassure nervous fans or investors.

According to Kelly Hrudey, blaming the players simply devalues the overall product. "It's like James Cameron saying don't go see *Titanic* because it's lousy because my actors are overpaid, they're bums, and the average fan can't relate to them. It seemed like the dumbest thing. We're a part of the owners' business and the fans have to like us."

The absence of an equitable working partnership hurts both sides. The owners control use of team logos while players retain rights to their own images, creating two separate licensing entities. Warily eyeing each other, the league and the players are unable to exploit promotional opportunities worth millions.

"When Bob Goodenow came in, he said the best way to show your mettle is to drop your gloves," says Ritch Winter. "So he did that just before the 1992 playoffs with the strike. The NHL realized what he was about. Then another new guy, Bettman, comes on the scene. He's got to drop his gloves to show his mettle. That was the 1994–95 lockout. Generally, in labour terms, everyone realizes that we don't have to do this after both guys have shown their willingness to fight. I mean, Donald Brashear and Georges Laraque don't fight every night. And yet we don't seem to be at that point yet where the sides respect each other's power."

Is there a more enlightened approach to labour issues in sport? NASCAR uses its drivers to cement the union of sport, sponsors, and fans—the cornerstones of the industry—in a way that provides a blueprint. Unlike hockey players, NASCAR drivers never miss an opportunity to promote their sponsors, and they're handsomely rewarded. When Geoff Bodine wrecked his QVC Thunderbird in the 1996 Daytona 500, he apologized to the fans and employees of the company for his failure to win the famed race and urged fans at home to "call the QVC shopping channel and order some merchandise, because we are going to need a new car." As Robert Hagstrom points out in his book *The NASCAR Way*, fans are keenly aware of sponsors and fiercely loyal to them: "Performance Research discovered that three out of four stock-car racing fans consciously purchase products of NASCAR sponsors." Tell that to Visa, official sponsor of the winter and summer Olympics. According to Performance Research, Visa paid $20 million for this right. After the 2002 games, 30 per cent of respondents believed that American Express had been the official sponsor. Do you know (or care) which credit card sponsors the NHL? Which computer firm? Which soft drink?

While no one advocates NHL players stumping for a particular beer or hardware chain between shifts, there's room for a closer marriage between the people who pay the bills and the men who cash the paycheques. With seats for NHL games costing up to $125, sponsoring corporations want more than a warm feeling from supporting the local squad. They want instant identification—à la NASCAR—with the stars of the sport.

Even if the NHL's governors reverse decades of intransigence on treating players more as equals, they must still deal with Bob Goodenow and his iron hold on the NHLPA. While Goodenow has made the union more democratic and responsive, he's the one who must be convinced that revisions to hockey's power-sharing are acceptable. NHL management believes that the determined Goodenow will do nothing to weaken his hold on a job that pays him an estimated $2.5 million a year until 2006 (a contract awarded by players to carry him through the predicted labour turmoil). Flexibility is not a word that springs to mind when players or managers discuss him. Thus, when a star such as Brett Hull or Jeremy Roenick fails to toe the party line of the Players' Association, it is big news. Hull's comment, seconded by Roenick, at the 2003 All-Star

Game that "75 per cent of players are overpaid" was a rare glimpse of discord within the NHLPA.

"He does what he wants," says one player of Goodenow. "He tells the players what to do, and he gets his own people on the NHLPA's executive board to pass his proposals. In that respect, he's not so different from the man he succeeded." Public pronouncements from players indicate support of his determination to resist, but in private few are happy with the prospect of losing a season or two from their peak earning years. Of course, maintaining solidarity in 2004 will be vastly different from keeping unity in 1994–95. With top salaries of $11 million and an average wage of almost $2 million, players now have much more to lose than they did a decade earlier, when average salaries were about $500,000. Things have never been so good for players; this time around it may be the owners who have less to lose from a lengthy work stoppage.

Goodenow has made positive noises about a new sharing agreement, but his comments are usually accompanied by a request to see unvarnished financial statements. Money from luxury suites, for instance, is not always included in a team's revenue. His members have echoed that desire for transparency. "With L.A. a couple of years ago," notes NHLPA vice-president and Flames defenceman Bob Boughner, "they were saying this new rink will be the key to our prosperity, and I don't think their payroll was much different than it is now. It's tough when you have owners who own more than one business. They own the cable-TV company and they own the hockey team and the money goes in one pocket and out the other. It's easy to mix and match numbers. You never know what to believe."

A financial report issued in Los Angeles in 2003 appears to reinforce the NHL's claims of poverty. Kings season-ticket holder Philip Propper, a portfolio manager and equity analyst, was dubious when he read that his Kings had lost $103 million since 1996. Propper, whose offices in Los Angeles are two blocks from the Staples Center, voiced his skepticism to the team. After all, hadn't *Forbes* said that the Kings had made $7 million in the 2001–02 season?

The forty-two-year-old Propper offered to study the Kings' books—as he does the statements of (then) AOL Time Warner Inc., Viacom Inc., and Walt Disney Co.—and post his results on the Web. "How could a team getting this many fans not be making money?" he asked the *Los Angeles Times*. He wanted to see the famous related-party transactions that NHLPA director Bob Goodenow talks so much about. How much were the Kings being billed for the operations of their parent company, the Anschutz Entertainment Group, which also owns the Staples Center and many other sports operations?

To Propper's surprise, Kings president Tim Leiweke agreed to his deal, with few strings attached. For ten hours over three days, Propper holed up with the Kings' financial statements, peppering Dan Beckerman, the team's chief financial officer, with questions. "Quite frankly, it was more thorough than most of the other audits we go through," Beckerman told reporters. Propper told anyone who'd listen that he was highly skeptical of the Kings' claims. "I went in with the bias that they were lying."

But in a twenty-one-page report he posted on Letsgokings.com, Propper whistled a different tune. He estimated that the team's over-all losses would be even higher than the published estimate. He said the team would post a cash loss of $12.5 million in 2002–03 (the Kings missed the playoffs), bringing Anschutz's losses since acquiring the team to $108 million. The biggest loss, $31.7 million, occurred in the 1998–99 season, he said, when the Kings also missed the playoffs. The cause of these financial woes, Propper believes, is player salaries. According to the figures he saw, the Kings' payroll has increased 19 per cent per year, revenues 15 per cent. Without a Stanley Cup, or even a finals appearance, since 1993, the Kings have struggled at the box office, averaging just 15,000 customers in the 18,118-seat Staples Center. Propper says it's a recipe for financial disaster.

Calgary Flames president Ken King says there should be no doubt about the veracity of the NHL's reporting. "The reality is grim enough. There's no necessity for us to take this information any other way. I consider it defamatory for anyone to suggest that we're not honest with the figures." The NHL could call the NHLPA's bluff by providing full financials, but as of summer 2003 they've chosen to show the books of just four teams to the Players' Association.

Goodenow is convinced that the rock-hard solidarity of the union will be sufficient to bring owners to the table before much damage is caused to players' financial status. But as NBA players discovered in their 2000 lockout, an association without the hammer of a competing league or disruptive picketing is no match for a determined ownership group bolstered by strike insurance, a huge war chest, and public sentiment. It would be a mistake to think that NHL owners are not desperate or determined enough to force a ruinous lockout upon their players.

Goodenow's warrior mentality—and his success since 1995—make a lengthy work stoppage appear inevitable. "The players didn't give him that new contract to reach an easy settlement before the last minute," says a prominent agent who supports Goodenow. "They hired him to fight for them, and that's what he'll do." Other agents are more cautious; they believe that back-channel negotiations—as when baseball avoided a labour stoppage in 2002—should be started now. With so much invested in their positions, neither Bettman nor Goodenow can be seen publicly backing down. But third parties can do horse-trading out of the spotlight and allow the front men to save face with their respective employers. As the summer of 2003 began, there didn't seem to be movement in this direction.

Predictions of what will happen come September 2004 run the gamut. "A work stoppage is going to happen," says Chuck Greenberg, an attorney for the Penguins. "There is too much at stake for both sides."

"I don't think there will be hockey in 2004," says TV personality Don Cherry. "That's the sense I get. When I see a guy like Kariya getting $10 million and scoring 52 points [in 2001–02], well, that's whacko." Then there's Neal Pilson, former president of CBS Sports. "You can write it down," he told the *Globe and Mail*. "There will be no labour stoppage. I think these [Buffalo and Ottawa] bankruptcies are occurring at a propitious time, because I think the message is very clear to the players and their labour leader that the league absolutely must have a restructured new collective agreement. I will, without hesitation, predict that the league will address its labour issues." Adds Rick Dudley, the GM in Florida, "Call me the eternal optimist, but I think they'll figure it out."

Three very different approaches to a new collective agreement are worth considering. The first, ironically, is to leave the current CBA virtually as is. Players would accept this solution in a heartbeat, and owners could make it work for them, too. Players have prospered more under the current deal, partly because NHL management neglected to press its advantages. As we've seen, skillful agents have raised the salary bar to $1.6 million for the elite players such as Jaromir Jagr; more tellingly, the average salary has risen a well-documented $1.6 million a season. Using the scarcity of free agents to drive up prices for Group Two free agents and then employing salary arbitration to enshrine these salary breakthroughs, the NHLPA clearly exploited the NHL's vulnerability in the first years of the new CBA. In the view of respected agent Don Baizley, "The current agreement should be ample to make this industry work."

The NHL could make the current deal work with minor modifications and a little discipline, as they have with more success in the past couple of years. The NHL has many levers under the current CBA, and in recent years clubs have begun to employ them more actively (while still blaming the players for the mess they created). Repressing salaries for Group Two free agents, walking away from salary arbitrations, holding the line on bonuses for all but elite entry-level prospects, keeping prospects in Europe unsigned till they are twenty-two or twenty-three—all these options are written into the current CBA.

The NHL could tweak the current agreement by reducing the number of rounds in the entry-level draft to create a larger p
cheaper players. It could also do away with maintaining its

twenty-five-man rosters and farm-team affiliates, reducing rosters to twenty skaters and two goalies. This, too, would free up a large number of players who would compete for jobs by reducing their prices. As a trade-off for guaranteed contracts, the league could limit the signing bonuses available to players, using a graduated scale to avoid the Fedorov and Sakic scenarios, which entailed balloon payments up front.

Owners need to recognize that, in a thirty-team league, there are going to be troubled franchises. The bankruptcies in Pittsburgh, Ottawa, and Buffalo wouldn't cause a moment's pause in most industries (think technology, or airlines, or the media), where survival of the strongest is the rule. But the current NHL is always compared to the more workable six-, twelve-, or even eighteen-team leagues of the past. When only one team can win the Stanley Cup, fans, owners, and the media must adjust their definition of what constitutes a troubled team. Teams will go under and franchises will move on occasion, but as Bob Goodenow reminds anyone who'll listen, you don't judge the prosperity of the Wal-Mart chain on their poorest stores but on their median outlets. It may well be that only twenty-four or twenty-eight clubs can reasonably operate under the current CBA.

It's not as if the 1995 CBA has been universally bad for revenue. Spurred by the need to pay players' market value, Bettman and his administration have learned to hustle in a way that John Ziegler never did. Until the economic downturn of 2001, the NHL continually pushed its revenue model higher, to the point that the league was bringing in $2 billion a year. (How much more is channelled through other businesses and through tax breaks is less clear.) And while the short-term challenges are considerable, Dean Bonham is correct when he says that market conditions and technology will benefit the NHL in the future, especially if the European gold mine is exploited.

The strongest argument for maintaining the current CBA is that, while the owners blame it for their troubles, there is security in predictability. After eight years, the advantages and disadvantages for both sides are clear. Major League Baseball owners spoke loftily about adopting a whole new system during their CBA negotiations in 2002, but when the moment of truth arrived they realized it was better to tinker with a known entity than to reconstruct a financial model that agents and the union might exploit before they did. If the NHL fully exploited its opportunities under the current CBA, it could still serve the owners well.

The current CBA already has provisions allowing for a Canadian currency equalization fund to help teams disadvantaged by the loonie. And the Canadian government might be more amenable to giving teams a national lottery if it's shown that the NHL has its fiscal house in order. Taxpayers in Canada and the United States have been loath to help businesses than can't help themselves. A lengthy, stable CBA would go a long way towards assuring government officials that moves intended to help the NHL wouldn't blow up in their faces.

Should the two sides seek a second option, it must address revenue distribution. Surely, say frustrated fans, there must be an equitable way to share $2 billion among thirty owners and seven hundred players. Assuming the NHL wants to maintain its thirty-team mix of large and small markets in even competition, a limited sharing of revenues is needed to prevent large inequities between clubs. Move money earned in the larger markets to the smaller ones, fans contend, and competition is protected. The NFL, for instance, shares its mammoth TV revenues equally, guaranteeing that Green Bay can compete with New York. But it also has an aggressive gate-sharing formula whereby teams share the home gate (after expenses) sixty-forty between the home team and the visitor. A study that applied the NFL split to the NHL's gate revenues from 2000–01 showed that the disparity between top and bottom teams would virtually disappear. It also showed that while lower-earning teams would receive a large boost from the plan, the top-earning teams wouldn't be unduly hurt. The study projected that Calgary would get a 26.5 per cent increase in revenues and Edmonton a 14.5 per cent increase, while Toronto would experience a decrease of 12.9 per cent and the mighty Red Wings a decrease of only 8.3 per cent.

To casual observers, this seems as a small price to pay for more equitable competition. But problems arise when revenue-sharing penalizes a well-run business such as Colorado (in a medium market) by transferring money to a poorly run operation such as the New York Islanders (in a large market). There needs to be incentive for creative, profitable clubs to move the market without knowing that their efforts are only enriching dysfunctional franchises. How, then, to design a revenue-sharing system that's fair to all teams but allows for growth in salaries for players?

A three-phase scheme has been proposed by Andy Bernstein in the magazine *SportsBusiness Journal*. Instead of establishing a hard formula to share revenues more equitably, Bernstein proposes assessing teams on the potential of their market and using the assessment to ensure both a payroll ceiling and a floor for every club. This market assessment would depend on population, media saturation, corporate support, and currency. A large market such as Detroit (a Stanley Cup contender) or Chicago (which hasn't won a Cup since 1961 and consistently underachieves) would still be assessed at the top end of the scale; Edmonton, Nashville, and Ottawa would be on the receiving end of the transfers. This market assessment would remove the need for assessing team revenues for the purpose of a salary cap—a contentious issue between owners and the players.

Those smaller-market teams would be forced to spend the money they receive on raising their payroll. Under Bernstein's plan, all team payrolls would have to be within, say, 10 per cent of the average NHL payroll. If the average payroll were $40 million, for example, all teams would have to have payrolls of between $36 million and $44 million. Any team coming up short or exceeding the top end would pay a graduated tax to the NHL. As league revenues increase, the average payroll could be increased. Bernstein argues that this scheme would allow for market forces to act on free agents while still keeping some restraint on salaries.

To entice players to accept the proposed structure, Bernstein suggests that all players become free agents after their first contract expires. Teams seeking to keep their stars after the first contract would be allowed to offer 15 per cent more than any competing offer from another team. Teams could access money from the market assessments to offer the extra money to keep their stars. This "loyalty" concept is one that's thought to be favoured by Gary Bettman.

Bernstein's plan is an innovative one, and Bettman has already floated the concept of market assessments instead of revenue-sharing for the next CBA. It will no doubt prove difficult for the commissioner to get owners such as Bill Wirtz and Mike Ilitch to accept the market-assessment idea. They seem to feel that breaking the NHLPA once and for all is a preferable strategy. The players, too, might balk if the average payroll were set too low or failed to move in concert with revenues.

A third proposal for a new CBA grows out of the notion that the best system is sometimes the simplest. Rather than hamstring hockey with a collective agreement that reads like the tax code, the NHL might consider a true free-market system. Hollywood doesn't imagine that every town with a multiplex deserves a major production studio. The Rolling Stones can't play every city with an arena and a passion for their music. The NHL could adopt the same view and follow a model based upon European soccer. In this model, teams would play at the level they can afford (as they're doing in practice today in the NHL). The twenty or so richest clubs—who can afford the price of a Joe Thornton or Jaromir Jagr—would play in a first division with few, if any, restrictions on what a player can make once he's past his entry-level contract. While salaries are largely uncapped, team rosters are limited, relieving the need to finance farm teams.

The next twenty clubs—those in the second division—would develop young talent and sell it up the line so they can afford to produce the next top young players. Their goal is basically to find and train good young players who will fetch a fortune in the future. In such a capitalist market, hockey wouldn't need luxury-tax schemes or Byzantine revenue-redistribution formulas to level the playing field for small markets. Let the first-division boys in their lucrative media markets decide what player costs they can bear. Hire the best general managers to assemble winning teams.

The advantages of this system? The quality of play would be enhanced. As in European soccer, the rich wouldn't have to carry weak-sister markets to placate politicians. The winner of the second division could be promoted to the first division each year, with the worst club in the top division dropping down. This would encourage teams to hire capable managers and scouts, not rely on the booby prize of a first-overall draft pick. To reflect the true supply of ready talent each year, the draft could be reduced to one or two rounds. The rest of the players would be free to sign at the level of their skill that year.

Fans would get the media buzz of three stretch runs, as teams compete for the first-division championship, to gain promotion to the first division, or to avoid relegation to the second division. This is how soccer has operated (successfully) for decades around the world, and how pro sports worked in North America before the advent of farm systems that artificially restricted the supply of available talent. Fans in large NHL markets such as New York or Toronto have little interest in paying $100 or $150 to see their team play the Columbus Blue Jackets or the Nashville Predators; they want to see other large-market teams with a history.

People in places like Edmonton, Nashville, Ottawa, and Buffalo initially wouldn't like being merely a producer of talent, as opposed to having a shot at the Stanley Cup, but the reality is that they're not going to survive when the NHL finally mines the lucrative European market. Given a choice between reduced status and no team at all, wouldn't fans of, say, the deposed Winnipeg Jets or Quebec Nordiques have opted for the former? Ticket prices in second-division cities would be decidedly cheaper, and fans would have greater access to local stars. If semantics are a problem, call the first division the Platinum (or Campbell) Conference and the second division the Gold (or Smythe) Conference.

This scheme has another advantage: rather than contracting, the NHL could expand to forty or fifty teams. Draft the largest American Hockey League cities—Quebec, Hamilton, Winnipeg, Houston, Salt Lake City, Milwaukee, and Hartford—and put them in a second division with Ottawa, Tampa Bay, and Pittsburgh. (The remaining AHL could constitute a third division.) That would mean forty or fifty logos to exploit, forty or fifty TV and radio markets to sell. The NHL would reach far more people.

The great impediment to such a model, of course, would be the NHLPA. The PA would frown on the film-industry model, in which Brad Pitt makes $2.5 million a film, a few supporting actors earn $1 million, and the rest of the cast are happy to earn in the tens of thousands. Under this divisional NHL system, the Players' Association would see a very few of its members earning perhaps $20 million a year while others made as little as $250,000 on the same team. Naturally, the PA would want to protect the earning power of its middle- and lower-class members. Such concerns are legitimate, but could be addressed by a lucrative pension fund or other post-retirement benefits.

These are three suggestions for CBA models. Others will no doubt be discussed as well, all aimed at finding a way to allow player salaries to rise with revenues while still guaranteeing some form of cost certainty to owners. Both management and the NHLPA will have to back off on a few crucial issues if a deal is to be made.

"Everyone in hockey wants to go to heaven," says one player agent, "but no one wants to die."

13

The Coming Storm

It's no exaggeration to say that, since Wayne Gretzky was traded to Los Angeles in 1988, the NHL has squandered almost every opportunity for growth that came its way. Failure to adapt its business model to changing conditions; an obdurate resistance to change from within; a fast-buck expansion process; a player-distribution system that has never worked the way it was supposed to; crushing debt from new buildings; contempt for its workforce—you name the challenge, the NHL has found a way to turn it against its own interests.

But, without question, one key failing in the fifteen years since the Gretzky deal has been the NHL's policy of allowing men trained as skaters and fighters to assume responsibility for spending the owners' money. (Ironically, Gretzky became one of the hockey products in management trying to sell the sport in a hostile environment.) This reliance on the hockey culture has been total. Even the owners who sign the cheques cannot overcome the immortal putdown: "How many games did you play in the NHL?" As a non-hockey person, Gary Bettman knows that his opinion carries little or no weight in hockey's inner sanctum on such issues as promoting skill or preventing injuries and violence.

Baseball statistician Voros McCracken, who was working for the Boston Red Sox, captured the unbending resistance to change in many sports in an Internet article. "The problem with major league baseball is that it's a self-populating institution. Knowledge is institutionalized. The people who aren't players are ex-players. In their defence, their structure is not set up along corporate lines. They don't have the mechanism to let in the good and get rid of the bad. They either keep everything or get rid of everything, and they rarely do the latter." Substitute hockey for baseball and you have a portrait of the NHL, a league that is willing to change but refuses to trust anyone from outside the "family."

As Michael Lewis points out in his book *Moneyball*, the institutional suspicion of outsiders means that sports are typically run at the whim of managers and scouts, most of them retired players, who cling to outdated methods. "In what other business do you leave the fate of the organization to a middle manager?" Lewis quotes former Oakland A's GM Sandy Alderson. The NHL, too, has been a captive of middle management such as Mike Milbury, Jim Rutherford, and Bobby Clarke, most of them graduates of the hockey monastery. Making short-term decisions based more on instinct than research, they waste talent selected in the draft, attach inordinate value to older, more expensive players when less costly options would work almost as well, and generally resist accepting wisdom from outside the tight circle.

Fuelled by abundant money and hubris, the system stumbled along in its haphazard fashion for fifteen years. But reality can be avoided for only so long. As the summer of 2003 arrived, the spending binge of the past decade had sent many teams into fiscal rehab. Almost every owner and general manager on Bettman's speed-dial was suddenly promising to follow the twelve steps to a clean balance sheet. Dallas owner Tom Hicks, who took his team off the market, spoke for all when he declared that his Stars would cut back his $66-million player payroll after their shocking upset at the hands of Anaheim. To prove it, he put $5-million centre Pierre Turgeon on waivers and let defenceman Derian Hatcher head to free agency. Just weeks removed from the Stanley Cup final, the Mighty Ducks stunned the NHL by not picking up the option on the contract of Paul Kariya and letting Adam Oates go free as well. Detroit let its star forward Sergei Fedorov walk to free agency when the Russian turned down a four-year, $40-million deal. Curtis Joseph, pursued with gusto the summer before by Detroit, was suddenly an outsider in Motown when Dominik Hasek announced his intention to return from retirement; there were no immediate takers for Joseph's $8-million price tag after the Red Wings' first-round loss to the Ducks. St. Louis lightened its payroll by dealing Cory Stillman, Val Bure, and Tyson Nash, and letting everyone know that Doug Weight and Pavol Demitra could be had cheap. Across the NHL, star players from Brian Leetch and Mark Messier to Teemu Selanne found themselves cast into the open market. It was also widely known that Washington would part with $11-million star Jaromir Jagr to anyone who'd take his bloated contract.

Tightening was evident elsewhere as well. Pittsburgh announced it was dropping ticket prices; Detroit and Dallas said they would hold the line on ticket increases for 2003–04. But perhaps the starkest indicator of change came on July 1, 2003, the day unrestricted free agents could make themselves available to all bidders. Exactly one year earlier, Bobby Holik, Bill Guerin, and Robert Lang landed huge deals on Canada Day 2003, only two small signings were announced, those of Jeff Hackett and Scott Nichol. The Ice Age seemed to be descending on the NHLPA's mighty fortress in preparation for the expiration of the collective bargaining agreement in 2004.

(Not everyone downsized: Colorado inked Don Baizley's clients Kariya and Selanne as free agents—Kariya accepting just $1.2 million—while Detroit snatched Derian Hatcher from the Stars for five years at $30 million. Carolina paid oft-injured journeyman Glen Wesley $2.7 million to return to the Hurricanes.)

The owners' sudden sobriety had many causes, perhaps none more compelling than the fate that befell the NHL big spenders during the 2003 playoffs. The prevailing wisdom dictated that you needed expensive stars to win a Stanley Cup. True, you could have a hefty payroll and still lose, but you couldn't win with a bargain-basement team. The record spoke clearly: since the back-to-back wins of the Pittsburgh Penguins in 1991 and 1992, teams with high payrolls had dominated. Detroit had won three Cups, Colorado two, Dallas, the Rangers, and Montreal (well-off in 1993) one each. Only New Jersey, with a middle-ranked payroll, seemed to defy the odds, winning three times. No small-payroll teams—Edmonton, Calgary, the Islanders, Tampa—had their names on the Cup. Teams such as Carolina and Buffalo did sneak into the final while riding a hot goalie, but they'd fallen short.

Owners, presidents, and GMs decried high player salaries, but in the next breath justified paying top dollar by pointing out they were only showing their commitment to winning. Few fans in a winning city complained about a large payroll when their heroes drank champagne from the Cup. But all that changed in 2003. The Rangers ($69.1-million payroll), Montreal ($48.6 million), San Jose ($47.7 million), and Chicago ($44.5 million) all failed to qualify for the post-season. Then, in two short weeks, the NHL's Goliaths collapsed at the hands of small-market Davids. In successive rounds, Anaheim ($39 million) eliminated not just Detroit ($69 million), but also Dallas ($61.6 million). Mighty Colorado ($60.1 million) was shocked by Minnesota ($20.5 million) in the first round. St. Louis ($63 million) was eliminated in the first round by Vancouver ($32 million). For good measure, the Wild shot down the high-flying Canucks, setting up a long-shot Western final between Minnesota and Anaheim. Toronto ($59 million) was dumped in the first round, as were the Capitals ($50.6 million), who were knocked out by Tampa Bay ($28.9 million).

The widespread destruction of the High Payroll = Stanley Cup equation shook the accepted notions of NHL management. Many clubs eliminated in the first round found themselves trying to pay huge payrolls with little or no playoff income after their early ouster.

With four rounds of playoffs worth as much as $15 million to a team, the first-round flops (and the teams that didn't make it to the post-season) were faced with crushing bills—bills that could only be paid by trimming big names and big salaries from the rosters of the Rangers, Maple Leafs, Red Wings, Capitals, Kings, and others. But there were few buyers willing to take on the $11 million for Jagr or Keith Tkachuk, the $10 million for Pavel Bure, the $8.5 million for Doug Weight, the $7.2 million for Ziggy Palffy, the $6 million for Owen Nolan or Pierre Turgeon, the $5.8 million for Tony Amonte, or the $5.2 million for Martin Lapointe. These players—plus others such as Eric Lindros, Peter Nedved, Luc Robitaille, and Roman Hamrlik—were all rumoured to be available to any team with an appetite for big salaries on long-term deals.

The second sobering memo to the NHL came via feeble TV ratings for NHL playoff games—this on the eve of negotiating a new network contract in the United States. Games went longer and longer—three overtimes in several cases—but fans at home were enjoying it less and less. The series between the surprising Mighty Ducks and the New Jersey Devils was the lowest-rated of any final in recent memory. CBC reported a similar slump for *Hockey Night in Canada*. Other players joined Brett Hull and Jeremy Roenick in blaming the on-ice product for the declines. Detroit's veteran centre Igor Larionov, who played on some great Soviet teams, said he was passing on the games altogether. "I haven't watched any of it because I know what kind of hockey it is," he told Tony Gallagher of the Vancouver *Province*. "I'm sure it's great for Minnesota and Anaheim because they are making heroic steps forward for their franchises, but it's terrible hockey."

Hall of Fame legend Guy Lafleur was similarly unimpressed by Team Dump-It-In (the Devils) versus Team Chip-It-Out (the Ducks). "We didn't throw the puck away for nothing like they do today," said Lafleur. "There's a big difference when you see a team that controls the puck instead of getting to the red line and dumping it in."

"The league is simply too coach-oriented," said former *Hockey Night in Canada* executive producer John Shannon, now running Leafs TV, the Toronto Maple Leafs' digital channel. "We see coaches, not players, reflected on the ice these days. Cautious hockey doesn't sell. We all want to see firewagon hockey with scoring chances and goals. That's why the Canucks are a fun team and drove the ratings this year. They're fun to watch—even when they lose 7–3, they're entertaining." Shannon says the Canucks are exceptional. "We don't talk about Marian Hossa or Wade Redden in Ottawa, we talk about Jacques Martin. We don't talk about Paul Kariya, we talk about Mike Babcock in Anaheim. There's too much emphasis on the coaches and how they're guiding everything on the ice.

"Someone once told me," added Shannon, whose paycheque comes from an NHL team, "that hockey's an instinctive game. And you can't teach instinct. Once you teach hockey players to think, they're lost. I think that's partly what's happened."

There are other reasons why the ratings have suffered. "I'm not surprised you're getting a one rating going head-to-head with golf on Saturday afternoons," says veteran TV producer Ralph Mellanby. "It's a very hard sell getting good network numbers in off-prime-time slots. They still need to consider the things our committee proposed years ago to get the flow back in the game. Why not have a penalty shootout to settle tie games in the regular season? Who needs another five minutes of play? The shootout is the most exciting play in hockey—and nobody understands those ot ties in the standings anyhow. Look at the All-Star Game: they were up on their feet, cheering to the end with the shoot-out.

"The players like it too. I can tell you one thing. From what I hear from [my son] Scott [Mellanby, of the Blues], they won't get resistance from the players if they try to bring the flow back in the game. They're just like the fans. They want to have fun."

With a new network-TV contract to negotiate, this dissatisfaction with the on-ice product was tough news for the NHL. So was the market for network-TV dollars, which was drying up in the straitened economic times following September 11. The NFL decided not to exercise an option to renegotiate its $17.6-billion deal with Fox, ABC, CBS, and ESPN, hoping a year or two might bring a better market. Not everyone thought it would. "As the appetite of the leagues has grown, it's increasingly obvious that the major networks can't sustain these rights fees," said former CBS Sports vice-president Jay Rosenstein.

Poor ratings and a sluggish economy are bad news for a business that wants to be paid like the big boys of sports broadcasting before any labour disruption in 2004. Many industry analysts said the NHL would be lucky to match the $600-million deal with ABC/ESPN. "The days of networks paying ever-escalating rights fees are over," CBS president Les Moonves told Bloomberg News.

Commissioner Bettman gave no hint about cost certainties when interviewed by Ron MacLean of CBC TV during the finals. Asked to comment on the Bernstein formula from *Sports Business Journal*, Bettman tap-danced away from specifics. "I'm not going to comment on the other systems," Bettman said. "It's too easy for people to speculate about things they really don't know about. We, in my opinion, need a system that links revenues and expenses so that all of our franchises can be healthy and competitive. It's very simple. I didn't say it's going to be easy to achieve and we have a lot of work to do with the players' union. But in concept, what we need, to me, is something very simple."

For his part, Bob Goodenow remained tight-lipped, other than to say, "Why is it all right for the players to give up something that's not in their best interest in collective bargaining, but it's not all right for the owners to do the same?" The intractability of the main protagonists in the upcoming drama continues to send dread through the industry. Agents worry that a headstrong Goodenow will take the players past the point of no return. Owners worry that Bettman will use the captive votes of his loyalists (he needs only eight voting governors to defeat any resolution he disagrees with), such as Boston's powerful Jeremy Jacobs, to stifle a settlement. If Goodenow and Bettman can't sit down together for a beer—in the time-honoured hockey way—what chance is there that the two sides will solve the economic riddles facing the NHL?

Yet there was also a feeling, in the summer of 2003, that there is simply too much to be lost by missing any action in the fall of 2004. For all Bettman's desire to outfox Goodenow and create a new paradigm for the NHL, he must balance that against the need to negotiate the new contract with nervous American TV networks, the enormous carrying costs on arenas, unsteady franchise values, guaranteed contracts, and a public that still hasn't forgotten the 1994–95 lockout. Goodenow, too, was faced with a hostile public and many players unwilling to kill the golden goose of salaries.

While there no doubt will be many dark days and worrisome moments leading up to September 15, 2004, the only likely conclusion is a gruelling negotiation wrapped up at the last minute. Calgary Flames star Jarome Iginla echoed the feelings of many players in the summer of 2003. "I think that it can get worked out," said the 2002 Art Ross Trophy winner. "I think there are things that need to be talked about and worked out, for sure. But I am really optimistic that, after the season, we will be preparing to play next season when it comes down to it." In 2002, Major League Baseball stared into the same abyss and pulled back at the last moment. The NHL would have to, also. If not, it risks undermining the rich traditions of almost ninety years, damaging a Canadian cultural icon, and leaving a stain on both sides that will be hard to erase.

14

UPDATE:
FIVE FOR FIGHTING

The biting February wind blew down Manhattan's glass and steel canyons, forcing up collars and pushing shoulders against the cold. There was a crispness that made it a perfect winter's day for hockey. But as the leaders of the NHL and its union gathered at a midtown hotel on February 19, 2005, there hadn't been a game for over four months. Instead of watching the greatest stars of the game perform, they would try to resurrect some semblance of the 2004–05 season. If there were a worst-case scenario for the NHL lockout, this was it. The credibility of Wayne Gretzky and Mario Lemieux—the Great One and Magic Mario—invested in a last-ditch proposition doomed to failure. In their days as superstars they'd rescued many a game in its dying moments, closing the deal on the Stanley Cup. Now, just days after the season had been called off by NHL commissioner Gary Bettman, they were being asked to end hockey's nightmare lockout, called into a meeting by two sides desperate to avert disaster in New York City.

When Bettman had cancelled the season on February 16, he'd suggested the league hadn't completely closed the door on a compromise. If the NHLPA would come up with an acceptable figure for a salary cap ceiling, moving closer to the league's drop-dead figure [believed to be

$42.5 million], then a 24-game season and playoffs might still be salvaged. No sooner had Bettman uttered this codicil than desperate representatives on the players' side started tossing out figures. "I think both sides took a step back the next day and realized 'we were that close,'" said Calgary Flames star Jarome Iginla, among the players seeking a reprieve. "And I think both sides realized that for the big hit hockey would take, maybe we needed to take another crack at it." Suddenly it became gospel that if the players accepted a $45-million cap, a season might be salvaged after all—and that Gretzky and Lemieux were the grease needed to get the gears moving again.

Sensing a thaw in the players' stance, NHL vice-president Bill Daly invited the NHLPA to chat one last time in New York City. The NHLPA put out a press release hinting that a settlement might be imminent. By the Friday evening, optimism ran so high that *The Hockey News* website declared (without evidence, as it turned out) that a settlement had been reached. Instantly other media outlets began circulating stories that Gretzky and Lemieux had brought the sides together. If anything had fuelled the wild rumour it was the presence of the superstars at the table. "I've said all along that the most important thing is coming to an agreement," said New Jersey Devils CEO and GM Lou Lamoriello. "Even after the season was cancelled it was just so important to get together as soon as possible. And I commend both of them for agreeing to do it. And now, get it done."

As with everything else in the lockout, the Gretzky/Lemieux tandem intervention proved another cruel deception for hockey fans frustrated that thirty owners and 750 players couldn't somehow divide $2 billion in revenues amongst themselves. In a battle where the league seemed content to take a year's hiatus from the costly player contracts it had so enthusiastically signed earlier and where the players were willing to surrender a season to prove their solidarity, Gretzky/Lemieux was a feint that was long on optics but short on substance. After all the excitement, neither side even made a new proposal at the meeting in New York City. Both management and labour left the table blaming the other. "I think there was a misconception that the two sides were close," NHLPA president Trevor Linden told reporters after the meeting. "I think, frankly, it came from the side of ownership and certainly general managers and some players and fans and media."

"This is the thing I'm really upset and depressed about, I mean what a terrible thing they did to our fans," Bettman told WFAN in New York. "This to me is the most horrific thing about what happened. I think this was a setup, I think it was done intentionally to try and cause the type of reaction that we saw all weekend."

Gretzky and Lemieux pronounced themselves baffled that no new proposals were offered after all the anticipation. "The only way that Wayne and I would have gotten involved is because we believed there was a new proposal coming from the Players' Association," Lemieux told the *Pittsburgh Post Gazette*. "We were told by some of the players we were talking to that there would be a new proposal on the table at the forty-five million [dollar] level."

"The union is still intent on negotiating for more than we can afford," Commissioner Gary Bettman told the league's thirty owners in a memo. "They put nothing new and concrete on the table. Unfortunately I was correct on Wednesday when I said we were much further apart then the media was portraying."

When Gretzky and Lemieux left the final negotiating session in New York after six hours of fruitless talks, it was clear that the 2004–05 NHL season was one cause not even their talents could redeem. The Stanley Cup was to go unawarded for the first time since 1917. That year the Spanish influenza epidemic had stopped the Cup. In 2005, it was an epidemic of labour madness. "I don't need aggravation from Bob Goodenow," Flyers owner Ed Snider quipped. "I might jump over the table and choke him to death. That would not be good. That's why they keep me out of negotiations. I am a throwback to the old hockey days."

Said Jeremy Roenick, who'd once suggested he could live with a salary cap: "It didn't get done, and that frustrates the hell out of me. It's very frustrating to know this may drag on another year." The cancellation moved Bettman's old boss, NBA commissioner David Stern, to level this withering critique of the NHLPA and Goodenow. "If those guys [NHLPA] had laid their cards on the table early on that a cap was something about which they would negotiate because football has one and basketball has one and baseball has a big tax— then there would have been a series of negotiations that have no doubt would have gotten the players and owners onto a page where they could have negotiated a deal.

"But, he [Goodenow] decided that the style was you don't give anything until what you perceive to be the eleventh hour and then in the pressure of the situation you can get your way. One of the worst miscalculations in the history of sports."

The implosion of the last-ditch talks in February 2005 was the result of militant elements on the two sides dominating the moderates, reducing the lockout to a war of attrition that would cost at least a full season or more. But it had been apparent as early as the start of the 2003–04 NHL campaign that hard-liners on both sides were spoiling for a fight to the death and moderates didn't care or couldn't muster enough support. For ownership, there were still deep divisions on how to run a business with wide disparities in earning potential and spending ability from team to team. Large markets remained indifferent to the huge gaps between their payrolls and those of small markets. Those small markets were adamant that they needed an NFL-type cap to rein in the profligate spenders in the league.

Bettman, bolstered by the eight votes he needed to defeat any opposition, astutely recognized the potential for division on his side and so concentrated on the one thing upon which all owners could agree: ridding themselves of Goodenow and union militants. (If any liberal-minded owners wanted to muse publicly about any internal struggles within the owners, they faced a $1-million fine from the commissioner.) Spurred by losses both real and imagined and by the sting of losing the previous negotiations, owners were galvanized by the equation of subtracting Goodenow equals happy times. In their minds, it was the NHLPA chief who caused the carnage, not them.

To position the players as intransigent, Bettman publicly complained that the NHLPA was not negotiating while the 2003–04 season was playing out, and that unrealistic salaries were driving ticket prices beyond the reach of average fans. His message got a receptive hearing in many quarters who view athletes as indulged and out-of-touch. But even as Bettman demonized Goodenow and the union, negotiators for the two sides in fact were meeting. An initiative called the Blue Fin Committee, consisting of representatives from both sides, met between March and June 2003 to discuss possible models for a settlement. But any talks between the sides foundered on the NHLPA's reluctance to accept the NHL's financial figures and accounting methods (based on four clubs' books supplied to the union by the NHL) and on commissioner Bettman's insistence on a salary cap as the only vehicle to solve what he described as the NHL's financial malaise. "We all put a lot of work into it," NHLPA deputy director Ted Saskin told the *Globe and Mail*. "It was very clear that from the forecasting we did, with the input and participation of league representatives, [that] the concessions we were offering would have had a significant, positive impact on league's overall finances."

Ironically, even as the sides were arguing about how to change the old CBA, teams were finally beginning to exploit the seven-year-old agreement. Just a year after small-market Anaheim had taken on former sad-sack New Jersey in the 2003 Stanley Cup final, the 2004 final featured two more small-market teams, Tampa and Calgary. Elsewhere, free-spending clubs such as Washington, Florida, the New York Rangers, Dallas, St. Louis, and Detroit were either not making the playoffs or being eliminated very early. As such, they were jettisoning costly veterans like Alexei Kovalev, Brian Leetch, Peter Bondra, Peter Nedved, Robert Lang, Ron Francis, and Sergei Gonchar wherever possible to pare huge payrolls that no longer seemed to work. Even the dreaded salary-arbitration system was tilting back to the owners' side as they finally used their levers in the

CBA. But Bettman and the owners, already locked into their position, described such evidence as an aberration, insisting (without evidence) that teams with big payrolls would prevail again. "We've had a car wreck and we want to buy a new car," Bettman said in Calgary. "The union wants—is insisting—on new tires for the wreck."

So the 2003–04 season played out with little negotiation and much rhetoric from players about staying the course till hell froze over. "The bottom line is, if they want a hard cap, we'll sit out for the rest of our lives," Toronto Maple Leafs union rep Bryan McCabe told the *Toronto Star*. "If they're not going to budge off of that, there's really nowhere to go." Said Montreal Canadiens goalie José Théodore, "I want to make the best deal available for both sides, but as long as they're talking about a cap, there's not going to be a season for sure. So as long as there's a cap, there's not going to be a season and we're ready to accept that."

While both sides stockpiled millions of dollars in war chests for a lengthy battle, the NHL in February of 2004 unveiled a financial report it had commissioned from Arthur Levitt, former chairman of the United States Securities and Exchange Commission from 1993 to 2000. At the NHL's behest, Levitt assessed the league's operating loss as $273 million for the 2002–2003 season. According to the study, only eleven of the NHL's franchises actually turned a profit for the 2002–2003 season, while the remaining nineteen reported losses averaging $18 million a team. Four of the nineteen teams suffered operating losses of over $30 million, two were in the $20–29.9 million range, six were between $10–19.9 million, another six suffered losses of $5–9.9 million, and one took losses of less than $5 million. Of the eleven profitable teams, only two saw profits of over $10 million, with four in the $5–9.9 million range, and five with just under $5 million in the black.

To hear Levitt, the NHL's future was bleaker than bleak. "I have to say, I would not underwrite as a banker any of these ventures, nor would I invest a dollar of my own personal money in a business that, to me, appears to be heading south," Levitt told a press conference in New York. "Regardless of how they get there, they are on a treadmill to obscurity, that's the way this league is going...Something's got to change...I can just look at what I see and can tell you from an investment point of view that it's a dumb investment. They've got a serious problem." Though Levitt himself is not an accountant, his report endorsed the accounting methods of the league that were so much disputed by the NHLPA. "I was given total carte blanche to go wherever I wanted to and ask whatever questions I wished to ask," Levitt said during the news conference. "I visited clubs, I spoke to owners, I spoke to financial officers."

Bettman quickly described Levitt's report a "super-audit" and brandished it enthusiastically as proof of his catastrophic predictions the previous few years. Some wondered aloud why Bettman seemed so happy to see a report that effectively damned his handling of the league's finances, suggesting that any other CEO would be fired for producing such a calamitous business statement. "This is supposed to be a business in crisis, in peril," said agent Michael Gillis. "They say they lost $237 million, and yet not one person in their management has been fired or replaced for incompetence. What does that say to you?" But Bettman was undeterred when asked why he shouldn't resign in the face of such results, saying that his willingness to get the paradigm changed was enough for his bosses on the Board of Governors.

The NHLPA—which had not been asked to participate in compiling the report—predictably dismissed Levitt's report. "We were given access to the UROs (United Reporting Operations) for thirty clubs, but were only able to conduct a thorough review of four NHL clubs," NHLPA executive director Bob Goodenow explained in a statement. "On those four clubs alone we found just over $52 million in hockey-related revenues and benefits not reported in the League's voluntary and unaudited URO process. If we are given similar access to all of the other individual teams' financial information, presumably used in the Levitt report, we will be in a position to provide further comment." That lack of an independent auditor was a familiar refrain for the NHLPA. "Everyone knows a good accountant can turn an $8-million profit into an $8-million loss, especially when owners have more than one business," said Bob Boughner, NHLPA vice-president. "It goes in one pocket, out the other."

Goodenow and the NHLPA also whispered that the NHL—as the least important of the major pro sports leagues in the United States—was being used as a test case by the other leagues as they prepared for their own labour confrontations. For instance, the NBA—where Gary Bettman was working when hired as commissioner by the NHL—extended its CBA for an extra year in 2004 to allow the NHL to go first at its players. No wonder. Eight NHL team owners also owned NBA clubs. Another was a partner with an NBA team owner in the arena their teams shared. Almost half the NHL club owners who owned their buildings or arena leases had NBA teams as tenants. Two NHL owners also had ownership of Major League Baseball teams. One owned an NFL club, one a pro soccer team. The cross-ownership interests didn't stop there. Five NHL owners had ownership stakes, or related business connections, in cable-TV networks that broadcast the games of several pro sports. One NHL team owner operated a concessions empire at buildings that host multiple pro sports events. A big CBA win by the NHL at the expense of its union would benefit them all, said NHLPA sources.

While Bettman's PR campaign rolled out, Goodenow stubbornly held to his bottom line: the NHL was not bargaining in good faith, and wanted simply to escape its legally binding contracts with players. As such, it would do whatever was necessary to break the union. The NHLPA said that only five or six clubs had serious financial problems, and that they only wanted what everyone else had in the hockey business: a free market to determine the players' worth. If owners couldn't do that without bankrupting themselves, then the fault lay with management, not players. So Goodenow warned his members to prepare for eighteen months to two years without a paycheque. There was no indication that Goodenow, confident after his previous CBA battles, had a fallback strategy should deadline pressure fail to defeat owners. Unlike the NHL, the union did not hire a PR firm to help it spin the issues to a public suspicious of "million-dollar" athletes in the first place. Its members would attempt (badly as it turned out) to articulate their issues with little or no help from communications experts. The result was often heavy handed—especially when a player deviated from the party line. When outspoken Jeremy Roenick proposed that a cap system within teams might work, he was quickly drowned out by the loyal rank and file. "Any time you deal with seven hundred players, there are a lot of different opinions, but hockey players showed in '94 they'll stick together," said a confident NHLPA president Trevor Linden. Neither did Goodenow do anything to enlist the help of other unions who might pressure the owners should a lockout drag on. The players were going to tough it out as they had in 1992 and 1994.

Finally, the PA did little to crunch the numbers or the methodology used in the Levitt Report, a PR success for the NHL whose figures were widely accepted in the media. Had the union done so, they'd have found fertile ground. In January 2005, almost a year after its release, the Levitt report's results were scrutinized by American journalist Russ Conway in the Lawrence *Eagle Tribune*. Conway revealed that Bettman's use of the words "super-audit" was without foundation and that Levitt himself was not accredited to certify an accounting procedure. "If anybody calls this a super-audit, you give them my number," Nelson Blinn, a thirty-six-year certified public accountant and member of the Banknorth auditing committee, told Conway. "This is absolutely, unconditionally not an audit. To pass it off as one is nonsense."

Richard Delgaudio, a professor of accounting and auditing at Merrimack College, explained the difference between an audit and a review. "An audit implies that you look at documentation and source documentation," he said. "A review is when you just kind of look things over to see if it seems right."

In other words, Levitt's team only performed a review, not verifying the accuracy of many figures supplied by the NHL—a far cry from Bettman's picture of an unimpeachable document (not one CPA signed off on the figures in Levitt). For instance, Blinn told the *Eagle Tribune* that accepting the NHL's own attendance and revenue figures was "another area of concern" in the report. "If you're an accountant working for a team or working for a company related in some way with the team, you're working for the same owner," Blinn said. "That's who pays you, so you've got his best interests in mind." Blinn added that if an independent auditor did the work, "Dollars to doughnuts, you'd get altogether different numbers."

Reporting the NHL's true profitability was crucial to the players' acceptance of a percentage of league revenues in any salary cap or luxury-tax scheme—a big problem in a league where twenty-two of the arenas are at least 50 per cent "owned, operated or controlled" by either the team, an affiliated business or related-party. Or where each club had its own reporting criteria—and often different reporting year-ends. Or where some owners such as Chicago's Bill Wirtz refused to disclose certain revenues at all.

While the NHL insisted the report made adjustments for these discrepancies between teams, the way they did so raised questions with Conway's experts. In one example, the *Eagle Tribune* reported that there were more than 2,600 luxury suites in arenas throughout the NHL in 2004. With rental fees, not including the cost of game tickets and concessions, they pulled in hundreds of millions of dollars a year—which might be expected to be reported as hockey revenue.

But in most NHL rinks, rental of a luxury suite also entitles the renter to admission to all other events at the facility—such as NBA, Arena Football League or National Lacrosse League games as well as all concerts, circuses, wrestling, and public events in the facility. Levitt investigators had no ability to independently examine the luxury-suite revenues for each club, so the report used a sample of eight clubs to create a formula that divided the revenue pie based on hockey's share of the total paid attendance—not per events—for all arena dates. In short, the formula treated all events as equal in the purchaser's mind. It didn't matter whether the box was actually used for any of the other events. Thus, the suite license or membership for an NHL game—diluted by other events—would have a lower reported value using the formula in the Levitt report. That assumption would reduce the hockey revenue reported in the Levitt report, making the NHL look like a worse investment than it is. (In those arenas where hockey is less of a draw—such as L.A.'s Staples Centre or Madison Square Garden in NYC—the opposite could be true.) In either case, the question was whether the method accurately accounts for actual hockey revenue or for the profitability of the arena itself.

The Levitt report then used the same method to determine hockey's cut of revenue from premium club-seat licenses, arena sponsorship and naming rights, and building costs, as well as suite revenues. The Levitt team did not benchmark revenue from concessions and other sources or general and administrative expenses, instead relying on the league's own in-house audits. In short the report was long on PR but short on facts the two sides could use as the basis for an agreement. "Unless they [NHLPA] agree with your definition of hockey revenue, what's the sense of doing it?" Delgaudio, a certified public accountant and nationally known lecturer on accounting, told the *Eagle Tribune*. "You're setting up the rules yourself, without the other person or the other entity agreeing, in this case the Players Association. And then coming up with that number and saying, 'See.' ... So the process didn't solve anything. It's one-sided. They used their own rules in coming up with a conclusion."

But questions about owners' true reporting of revenues didn't end there in Conway's critique. Take the tax case involving the Boston Bruins and owner Jeremy Jacobs—a key supporter of NHL commissioner Gary Bettman and the lockout. According to records of the Massachusetts Appellate Tax Board, the state claimed the Bruins and Jacobs under-reported taxable income on ticket sales and broadcast rights between 1991 and 1994. The Bruins argued that they shouldn't pay Massachusetts taxes on all of their home-game revenue, because they are obligated to play half their games out of state, incurring expenses but making no money. The Massachusetts tax board rejected that argument. It also rejected the Bruins' claim that they shouldn't be taxed on all the team's broadcast revenue, because a third of the revenue came from out-of-state viewers receiving the broadcast from a rented satellite floating "22,300 miles above Earth's surface and 1200 miles west of Mexico's Baja California coast." The Bruins and Jacobs were hit with a bill for $3.2 million in back taxes and penalties.

Then there are the New York Islanders. The NHL's due diligence process for prospective owners was publicly exposed after approving the sale of the Islanders in 1997 to John A. Spano Jr., who left a trail of bounced checks before dropping out of the Isles' bidding. Spano passed an NHL background check that cost the league just $750 (his deal to "buy" the team was for $165 million). Instead of going to the NHL, Spano went to prison on wire fraud charges. The 2003 bankruptcies in Buffalo and Ottawa were often cited in press conferences by NHL Commissioner Gary Bettman as indicative of the fragile financial state of the NHL. "We've saved a number of franchises from bankruptcy," he told a press conference in Calgary in 2004. "We've kept a number of other franchises from going into bankruptcy."

But neither the Buffalo nor the Ottawa bankruptcies was caused by hockey operations. The Sabres went bankrupt in 2003 when former team owner John Rigas and his son were convicted of fraud for systematically lying to investors of their company, Adelphia Communications. In Ottawa, the franchise was crippled by debt related to arena construction problems and paying for a highway interchange to serve the Senators' arena. As a result of these and other examples of NHL accounting, many players and agents remained skeptical of the NHL's accounting even after Levitt. This was all rich PR ground for the NHLPA in defending its arguments against a salary-cap system. But Goodenow did not exploit this until late in CBA talks when the 2004–05 season was cancelled and the union was effectively compromised.

So the NHL peddled Levitt, the players dug in and the clock ticked toward a confrontation. In July 2005, the owners proposed six ideas for a new system—including having the NHL's head office negotiate all individual player contracts. Predictably, the NHLPA saw them all as salary caps by another name. The Players Association then proposed a luxury-tax system that was instantly shot down by the league. "I'm very frustrated and concerned right now because I think we're engaged in a charade," Bill Daly told reporters after an August session with the NHLPA. "The union is not willing to negotiate with us." Shot back Linden: "It is clear the owners remain stuck at trying to get a salary cap. At some point the owners need to understand the players will never accept a salary cap or any system arbitrarily linking payroll to league revenues."

As the teams assembled in Montreal for September's 2004 World Cup of Hockey, there was a palpable sense of resignation in the air. "If we aren't playing soon, it's too bad because we have the best players in the world at this tournament," said Canadian defenceman Robin Regehr. "They're all ready to go and provide some great hockey. We'll just have to see where it goes. But it's a little disappointing that we can't take the lessons from this tournament forward right away." There were rumours that Daly and Saskin had hammered out a deal late one night during the tournament at Montreal's famed Crescent Street bar, Hurley's, but such proposals were reportedly quashed with equal vigour by both Goodenow and Bettman.

Having cornered the union on its unequivocal stand against a salary cap, Bettman announced the lockout of the players on September 15, 2004—the night after the World Cup ended with a win by Canada. The Cornell grad had been preparing himself and his business for this moment, almost since the day the previous CBA was signed. Unlike 1994–95, he didn't face the pressure of losing lucrative U.S. network–TV dollars should the NHL still be out come January (he'd signed a cost-sharing partnership with NBC this time to remove that negotiating stick). Plus he had a kitchen cabinet of at least eight clubs, enough to defeat any attempt at the appeasement seen in 1995. No wonder he sounded cocky. "To use a hockey term, they're instigating a fight," said the commissioner. "They think they can win this fight. And that will get them to keep the most. They're wrong. And time will tell. And time will show."

"That's just absolutely ridiculous," thundered Goodenow, who called Bettman the "owners' commissioner." "He never once acknowledged, not that he would, that we came forward well over a year ago with very meaningful proposals. He recited a number of times erroneously through his comments that we haven't acknowledged some of the issues when in fact we most definitely have. Strictly in hard dollars our proposals amount to savings of well over $100 million." Said player rep Todd Marchant, "When they come back and say hard cap or nothing, that's not negotiating, that's not trying to get a deal done. That's trying to be the bully." But Hall of Fame winger Mike Bossy hinted that, even among some former players, the NHLPA was out of touch. "There were a lot of players that were being taken advantage of in my era," Bossy told the Saskatoon *Star Phoenix*. "[A]s there were in the era before me. I don't think that any hockey player is being taken advantage of now."

Much of this rhetoric flew over the heads of hockey fans, who had already ignored the bickering when opening night for the 2004–05 season came and went without a settlement. And so the league and teams laid off up to half their employees while more than 150 NHLers signed on with European clubs—with the list growing to 350 by mid-January. The NHL advised teams that home games may be cancelled so buildings could book dates for other events on a forty-five-day rolling basis.

As the lockout began, the teams could be safely assigned to categories. Some couldn't lose money if they tried. Others have to exercise a little caution. Some need to be maximize every dollar. But only one category was in any danger of failure. They broke down roughly this way on the eve of the lockout:

1) Filthy Rich. These teams own or control their own building (often they own the surrounding real estate, too).
They are either owned by or have very close working
relationships with their TV partners. Their owners can run
the team as a hobby. The lockout is irrelevant for them.
Members: Boston, Toronto, Philadelphia, Chicago, NY
Rangers, Detroit, Colorado.

2) Comfortably Rich. The upper-middle class of the NHL
with combinations of the Filthy Rich's assets, but not all.
Montreal, say, would be in (1) but for Quebec's ridiculous
taxes. St. Louis, Dallas and L.A. the same but for wild
spending by their GMs on unproductive free agents. The
lockout could help them somewhat, but they don't need
it. Members: St. Louis, Columbus, Minnesota, Dallas,
Montreal, L.A., San Jose, Vancouver.

3) Middle Class: Each club has one major challenge—either
their building, TV revenue, the Canadian dollar, corporate
support—but can work around it with savvy management. They need occasional playoff success for profit. For
example, the NY Islanders need only a new building and
creative leadership to escape the Fiscally Challenged dog-
house. Calgary has reduced pressure from Canadian
dollar but smaller population base. A hard-cap CBA will
help these teams but they're in no real danger long term.
Members: New Jersey, NY Islanders, Ottawa, Buffalo,
Washington, Calgary, Tampa Bay, Anaheim.

4) Fiscally Challenged. These teams have a fatal flaw, either
location, building or population size that make them
chronic problems. Ironically, they're not the biggest
money losers as the lockout begins. They can only succeed with a winning team. With no stalking-horse city
willing to pay $80 million for them, they're stuck—and
so's the NHL. Members: Pittsburgh, Edmonton, Carolina,
Atlanta, Anaheim, Nashville, Florida, Phoenix.

With no games being played, pressure was ratcheted up for both sides. But as they had in 1994–95, the players caught most of the flak from fans and media. An Ipsos-Reid poll conducted for CTV, TSN, and the *Globe and Mail* in the fall of 2004 found that 52 per cent of Canadians blamed the players for the impasse, while only 21 per cent blamed the owners. Without the million-dollar fine imposed on owners for speaking out, the players were the first to show signs of dissent. Flames defenceman Mike Commodore was the first player to break from NHLPA line, saying he would play under a salary cap if it was fair to both sides. Montreal winger Pierre Dagenais told *La Presse* he, too, would play under a salary cap. Brian Pothier and Rob Ray echoed the sentiments. Their comments drew heated reaction from other NHLPA members; within days Commodore and Dagenais were said to be having second thoughts about their acceptance of a cap. Still, the hints of discord grew, with suggestions players were being kept in the dark on issues by the union. Twice that fall, Goodenow convened "information sessions" to brief players on the reasons for the non-existent talks.

Still, Goodenow stuck to his 1994–95 strategy, confident that his members would stay united. As such, he let another PR opportunity [to] pass without comment when *Forbes* magazine released its annual estimate of franchise values. Despite Bettman's claims of mortal peril for the NHL, Forbes insisted that "hockey franchises are now worth an average of $163 million, up 3 percent from last year and 31 percent higher than when we first valued them six years ago." And what about the NHL's claim of $224 million in total losses, a number rubber stamped by Levitt? "The thirty teams in the NHL lost a combined $96 million (before interest, taxes, depreciation and amortization) on revenue of $2.2 billion during the 2003–04 season, with seventeen teams posting a loss. The prior season the NHL lost $123 million on revenue of $2.1 billion."

Forbes also scoffed at the huge losses reported for some big-city markets. The New York Rangers reported a $45-million loss (*Forbes* said it was more like $3 million) while the parent company MSG somehow made $57 million. The Kings claimed to have lost $100 million in the past ten years, but Staples Center—owned by Philip Anschutz, the Kings owner—generated about $50 million in revenues in one year. While the NHL howled about "irresponsible journalism," *Forbes* had said that a well-managed team, owned by rich people, playing in its own building with a decent TV package has to work very hard to lose money. (A number of clubs had worked diligently at doing just that.) But Goodenow let the *Forbes* report pass with little public comment. Meanwhile, both sides rejected the call for mediation or arbitration as a means to solve the lockout, insisting both sides knew the issues.

By December, with no negotiations in three months and pressure building on players, Goodenow moved to appease his members' impatience with the stalemate. The NHLPA offered a dramatic 24 per cent rollback on salaries and 20 per cent tax on payrolls over $45 million. The owners would also receive concessions for entry-level contracts as well as arbitration rights. The NHLPA proposal promised to save the league up to $600 million in salaries. NHLPA executive director Bob Goodenow called them "significant, significant changes" that achieve the NHL's goals of reducing payrolls to $1.4 billion. It took the NHL five days to formally reject the pitch, but the 24 per cent rollback on existing contracts would now represent the floor in all further discussions between the sides. The other lasting impact was that of furious NHLPA members who asked when the NHLPA's negotiating team had been mandated idea for such a major giveback. The seeds of discontent with Goodenow's strategy were sown for many with the rollback concept. Even Marvin Miller, the man who made the MLB Players Association into a force, was unhappy with the hockey players' givebacks in the December proposal, calling them hasty and ill-advised.

Bettman, too, had issues with a number of his owners who could not understand why they had to lose money and goodwill to save a few chronically weak partners. When it looked as if dissident owners might use a January 2005 Board of Governors meeting to challenge him, Bettman simply cancelled the meeting, citing a lack of progress in negotiations as reason for the cancellation. Plus he hinted at a strategy of replacement players should a new CBA not be reached by the fall of 2005. Meanwhile, his patron, Boston owner Jeremy Jacobs stoked the public resentment of players with a tirade against their work ethic that harkened back to earlier generations before player independence. "They're comfortable, they're presumptuous, they know they're going to play, and they don't have to fight for the position," he told the *Boston Globe*. "There should be a way of handling that, there should be a way of perhaps sending them to a Providence for a couple of games or so until they build back the energy and the desire to play."

Whatever the merits of Jacobs' plea, the pressure was mounting in the players' camp as January ended with no progress in sight and a whole year's salary almost gone. Dallas Stars captain Mike Modano mused to a reporter that the players would probably crack first. A contrite Modano quickly corrected himself. "I think that whole clip was a little turned around, I talked to the fellow for a while last night, there were some things said that led to that result of 'us cracking,' but I really can't see that happening. Our guys have stayed strong, they have stuck together...the future of the game relies on that." But while Modano tapdanced, brother members of the NHLPA were making direct contact with management to establish a dialogue. Toronto's Tie Domi met with his owner Larry Tannenbaum and Penguins player/owner Mario Lemieux, while Calgary star Jarome Iginla and Blues defenceman Chris Pronger also tried to find ways to ownership around the stalled talks. In a nationally syndicated rant, Boston legend Bobby Orr—now an agent—scolded both sides for their intransigence in talks and urged Bettman and Goodenow to put egos aside for the good of the game. In labour jargon, the players were blinking first.

Seeing signs of panic from NHLPA membership, Bettman finally could promise his owners a win—possibly a rout—if they just showed some "spine" (to use one of Bettman's favourite words). So the NHL refused to budge on its core issues. Whether in formal meetings in Toronto, New York or, Chicago or clandestine talks elsewhere, the struggle between owners bent on a salary cap system and a union adamantly opposed to one began to tip in favour of owners. Internally, the NHLPA was racked with disagreement between hard-liner Goodenow and forces now open to compromise. Then, at secret meeting in Niagara Falls, N.Y., in mid-February between Bill Daly and Ted Saskin, the Players Association suddenly abandoned its core issue against salary caps in exchange for the owners de-linking player salaries to league revenues. The NHLPA proposed to play under a $52-million salary cap while the league proposed a $40-million salary cap with no "linkage" to revenue.

The stunning giveback seemingly came from the blue and left the Players Association's position in tatters. "Am I excited about a salary cap? No. But it's about trying to get a deal done," said Calgary star Iginla—one of the union moderates. Buffalo player rep Jay McKee, a hardliner, was more direct. "It's not so much that I'm angry that they offered a cap. I'm angry that why now?" McKee said. "Why not last June, last July?" With Bettman's drop-dead date on the 2004–05 season just days away in mid-February there was no immediate answer to McKee's question. But in subsequent weeks it would be asked many times by many players. Goodenow's inability to answer it to their satisfaction would destroy his credibility with much of the membership.

Having breached the NHLPA's invincibility with this massive give-back, the NHL pushed to find contract language plus payroll ceilings and floors that worked in time to save the 2004–05 season. Lemieux and Gretzky were summoned a few days later to rescue the day. It was a rescue that failed—in large part because the sides still couldn't agree on what constituted revenues in the league.

For all intents, the once-powerful NHLPA was fractured irretrievably on February 19, 2005, leaving Bob Goodenow in an exposed position. The most hated man in NHL management circles had predicated his lockout strategy on two pressure points. He told players

and agents their leverage would come, 1) when the NHL had to cancel the 2004–05 season, and 2) when the NHL had to cancel the
2005–06 season. Nothing more, nothing less. Only when those
moments came, said Goodenow, would Gary Bettman cry uncle and
get serious about talking. There had been good reason to believe
this gambit would work based on the last labour stoppage in
1994–95. Then, NHL owners stuck with arena leases, debt loads and
a new Fox TV pact cut a deal in January 1995 to save the season.
But the union strategy of repeating the '94–'95 tactics was so public and the dislike for Goodenow so palpable among owners, there
was every reason to believe Bettman would cancel the entire season
just to rid the NHL of Goodenow.

This obsession was the glue that held the disparate markets and
feuding owners together through much of the lockout. So when
Goodenow was forced to tell his members in February 2005, "Just
wait another eight to ten months, we'll get them then. See you in
September," he hit a dead end with his membership—many of whom
already felt marginalized during the talks. To give Goodenow his
due, he had repeatedly told the membership to be prepared for a
two-year lockout. He warned them to save up money for the long
haul. He hadn't sugarcoated the possibilities. But it's one thing to
hear about root canal and another to undergo the surgery. Players
learned the reality behind Goodenow's words that February day, and
while they still professed solidarity, they did not like losing a full year
of salary. Someone would be made to pay for that.

Sensing discord, the NHL ramped up its pressure on players in the
weeks following the cancellation of the 2004–05 season by talking
about using replacement players in the fall of 2005, an idea they
abandoned in late April when it became clear they were going to
score a big win in negotiations. The breakthrough came when the
union finally pursued the reality of NHL revenues—such as the ones
contained in Russ Conway's articles. Before the sides could be partners in a salary-cap system, they had to agree on precisely what
constituted NHL revenues (by the time the process ended, the union

claimed it had found $200 million more in revenues than the NHL had been admitting). More than anything, it was this process of mutually agreeing on the revenues of the business that broke down the impediments to a solution. The marginalization of Goodenow by his former loyal lieutenant Ted Saskin and president Trevor Linden also sped up the process, confirming that the NHLPA was in full retreat and willing to give back big time on all the major issues.

If the two sides needed any reminder on what awaited them when they resumed play, they got it in May 2005 when ESPN announced it would not pick up a $60-million option to retain NHL broadcasting rights for the next season. The league would now have to restore its profile in the ultra-competitive American sports without the support of the U.S. cable sports giant. It subsequently signed a three-year deal worth $200 million with Outdoor Life Network, owned by Comcast, a company owned by Flyers owner Ed Snider. But ESPN is in ninety million homes while OLN is in only sixty-three million households—reminiscent of John Ziegler's disastrous decision to spurn ESPN's huge audience for SportsChannel America's big cheque in the early 1990s.

The ESPN deal was the final vestige of Bettman's heralded $600-million TV strategy negotiated with ESPN and its parent company ABC. In its place would be the OLN deal and a two-year deal with NBC. Under the agreement, NBC would take the first portion of income from advertising to cover production expenses, while the NHL takes the next portion and the two split additional revenue equally. NHL officials said this was the direction they wanted to take their TV package. "The future for us on (U.S.) national television couldn't be more bright," Bettman said in announcing the deal. "We couldn't be more thrilled." Nonetheless there were no guarantees of revenue. (The NHL's gamble on OLN quickly turned sour when the NFL decided against placing games on the Comcast channel, thereby marginalizing it further.)

By June 2005 the first reports of a CBA solution were making (premature) appearances in the media—and with them stories of a badly fractured NHLPA with Goodenow and few loyalists pitted against Saskin, Linden and the compromise faction on the other side. It would take till July 13 before a final deal was concluded and ready for votes by the Board of Governors and the NHLPA. As in 1995, media observers would conclude that the NHL had beaten the players in the talks. This time, however, they would likely be proven correct. Against the advice of Goodenow, a humbled NHLPA had accepted the unthinkable: a $39-million salary cap (with a $22-million floor), a link to overall NHL revenues, a 24 per cent rollback on all existing contracts, a $7.8-million ceiling on individual contracts, an escrow system where players made up the difference of any salary overruns over 54 per cent of NHL revenues, two-way salary arbitration, significant restraints on rookie salaries, punitive restrictions on player movement between the NHL and the minors.

The only feathers for Saskin and Linden's cap came in free agency, where within a few years, players could gain unrestricted status as early as twenty-five years old. There were also provisions for revenue sharing where the top ten money-making clubs donate to a fund shared by the bottom ten teams. And the new CBA effectively made revenue partners with the owners. "The way I look at the situation," said player agent Ritch Winter, "is that when the players agreed to this new deal, they automatically became partners in the growth of the NHL with the owners. With salary caps, we now have a vested interest in seeing the teams grow revenues dramatically over the next few years. That's how we'll make as much or more money as we did in the past—despite the ceilings. And if any of those owners think they're going to sit back and do business as usual, they've got another thing coming. We'll be pushing them for growth."

On July 21, 87 per cent of the "owners' new partners" who cast ballots did so in favour of the agreement. Out of 532 votes cast, 464 players voted in favour and 68 voted against. The next day, the Board of Governors unanimously endorsed the new deal.

The reaction from a ravaged industry was mixed as Bettman and Goodenow posed together at a press conference in New York. "Well folks, it's over," said a triumphant commissioner Bettman. "Let's drop the puck on a fresh start and a wonderful future for the National Hockey League." But Bettman could afford to be magnanimous. Others on management's side were less joyful. "At the end of the day everybody lost," said Gretzky. "We almost crippled our industry. It was very disappointing what happened. For everyone to say 'all right, let's forgive and forget, let's move forward,' that's all fine and good, but it's a lot easier said than done. It's going to take a long of time, it's going to take a lot of hard work.

"We disappointed a lot of people and I don't just mean the average fan. I'm talking about TV partnerships, corporate partnerships, the fan, the guy who goes to one or two games a year with his son. We've got a lot of work ahead of us. It's not going to all change and be all nice overnight." New Jersey president/GM Lou Lamoriello, one of the architects of the new CBA, was straightforward. "There's no question, we all have to be honest, I don't think there's anything that we can sugar coat. We went through this process for a reason, maybe some people agree or disagree, but it wasn't by any means out of spite or out of anything other than the sheer economics of where our game had gone. I really believe that we will come back with a tremendous amount of excitement and enthusiasm. It's time to move forward and not look back."

On the players' side, the settlement was greeted with sadness, disbelief, and bitterness. "I think the biggest thing I learned is that I probably shouldn't use the word 'never' as much as I did," said Scott Walker of the Nashville Predators. "Ultimately we have a cap, and guys like me said we never would have one, so maybe we're eating our words in some sense." Flyers forward Turner Stevenson was blunt: "Why did we sit out all year to do this?" Chicago's Matthew Barnaby was sanguine. "Am I mad? No. I want to get back to work. But at the same time, I'm just a little disappointed that it went this far to play poker and to have someone call your bluff." "I don't like the rollback, no question," said Columbus player rep Todd Marchant, whose salary dropped to $2.47 million from $3.25 million. "No one's happy about that but it's something we had to do." There was also discontent with the union's strategy. "There are seven hundred guys trying to call one number, trying to talk to Bob," said Lightning defenceman Brad Lukowich. "My feeling is I'm confused and disappointed. I thought the players were tougher on this." Opined Bobby Hull, Hockey Hall of Famer, "I'm not so sure (the players) got proper guidance from the guy running the Players' Association (executive director Bob Goodenow)."

But the prevailing sentiment was get-back-to-work. "I don't think the deal that we're going to get would have been ratified last summer," said goalie Sean Burke. "But I just think we've been worn down to the point where at this stage the deal would really have to be incredibly bad for the guys not to vote it in. At least that's the sense I'm getting." "We can't drag our feet any longer," said Keith Primeau of the Philadelphia Flyers. "More than anything, guys just want to return to playing."

Less than a week after his membership signed a deal he had privately opposed, Goodenow was cashiered, with Saskin being hastily handed his job in a late-night decision by select elements of the NHLPA's executive committee. Within days, there were protests at Saskin's controversial accession and $2-million salary demand. (In spite of the losses, there were healthy raises proposed for a number of other NHLPA staffers as well.) With Goodenow's departure also went a decade of militancy and success for players. Saskin quickly established that however long his leadership lasted, it would not be based on the same antagonism that characterized the prior relationship. He appeared at NHL Board meetings, something not done since the days of Alan Eagleson as union director. He made little or no protest when respected veterans Alexander Mogilny and Dan McGillis were sent to the minors to clear cap space for New Jersey.

So what had changed as a result of a full year wiped forever from the books? For one thing, the style of play. Clearly, after years of deriding complaints about playing style from Brett Hull, Mike

Modano, or Mario Lemieux, the NHL acknowledged it had strangled the growth of its game by allowing it to becoming too defensive. So, at the instigation of Detroit's Brendan Shanahan and others, new rules freeing up the game were introduced to add scoring in September 2005. For the most part, the elimination of the red line for two-line passes and an extensive crackdown on obstruction and goalie equipment succeeded in juicing offensive numbers. So, too, did the arrival of the best rookie class in decades, as Alexander Ovechkin, Sidney Crosby, Marek Svatos, Peter Prucha, Dion Phaneuf, Thomas Vanek, Jeff Carter, Mike Richards, and goalie Henrik Lundqvist electrified crowds. For some, the lockout was justified if only because the league accepted it had to speed up the game and eliminate the petty fouls that choked its flow.

On the management side, however, little seemed changed as only two of thirty GMs were replaced going into 2005–06—and one, Brian Burke, simply moved from Vancouver to Anaheim. The general managers and owners who'd brought the NHL to this drastic course of action quickly reverted to type. Given a short window in August to absorb the salary cap implications for signing players, many fell into the same traps of overpaying for past performance and offering long-term commitments for veteran talent. With a $39-million salary cap, many teams hastily filled rosters, seemingly oblivious to the implications of awarding guaranteed money under the restraints of a cap. Thirty-something defencemen such as Chris Pronger, Adam Foote, Derian Hatcher, Adrian Aucoin, Mike Rathje, Roman Hamrlik and Sergei Gonchar were once more inking lucrative three-, four- and five-year contracts—deals that teams could not renegotiate until the last year of the term.

Meanwhile, with unrestricted free agency now available as early as twenty-eight, clubs scrambled to keep the so-called "franchise" players such as Jarome Iginla, Vincent Lecavalier, Markus Naslund, Martin St. Louis, Rick Nash, Joe Thornton, Jose Theodore, Glen Murray, Mike Modano, Milan Hejduk, Miikka Kiprusoff, and Marian Hossa off the free market. Prize free-agents Scott

Niedermayer, Peter Forsberg, Pavol Demitra, Miro Satan, Sergei Gonchar, Paul Kriya, Ziggy Palffy, and Nikolai Khabibulin similarly enlisted in multi-year deals.

Given a one-time exemption from the salary cap, some (but not all) teams took advantage by terminating veterans John Leclair, Tony Amonte, Alexei Zhamnov, Derian Hatcher, Darren McCarty, and Ray Whitney were paid off and sent packing. Other teams, however, declined to buy out pricey veterans. So Jaromir Jagr, Keith Tkachuk, Doug Weight, Ed Belfour, Bill Guerin, Alexei Yashin, and Sergei Fedorov were retained under their old deals, their weighty contracts occupying much valuable cap space. In the orgy of spending, it wasn't long till many clubs were up against the salary cap. A quick perusal of the payrolls of NHL clubs just a month into the new CBA showed the New Jersey Devils were only saved under the $39-million payroll cap because Patrik Elias was recovering from hepatitis A. Philadelphia only slipped under the cap when the L.A. Kings thoughtfully took Jeremy Roenick ($4.94 million) off their hands. The defending champion Tampa Bay Lightning had $20.5 million tied up in just their top four players—with just one of those contracts renegotiable in the next three years. Toronto, Detroit, Colorado, Vancouver, St. Louis, Los Angeles and Dallas were all reduced to virtually no wiggle room, hoping to dump pricey veterans off to clubs that still possessed cap space. New Jersey took to demoting Mogilny and McGillis to the minors where they paid their salary but it did not count them against the salary cap in 2005–06. In a bizarre turn, Vancouver flipped goalies back and forth, sometimes on a daily basis, to keep below the cap. Meanwhile, Columbus sent five players to the minors during one long break to stay under the cap.

Clubs made accommodations to survive in the short term, but as the new CBA progresses it will learn it will be increasingly difficult for free spending teams to find a friendly corner in which to unload a Chris Pronger ($6.26 million) or Derian Hatcher ($3.5 million), Sergei Gonchar ($5 million) or Martin St. Louis ($6.5 million), when their salaries no longer bear any relation to their value to the team.

Buyouts count against the cap and long-term deals cannot be rene-gotiated before the final year of the contract. And recallable waivers make it extremely difficult to finesse minor-league demotions. Plus, many small-market teams kept below the halfway point between salary floor and ceiling, thereby avoiding the possibility of paying into any equalization schemes.

Chicago owner Bill Wirtz was one of the first to recognize the mistakes his club had made in hastily inking high-priced free agents Nikolai Khabibulin, Adrian Aucoin, Jassen Cullimore, Jaroslav Spacek, Martin Lapointe, and Matthew Barnaby. But instead of blaming his perpetually inept management headed by Bob Pulford, Wirtz blamed the new style of play. "We made mistakes on our free-agent signings because we didn't think the game would change that much with the new rules.... We signed the free agents, and then we had the rule changes...with the red line out, that has changed the game. Speed is the greatest requirement," said Wirtz.

But Wirtz had plenty of company as clubs got their wish for a hard salary cap. By the trading deadline in March 2006, almost every club was juggling (with varying success) the new responsibilities of improving their club while also staying under the $39-million ceiling. After re-signing their stars Vincent Lecavalier, Martin St. Louis and Dan Boyle to lucrative, long-term deals, Cup champion Tampa Bay had virtually no cap space for a new goalie. Others such as St. Louis were hanging onto the high-priced Keith Tkachuk just so they could reach the $22-million payroll floor. What all parties agreed upon was that no one had a clear feel where the new CBA would take them. "This whole year, you think you know what's going to happen, but you end up turning around going, 'What happened?'," Pittsburgh GM Craig Patrick told the *Globe and Mail*. Salary-cap nirvana proved more like a budgeting hell for many teams.

The rules changes penalizing obstruction, slow play and defence-first did bring a little heaven to the league in its first season back, putting scoring back into the game. But the NHL's promise of bold new marketing initiatives to go with the hot property stalled in Year

One of the new reality. While everyone in the business acknowledged that EA Sports' use of bright new stars was needed to attract fresh markets and young fans, the league aimed its initial marketing thrust at the traditional fans whose taste runs to macho-soaked hockey. In an attempt at translating Sun Tzu's *Art of War* to hockey called "My NHL," the league jumbled a half-dressed sorceress, an actor/ hockey player in a fictional NHL uniform, and a smiling, tow-headed youngster, all in a frozen homage to *Crouching Tiger, Hidden Dragon*. Subsequent commercials in the series continued the theme of actors playing hockey in anonymous uniforms—all accompanied by an overworked paeon to the ancient Chinese philosopher/warrior. Where were the new stars such as Ovechkin and Crosby who were to take the game into a new generation? Why was the league glamourizing the martial aspects of the sport at the same moment it was reducing fighting and restoring some artistry to the game? Why mix a tempting vixen with a young boy in the same commercial? The promotion was either ridiculed or ignored. The best that Bettman could offer about the promotion was that it had sparked debate and wasn't that the purpose of a commercial?

If the "My NHL" marketing thrust was engaging people's attention, it was hard to tell from the TV ratings in the United States. While hockey-starved Canadians rushed back to the opened-up game in record numbers, Nielsen numbers showed that most Americans simply ignored the sport with pitiful NBC and OLN ratings for most of the year. Before the lockout, regular-season ratings on ABC had declined 21 per cent since the 2001–02 season; the 2004 Stanley Cup final ratings were down 21 per cent from 1999–2000. The first OLN telecasts scored lower than 1.0 in the Nielsen's and stayed stalled for most of the season. (Prompting Norman Chad of ESPN to say, "OLN no longer uses Nielsen ratings for its NHL games; it simply asks viewers to sign in to its guest book.") According to the L.A. *Times*, forty-two of OLN's 57 regular-season broadcasts received a 0.0 rating in greater metro L.A. (representing fewer than 1000 households). "OLN's national telecasts averaged only a 0.2 during the regular season," reported the *Times*, "and are averaging a 0.4 during the playoffs, which translates to only 246,000 homes. For the playoffs in 2004, ESPN was averaging a 0.7 (580,000 homes) going into the conference finals."

Despite the TV numbers, Bettman remained bullish on his new league, issuing public relations bulletins about record attendance figures, even though arenas outside of Canada often appeared half-full and the advertised numbers were bloated by giveaways and papering the houses in some cities. Boston's season-ticket number slumped to a reported 4700 in one of America's best hockey cities; Chicago played to half- and one-third filled stands at the United Center; Florida was giving away tickets as promotional incentives in real-estate sales. Neither Nashville nor Carolina was able to sell out playoff games. Still, the commissioner announced that NHL business was so good that the salary cap would be boosted in 2006–07 as high as $46 million per team. What he failed to say was that outside the OLN money delivered by Ed Snider, much of the "new money" found in the business was a result of currency gains made by a bullish Canadian dollar (up 30 cents since 2003) and resurgent Canadian cities such as Calgary and Edmonton. The numbers were also boosted by ultra conservative accounting when the initial cap numbers had been estimated.

Restoring franchise equity had been another crucial thrust of the lockout strategy. The league made positive noises about new investors with deep pockets in its first season under the new CBA. Bettman bragged of being offered $250 million for a franchise and spoke of teams' values appreciating dramatically. "The NHL is one of the best buys in professional sports right now," Los Angeles Kings president Tim Leiweke told Bloomberg News. "We have no plans to sell. And you don't see many other teams on the market, either. It's clear...that the value of our asset is worth at least 50 per cent more than when the labour agreement was finalized." And some in the business of evaluating teams painted a glowing picture. "I know of one franchise that was recently offered a 60 per cent premium over its pre-lockout valuation, and I'm working with several investors who are sniffing around for an opportunity," Gordon Saint-Denis, managing director of the sports advisory and finance group at CIT Group Inc., told Bloomberg News.

But to others, the reality of the expansion $80-million sale value proved questionable in the first year back. Anaheim sold for a reported $70 million and St. Louis stayed on the market the entire year before being sold for $150 million. (In both cases the arena was included in the purchase and constituted the greater part of the value.) At this writing, Pittsburgh continued to founder without a new arena deal. "The salary cap will help mend the league's balance sheet," noted *Forbes* in November 2005. "But it still remains to be seen whether the teams in Atlanta, North Carolina and Nashville have enough fans to survive." It was clear that however well the CBA improved the immediate prospects, it would still depend on the NHL's [dubious] management class not reverting to old habits. One consolation for NHL GMs: With league salaries capped at 54 percent of league revenues, any overruns by teams will be made up by the escrow payments clawed back from players. That, thanks to the deal Ted Saskin accepted for the players. So a Chris Pronger may repay as much as $700,000 of his salary to compensate for the exorbitant signings that followed.

So how to sum up the spectacular rise and fall of the NHLPA and Bob Goodenow? It can safely be said that if the league hadn't had Goodenow, it would have had to invent him. Through hubris and bad timing, the NHLPA and its director provided a convenient rallying point for an ownership group that needed to deflect attention from their abysmal handling of their business the previous fifteen years. By giving a self-satisfied union enough rope, the NHL managed to rid itself (for now) of militancy in its workforce and buy time to apply proper business principles to its management structure. (For anyone who thought the lockout was about more than crushing Goodenow: The average 2005–06 player salary under the NHL's newfangled economic structure was approximately $1.6 million U.S.

The NHLPA proposal with the 24 per cent rollback offered in December 2004 had promised a $1.3 million average player salary.)

Whether the owners and managers had learned their lesson— and some early contract results suggested they had not—would not be known until the new CBA had been operating for several years. Evidence from the much-admired NFL suggested that no cap or luxury-tax system could permanently defy the reality of vastly unequal local markets. The resentments and jealousies stoked by unbalanced forces will always haunt leagues that expand past a workable number of cities. Adding to the league's burdens, it was now a partner with its players, who will drive the NHL to maximize its revenue oportunities—something they have repeatedly failed to do the past decades. How the NHL copes with the next such crisis— without a whipping boy like Goodenow—will eventually say whether the lockout of 2004–05 was a proper correction of the market or simply a delaying tactic before tackling its real issues head-on. Or as influential Las Vegas oddsmaker Robert Walker observed when asked about the NHL's prospects in 2006: "Just because you call yourself a major sport, doesn't mean you are one. The NHL's not a major sport. Sorry."

Index